William Charles Edmund Newbolt

Religion

William Charles Edmund Newbolt

Religion

ISBN/EAN: 9783337261405

Printed in Europe, USA, Canada, Australia, Japan

Cover: Foto ©Lupo / pixelio.de

More available books at **www.hansebooks.com**

RELIGION

BY THE REV.
W. C. E. NEWBOLT, M.A.

Canon and Chancellor of St. Paul's

LONGMANS, GREEN, AND CO.
39 Paternoster Row: London
New York, and Bombay
1899

EDITORS' PREFACE

THE object of the Oxford Library of Practical Theology is to supply some carefully considered teaching on matters of Religion to that large body of devout laymen, who desire instruction, but are not attracted by the learned treatises which appeal to the theologian. One of the needs of the time would seem to be, to translate the solid theological learning, of which there is no lack, into the vernacular of every-day practical religion ; and while steering a course between what is called plain teaching on the one hand and erudition on the other, to supply some sound and readable instruction, to those who require it, on the subjects included under the common title 'The Christian Religion,' that they may be ready always to give an answer to every man that asketh them a reason of the hope that is in them, with meekness and fear.

The Editors, while not holding themselves precluded from suggesting criticisms, have regarded their proper task as that of editing, and accordingly they have not interfered with the responsibility of each writer for his treatment of his own subject.

W. C. E. N.
F. E. B.

CONTENTS

CHAP.		PAGE
I.	RELIGION	1
II.	ORTHODOXY	22
III.	MORALITY	45
IV.	THE HIGHER LIFE	72
V.	THE HIGHER LIFE—*continued*	98
VI.	THE GREAT IDEAL	112
VII.	THE OBSTACLES TO RELIGION—EXTERNAL	125
VIII.	THE OBSTACLES TO RELIGION—INTERNAL	154
IX.	DOUBTS	177
X.	DIVINE HELP—THE ATONEMENT	204
XI.	DIVINE HELP—THE CHURCH	228
XII.	THE EXPRESSION OF RELIGION—WORSHIP	253
XIII.	THE EXPRESSION OF RELIGION—GOODNESS	277

CHAPTER I

RELIGION

> 'Morality is conformity to a law of right. . . . Religion is essentially a relation towards a Person.'

It is a strange world on which the little infant gazes as he first opens his eyes. The first voice which he utters is a cry,[1] and only gradually he learns to smile,[2] as there dawns upon him the opening sense of possible satisfaction as the end of ungratified desire. Day by day, as he lives and grows, and his sensibilities begin to awaken, he finds himself penetrating into fresh rooms of an enchanted palace, filled with new mysteries, and guarded by a strange apparatus of pleasure and pain. As he compares his experience with that of others, he finds that some seem to be led on by malignant beings only into fresh developments of pain and want, while others are guided by fairy hands into opening visions of delight, pained only by the stumbles of too great eagerness, or by the mistakes which prudence soon learns to avoid. He may go on, if he pleases, simply leaning on the experience of others, and with his hand on the clue of obedience be led by a graduated path into the fulness of life. But as soon as a real sense

---

[1] Compare Wisdom vii 3.
[2] So S. Augustine *Confessions* i 8 'Post et ridere cœpi'; and compare Mr. Keble's 'Cradle Songs' in *Lyra Innocentium* 'The first smile.'

of his own personality and the powers of reflection awaken within him, three questions occur at once, and demand an answer. First, Has the world an owner? does it belong to him, at least the little space which he occupies, or to some one else? Secondly, Is there any scheme or ordered plan which regulates its many and strange vicissitudes? If so, in the third place, What relation has he to that scheme, why is he there, and when will he leave it? is he there by chance, just to flit about in the sunshine from pleasure to pleasure, and die at the first nip of adversity? Or has he a place in an ordered plan, a place which no one else can fill, and in which his actions are of great and lasting importance to a scheme outside himself?

And so accordingly he sets himself to inquire. He asks those without who have hitherto professed to teach him, he interrogates his consciousness within as to what it has to tell him; and the answers which he receives are various.

A certain number of people tell him that this world has no owner, and contains no secret beyond the reach of human intellect to discover; that it is, as it were, a vast piece of common land, or rich gold-field, in which ownership is secured by possession; that every one should set to work to measure out his own claim and make the best of it; that all which contributes to this end is good, and all which militates against it is bad; that the two regulating powers—that is to say, the only two to be reckoned with—are matter and force; that he must learn by experience carefully to estimate their strength and direction; that a mistake is a serious thing: to make a mistake means to receive a blow as if from an unseen adversary, and that a blow without a word. Further, that he must resolutely set himself to repress the obstinate questionings of an intellectual restlessness, which will always be seeking to set up an imaginary owner for the world, as a child will clothe trees and shrubs with the attributes of giants and fairies, the offspring of his own imagination. Further, that he must not allow himself to be led astray by systems of Religion so called, in which men in the infancy of their development have invested the creatures of their imagination with divine attributes, first personifying their own fancies, and then erecting them on a throne. That these fancies have lived on into modern times is no argument in their favour. They have been adopted by successive generations without thought, and are being gradually pushed on one side by the slowly advancing force of intellectual culture. The world has no owner in the shape of God; the dwelling on a so-called spiritual world, or living as for another, is a sheer waste of valuable force, which ought to be expended in developing the rich claim which chance has brought within reach. The voice is loud and persistent; it rises in ever-increasing volume; it is only a theological narrowness which seeks to label it as the voice of the Fool. It is the voice of the wise, and the voice which will prevail: 'There is no God.'

Others, again, will tell him that so far his first impressions were right, that there is a great Being somewhere, a mighty First Cause which once in the beginning erected this palace for the abode of man, and filled it with resources which would ever evolve fresh powers of beauty and beneficence; that He is a Being who neither can be known nor seeks to be known; that having once set the world in motion,

He has left it to itself to follow a fated destined course; that He is not touched by human woes, or pleased with human happiness; that we stand in no need of Him, and He in no way needs us. Prayer to Him and worship are both needless and a waste of time. At the best, as far as man is concerned, He is represented by an empty throne, before which we bow in passing, as the figure-head of a strictly limited monarchy. There is a God, it would be rash to deny it, but for all practical purposes He is banished from the world. In following the laws of nature, and the order which was meant to regulate our progress, we shall be recognising in the truest way the ownership and supremacy of God.

Others will tell him that of a certainty there is more in the world than that which meets his eye; that underneath all the unfolding beauty before him, even in his own inner self, there is a great principle of life welling up into myriad forms, and that this is God— no Person dwelling apart from the world which He created, but its very inmost soul; that He is identified with the world; that He is, as it were, hidden in every room of the palace of life, filling up the cup of its pleasures, and working within its most solemn terrors; that He is within man himself, to enable him to appreciate what is around him. The world is, as it were, magnetised with God, and hence life itself, however lived, is one vast Religion.

Can we, in looking back over our experience, be satisfied with any of these answers to very momentous questions? We feel there must be an owner to whom all this vast and complicated system belongs, that we need a clue to its mysteries, and a protection amidst its strange and unsuspected dangers, and a guide that we should choose the best, and not fail of the end for which we came ; while we grope our way to Him, Who we feel cannot be far away from creation, which is still warm with His touch.

We find on looking around us how universal this feeling is. The very multiplicity of religions, strangely diverse, yet strangely alike, exhibits men separated as it were into exploring parties, feeling after an owner of all this complex world, lest perhaps all unconsciously they should be insulting a hidden Power by a neglect to recognise Him. It is a feeling which men seem unable to shake off, that they are occupants of a possession which does not belong to them. And joined to this there is an intense desire to know what it all means. The three sights which startled Gautama are still to be seen around the richly-loaded tables of this world's good. Men die while yet clutching with their hands the treasures which had invited their labour and fired their ambition. Or they sit with no enjoyment at its feast, out of correspondence, out of sympathy with its fullest allurements, as age creeps on with its chilly paralysis. Or they lie panting with parched lips, like a thirsty man on the salt sea, like a hungry man with a bag of gold. It is not all an even progress from good to better; there is fate and chance and disaster; there is a hand moving the machinery of life which sometimes strikes and kills. The faces are always changing; old ones pass away, new ones come on. Where have the old ones gone? whither are the new ones going? It is ill trifling with machinery connected with an unseen God, the mechanism of which we cannot understand. The religions of the world are stamped with the puzzled uncertainty of men who long for assurance. They furnish a working hypothesis for a time, and then break down; but they all show the widespread feeling of mystery and uncertainty which craves for a solution. Added to this, there is the strange feeling that a progress through the world which shall not be conspicuous for disaster is only possible to one who has learned the principles of self-restraint; that free as he is in his choice, a man who will succeed must have learned not to touch. And so vast systems have grown up, regulating desire, and guiding choice, and applying the principles of restraint to the daily work of life. Along each and all of these ways men have started out to look for God; to find an owner to whom all these riches belong; to find a clue to the great enigma, so that man may no longer stumble on his doom without knowing it; to obtain a sanction for the restraints of morality, either from great universal laws, or the positive precepts of a guiding mind.

I

We are sure, therefore, of sympathy, and of finding ourselves in company with a large band of earnest men in all ages, if we resolutely set ourselves to seek an owner for this world, if we refuse to believe ourselves mere lucky tenants of a rich claim, with no other good but self-interest, and no other evil but a false step; if we believe that there is a plan of life, and true and right rules to guide us in the regulating of it; if, in one word, we abandon the life of chance, and seek earnestly and sincerely for Religion. For what is Religion? It is variously defined and described. Some would connect it with a word which suggests an anxious pondering over the things which belong unto God. Others again, by a doubtful etymology, would understand that which binds us to a great and invisible Lord.[1] Again, it has been described as consisting entirely in the recognition of our dependence on God, or as being in its essence 'the sense of an open secret which man cannot penetrate'; or 'the seeing in Nature a somewhat transcending Nature'; or 'a binding back, a restraining of men, an arrest of their natural impulses and desires.'[2] Or, to sum up, 'Religion includes in its complete idea the knowledge and the worship of God.'[3] All these bear witness to the same idea; they represent man waking up to a Presence outside him. They show to us once more man listening to the voice of the Lord God walking in the cool of the garden, which serves at one time to nerve his sense of defenceless dependence, at another to quicken his consciousness of sin. Religion which is worth the name has found out the Lord and Giver of all life. As in the days of the patriarchs, so now, it is to walk with God, Who can provide, protect, instruct, and punish. Religion is the attitude towards God of one who has discovered His ownership, His wisdom, and His power. 'Blessed is the man whom Thou chastenest, O Lord: and teachest him in Thy Law; that Thou mayest give him patience in time of adversity: until the pit be digged up for the ungodly.'[4] We are face to face now with the underlying basis of true Religion,

---

[1] Liddon *Some Elements of Religion* p. 19.
[2] Farrar *The Bible* pp. 157 158.
[3] Liddon *Bampton Lectures* pp. 6 7 note.
[4] Psalm xciv 12 13.

that, in contradistinction to morality, it is a relation to a Person. If a man could truly say to God, 'Nevertheless I am alway by Thee,' he would be religious; if he could add, 'Thou hast holden me by my right hand,' he would be feeling the benefits of Religion.

Has then God ever come forward to meet men? Has there been any advance on His side, any greater certainty than the feeling of a gap which He alone can fill, of an invisible hand which belongs to an unseen Providence, of judgment and justice which belong to a hidden Power? In seeking for personal fellowship with a Personal God, shall we find any advance to meet us on His side? Longing as we do to be religious, can we attain to any certainty in the object of our Religion?

There is a body among us which claims to be the mouthpiece of God, to hold in its hands not only the clue which is to guide us through the paths of life, but to have constant and real communication with Him; which possesses the record of His long dealings with the world, showing why all things were created, and what purpose they serve. These tell us that God has laid aside portions of the thick veil which hides His Presence, and that the records of His Revelation have been committed to writing, and are the treasure and tradition of the Church.

Three times in the history of the world God has revealed His Name, and, besides many shadowings and symbolical indications, He has once revealed Himself in human form; passing through the world like one of the ordinary travellers whom we encounter in our daily path, meeting and assimilating pleasure and pain, passing through the mysteries of birth and death; strange in His choosing, unpopular in His methods, despised and rejected of men, but now acknowledged, by those best qualified to speak, to have used this world as no one else has been able to use it, according to its purpose, and avoiding its subtle dangers. This great Revelation must be looked upon later, more fully and in greater detail. But what of the revelations of Himself which God has condescended to give us? How do they help us? What have they to tell us? God has revealed His Name. This is what we are told, and this we find in the records which are given to us to use. The Name of God stands to us for certain revelations which He has been pleased to make of Himself to man; certain discoveries which represent to us just as much of the divine Nature as we are able to apprehend. And accordingly we notice that these are not Names which man has given to God, as he has stumbled upon a manifestation of divine Power, and, like Jacob, has set up the pillar which shall localise his dream; but, on the contrary, they are Names which God has of Himself given to Himself, and left them with man.

In the early history of the world God announces to us that He was pleased to reveal Himself to the patriarchs by a special Name signifying omnipotence: 'I manifested Myself to them in the character of El-Shaddai, the Omnipotent God, able to fulfil that which I had promised.'[1] The omnipotency of God was the sum of their creed; there were not gods many, nor lords many; this world does not belong to many and rival owners, there is no divided empire of good and evil, but God is all-powerful, He shares His throne with no rival. This is a revelation which we welcome even at the present day, when the soul in its struggle with

[1] See *Speaker's Commentary* on Exodus vi 2 3.

evil is tempted to think there are some things too hard for the Lord. Coming down the course of history, God manifested Himself in the character and attributes of Jehovah to Moses, a Name which declared the nature of God, as underived eternal existence, ' the Cause of all being, governing the past, the present, and the future,' until we come down to the period of the Incarnation, when the Incarnate God, before leaving the earth at the Ascension, gave to the Church the new Name of God—God the Father, God the Son, and God the Holy Ghost, which contains in sum the Christian revelation of God. So God has revealed Himself out of the gloom. He wills us to look upon Him as the Almighty; there is only one Being to reverence and fear in passing through the rich storehouse of this world; with Him we need not fear its blows or its smiles. He is Almighty, all belongs to Him; He is the Lord, standing outside it all, in the mystery of His Being. He is in the mystery of the Trinity; Father, Son, and Holy Ghost.

The Names of God, therefore, are points of extreme solemnity, points of observation whence we gaze out by faith into the immensity of Heaven; wellnigh points of worship, where whenever we speak God's Name we worship Him. It is impossible, therefore, to treat these revelations lightly, as if man by himself could attain to the same results by careful investigation and earnest speculation. If we find, as we do find, that an idea of the Unity of God, or even traces of the highest moral aspirations of Christianity, are to be discovered in purely heathen systems, are we to say that Revelation has no more to offer; that this great Name of God, which has been traced for us by the finger of the

Almighty Himself, carries us no further, and opens up no clearer vision of the mutual relations between man and his Maker? Surely, to say this would be as if a man were to rise from the contemplation of some splendid example of self-elevated genius, and say that education and training are altogether unnecessary, because some men have risen to position and eminence without them. A great writer has described more truly the imperfect vision of those who only guessed at the forms whose shadows they saw reflected on the veil undrawn by Revelation. 'They looked with unsteady and wavering vision; they saw, and they saw not; one impression came and was chased away by another. They seem like men striving after a great truth apparently within their reach, but really just beyond it. Serious questioners, I do not doubt, many of them were, of what they saw of their own selves, of what had been handed down to them from their fathers. Seekers after God they may have been, but who will say that they were finders?'[1]

Surely it is at the point where the human eye fails to penetrate, where the clouds chase each other down the mountain-side, and all further progress seems barred by gloom, that to the godly there ariseth up light in the darkness. The hand of God lifts up the veil of cloud, and shows that there is an end to the path which it seemed so hopeless to pursue. In the perplexity of speculation, in the bewilderment of the moral conflict, under the showers of blows which beat a man down in his struggle with what seems to him only blind chance, then the revelation of God in His irresistible strength, in the tenderness of a Father, the power of a Saviour,

[1] R. W. Church *The Gifts of Civilization* p. 314.

the strength of a Comforter, adds renewed vigour to
his faltering steps. He can reverently bow his head,
he can raise his eyes to heaven, and, as he murmurs
' God is where He was before,' pass on his way, as one
who has seen a vision, and is comforted by a knowledge
which has given him strength. God has spoken, we
thank Him for it, to the ear which strains to catch the
sounds of His Presence. ' The invisible things of Him
from the creation of the world are clearly seen, being
understood by the things that are made, even His
eternal power and Godhead.'[1] But He has also spoken
plainly in words of direct and special Revelation, and
has told us that we guess aright. There is a great
Owner to this world, Who is omnipotent, self-existent,
and a Trinity of Love and Power, with Whom we can
go forward confident in His protection and certain of
His love.

II

If we are thus able to find an Owner to Whom all the
wealth belongs, Who meets our instinctive longings with
partial manifestations of His Presence, lingering long
enough that we may thank Him, and close enough
that we may hear Him—is there further a plan and a
purpose in all around us discoverable to us? We see on
every side much to perplex, and even to dismay; some
calling upon us to admire a scheme of beauty and
beneficence; and others tell us that underneath this
fair outward show there is little but heartless cruelty
and a pitiless treachery; that the good things are
poisoned, and beauty only a lure to land us in destruction. No one can deny that this world around us is a

[1] Rom. i 20.

difficult puzzle, full of hard problems. Is it to be explained? Is there any clue to its apparent contradictions? Is there anything which serves to explain why the strait and stony path is always to be chosen in preference to the broad and sunny road? Why do so many sink down baffled, poisoned apparently by the good things which they eagerly followed? It must surely be of the very last importance to discover the meaning of this arrangement which we call life, and the best way of passing through it, not only without disaster, but with the fullest share of the bounties which it has to offer. Here once more the Owner Who has proclaimed His presence has revealed to us also the plan and purpose of this which we see around us. This world was created for God's glory, it was designed to work out a great purpose. Just as an artist will seek to express himself in some work of art which represents to him the beauty or the design which he struggles to bring into life, so this world was meant to be the expression of the beauty, the love, the beneficence of God, preparing the way for another, developing into a still richer state of perfected life. The instrument chosen for the evolution of this great idea was Man; under his care the garden of the world was to be tilled, and dressed, and made fruitful, and the eternal city, the new heavens and the new earth, wherein dwelleth righteousness, were to be developed. But here the plan of God was changed, not destroyed, by the failure of the agent. Man, placed here as the agent of God, failed in his allegiance and marred the Divine plan. Hence there is discernible in the world a flaw, an imperfection; there has been a fall which has dislocated the original beauty and simplicity of the design. Now there is much that is broken, imperfect, harmful; man has to steer his way between opposing dangers, and carefully examine all that crosses his path, lest what is harmful shall be disguised under the shape of blessing. He himself is not the same being he once was, nor the same being that he might have been; more resourceful, more in sympathy with the world, more developed, he obeys God with greater difficulty, and is easily led to forget the end of his sojourn here, viz. to carry out the will of God. So that the spectacle we have before us is that of a world designed to exhibit God's glory and to prepare for another under the administering hand of man, now perverted and damaged, but still being led on to carry out its original purpose. Man is still the agent of God; he passes through the world in ceaseless relays; each generation as it comes adds something to the completeness of the city which hath foundations, which is rising in its solidity beyond. This world is like a workman's city which has grown up round some great building, into which at some future time the race is to be moved. The tendency is to forget both the work and the transitory nature of our present home. Men get satisfied with their huts, and despair of the unfinished palace. They sit down satisfied with the good things to be picked up here, and forget or despise the fuller blessings to be attained hereafter. So that this world, as it is explained to us, is shown to be the temporary home of man, in which he is placed by God to work out the plans and the fuller development of God's glory. Its dangers and its failures are to be explained by the fact that man has gone very far away from the original plan of God. Self-will, self-gratification, rebellion, once ruined, and still mar, the perfection of His plan. The eternal city rises slowly, the workman's town echoes with the cries of labourers who have forgotten the end for which they were placed there, and have lost themselves in pleasures which only do them harm. Religion, therefore, while it binds us to the Person of God, makes us more and more careful to follow out His plan. His glory, not our own gratification, must be the first thought. The city which hath foundations, not the world which has become a mere workman's city, must be the first aim. And so Religion at once puts us into a richer and fuller relationship; our aims are higher, our correspondence with the things around us is more complete. Day by day, beyond the hoarding and the scaffolding-poles which shut in the horizon, we have had visions of the rising walls and the soaring turrets. Our houses here are built up of fragments of ruined beauty, the ground is strewed with splinters, and poisonous with its long years of decay; but its fragments have to be rescued, its treasures, bruised as they are, to be developed, its costly fragments to be restored to their original purpose, not selfishly clutched as ornaments for a home which must shortly come down. This world is so beautiful because it is full of fragments of a city once built for the glory of God. It is treacherous and deadly because it has been shattered and ruined; the new city must be built up of fragments, not developed, as the more from the less perfect. Man is still here; once he was the agent of the perfect will of God; still he labours, impaired and feeble as he is, to reach out after that will. Religion exhibits the plan and clue. We are put here to promote God's glory, to build up out of a broken world the eternal city, which will be the final home of man. This world is not for human gratification; it is for the glory of God. It is not governed by chance; it is directed by a plan, which has never faltered, however much it may have been modified by the faithlessness of man.

III

If this world is created and upheld by a Great Being, for Whose glory it was created, clearly one function of Religion will be rightly to adjust our personal relations toward Him. We have dismissed the thought of chance, we see clearly the unworthiness of mere selfish gratification, which clutches at the *maximum* of pleasure, and hopes for the *minimum* of pain, and we are brought face to face with responsibility. Life is a serious matter, in which we have a definite place, a distinct vocation, a separate work. We know it, we feel it, we grow to it; and yet how hard it is to realise it! Sometimes we are tempted to say that Life is a drama, where there is a leading part for one or two striking actors, where no one pauses to think of the brilliantly-dressed citizen, or the soldier with his picturesque armour, or the moving medley of the stage-mob, mere picturesque adjuncts and nothing more. The world, we are tempted to say, depends on a few great men, the ordinary man will at least escape notice, and not be asked for an account of his less than one talent. Vocation and duty, and the obligations of Religion, are for the great and the few, not for the many who come and go and are forgotten. And yet, if we look into the same Revelation which spoke to us of God, we shall see in the records of His dealings with man that one fact stands out clearly before all others, and that is God's intense care for the individual. He is not like some general carrying his point, at a tremendous sacrifice of life, at any sacrifice, so that he may carry it. He is not the miner just sifting out a speck of gold from a heap of refuse and discarded toil. The care for the individual stands out clear and distinct in this unfolding of His will. Let us look at some simple statement such as this: 'He slept with his fathers, and his son reigned in his stead'; or at the grim record of some act of sin, where the sinful act is prefaced with the pedigree of the sinner, and linked backward and forward with the past and with the future. So the record of Korah's sin begins thus: 'Now Korah, the son of Izhar, the son of Kohath, the son of Levi, . . . took men.'[1] So Achan's sin, again, is bound up with his ancestry: 'But the children of Israel committed a trespass in the accursed thing: for Achan, the son of Carmi, the son of Zabdi, the son of Zerah, of the tribe of Judah, took of the accursed thing.'[2] So again mysteries lie in those long strings of names which form the genealogies. What interweaving of destinies goes on! The individual who has failed in the eyes of the world lives and dies and reappears in some brilliant life descended from him in this chain of existence. Or some lingering taint runs like a deadly plague, in a course which reaches to the third and fourth generations, where men only trace its passage by ruin, upheaval, and blighted hopes. The effect of the individual life has lived on. Life is too great a thing to be cast into this seething mass of existence and leave no trace behind it. The knowledge

[1] Num. xvi 1.   [2] Josh. vii 1.

of God, and the exigencies of His plan, extend to every life, however humble, which appears in the world of His creating. And out of this stands forth the great truth which serves to shape our course and quicken our purpose. 'Every life that is lived has its message to the world.'

In view of the Great Presence before whom we stand, and the plan which is carrying us along with it in its rapid evolution, it is the function of Religion constantly to recall us to ourselves, with the warning cry, '*Unde, quo, quomodo?*' Remember whence you came, and whither you go, and the way in which you are speeding. What is the part which as an individual you have to play, and how are you doing it? And on looking round we find that after all we are not the absolutely isolated phenomena which we thought ourselves to be. We are, saving of course to the utmost our free-will, marionettes rather than players, marionettes, it is true, capable of resisting the guiding hand, and frustrating its main purpose; and we are held in check, we are guided and directed by three strong cords, as it were,—by divine purpose or destiny, by heredity, by circumstance or, as it is called, environment.

When we talk of destiny we do not mean a blind irresistible fate, which hurries us on towards a certain goal, to which our very struggles lend velocity. In spite of argument and proofs, man can always at the end point to his absolute conviction of the certainty of his own freedom. Demonstrate to him that he is bound by fate, he can only reply that he knows that he is a free agent. But purpose or destiny means, rather, that in the end we cannot resist God's will; we plunge madly out of the path, we rush down a labyrinth of trees, we hide from God; for years we are successful, we get further and further away from duty and from God; yet at the end, behind the trees, there is the encircling wall of His will. We are free within limits. But either we must consciously play our part in union with God, or He will use us for some divine purpose of His own, in spite of ourselves: Gibeonites in the house of God. We came into being and were placed in this world without our consent; we shall leave it without being asked. We are moved here and there into places and conditions of which we have little cognisance. The purpose of God is a presence which we feel at hand, when, like a child who totters along in his first endeavours to walk, we stagger forward; it starts us, it catches us, it takes us up. God makes us feel that we have a work to do, and that we are immortal until that work is done.

And if the purpose of God shapes our life, He shows us again what a strong controlling force we have in heredity. We are one in a series, all known to Him.

The torch is put into our hand, we have taken it, it may be from a hand stiffening in death, and we have to pass it on unquenched. We do not enter on this wonderful scene, with its rich store, disconnected, and with only a selfish claim: we are the child of the ages, an inheritor of the past, which has filtered down to us, through one particular channel, with its good or ill, with its warp or bias. It is a scene in which the actors only change, and history is behind them. A long chain of life hangs on the one link of our individuality. God has shown us sometimes how much depends on a life. Joseph in the pit, in his exile, in his prison, is bearing up the chain of life, which links on to Abraham, and back from him to the parents of our life. That young man, despised, persecuted, and lowly, is sent on to preserve life; and we see the chain stretching out from him through Moses, through David, now resting on some Ezra or Nehemiah, now taken up by some prophet, until the destiny of the world is buoyed at last to a virgin called Mary, at a despised Nazareth. There are strands of destiny which run across the humblest lives, which elevate the individual to his true importance. The Personality which Religion displays to us, walking in the midst of His work, tells us clearly that there is no such thing as an unimportant individual.

And the third bond which steadies and directs our life is environment. We are each placed in the spot where we can best work and best be developed. We have a station in life, as we call it. Out of our surroundings our life has to take its material, and through its surroundings lies its perfection. When Solomon's temple was in building, it was made of stones shaped and prepared before they came thither; the temple sprang up noiselessly out of perfected material; one laboured in the quarries, another in the forest; one excavated, another carved and ornamented; wherever he was, the work before him drew forth his powers, and he sent up finished work to the temple. So we are held down, as it were, to certain work, hedged in by a certain environment, in which we must labour. Discontent, jealousy, neglected duty, misapplied trusts, mean that we have lost our cue in life, missed our aim, and forfeited our excellence. The eye is saying to the hand, 'I have no need of thee,' the hand is saying to the foot, 'I have no need of thee.' All around us there is a vision of order in its regulated force, of peace in 'its tranquillity of order'; and life which God has given to us puts us in our place in the great worship of the universe. 'Blessed are the eyes which see the things that ye see: for I tell you, that many prophets and kings have desired to see those things which ye see, and have not seen them; and to hear those things which ye hear, and have not heard them.'[1] So Religion appeals to us with all the seriousness of a mission and the gravity of great responsibility. 'Lord, what wouldst Thou have me to do?' Religion has displayed to us the presence of a Personal God, and divine service is to carry out His Will.

[1] S. Luke x 23 24.

CHAPTER II

ORTHODOXY

'Gospel means "good news," and not good advice.'

If Religion is the working principle which regulates life, if it supplies the clue which is to guide us through its mazy paths, it is evident that it can never be an unimportant question, an indefinite apprehension of a supernatural background, a hazy sentiment varying with the individual. Accuracy in so vital a matter will be of the very last importance; and if God Himself has spoken, a faithful and intelligent grasp of what He has said will be the aim of every one who seeks to guide his course aright in a subject which so nearly concerns him. And accordingly we find that Christianity, which we are led to believe is the last perfect and final expression of God in this particular, as enshrined in a teaching and dogmatic Church, is so precise and clear in its definition and outline, that it does not hesitate to state that a right faith is necessary to salvation. That is to say, in view of the complications and dangers of life, the only chance of emerging with safety and gaining the path will be found in exact obedience to the revealed will of God.

And yet as the stern uncompromising requirements of Christianity become more and more evident, exploring parties, as we have seen, break away hither and thither, carrying out this or that portion of the directions supplied to them as they think best, while, on the other hand, a large number set to work to simplify these regulations, to prove, if they may, that a great deal which passes for Christianity is of purely human origin,—that Christianity, as it emerged from the hands of Christ, was a very simple thing, in which a strict morality was announced, if not absolutely new, at least immensely in advance of any practical scheme which the world had as yet essayed; that the language of mystical rapture in which Christ so often spoke was susceptible of grotesque perversion in the minds of men, who only imperfectly understood it. Picturesque words and picturesque rites alike were employed to convey this scheme of morality, which were susceptible of a very real meaning to oriental mysticism, but not to be translated into the prosaic language of our day—so that it has been the fate of the simple teaching to be overlaid with legend and corrupted with misunderstanding; that the death of Christ was the ordinary seal of martyrdom to a life too pure and good to be understood by those who surrounded Him; that His resurrection only meant a spiritual reunion with His apostles in a nearer state which death made possible.[1] And then came the inevitable apotheosis of the divine hero, the attempt to fasten down spiritual sayings by a stupid literalism; and then, as men lived further and further away from the events, Church Councils, heated disputants, religious writers, made the matter more complicated still; and now we have a tangle of theological distinctions,

[1] See Wendt *The Teaching of Jesus* vol. ii p. 274.

supernatural accretions, sacramental systems, and a Church to keep them alive, from which every one, at all events, who earnestly wishes to get at the truth, must break free and return to the simplicity of a life which, after all, was only the example of One Who studied more completely, out of pure native piety, the objects and obligations of religion as expressed in a human existence lived under the eye of God.

If this be a true estimate, the sooner we dismiss creeds and dogmas and all the exact system of the Church the better. And yet any unbiassed mind must feel the unreality of such a statement as this. The words and the life of our Lord Jesus Christ, taken by themselves as a mere biographical study, are obviously inadequate to explain His unique position, or to account for that lengthened shadow which falls from His Person over the civilised world, taking the shape of the Catholic Church. We have, as a matter of fact, our blessed Lord's own presentment of what we know as Christianity, which He ordained to be the lesson constantly to be used by His Church in bringing in fresh disciples to His fold. It is this: 'Go ye therefore, and make disciples of all the nations, baptizing them into the Name of the Father and of the Son and of the Holy Ghost: teaching them to observe all things whatsoever I commanded you: and lo, I am with you alway, even unto the end of the world.'[1] We may call this, if we like, 'a subsequent gospel tradition,'[2] but the authenticity of the passage is undisputed, and in it we see Christ presenting His message to the world in the terms of the deepest

---

[1] S. Matt. xxviii 19 R.V.
[2] Wendt *The Teaching of Jesus* vol. ii p. 349.

mystery of the Faith. Here is no appeal to a hesitating humanity, trembling at the brink of truth, to enter cautiously, one foot at a time, through Deism up to a Personal God, through a Personal God up to a Divine Christ, through a Divine Christ up to a further teaching of the Holy Spirit; it is rather the great plunge of faith which is demanded, the belief in the mystery of the Holy Trinity, enterprised through the medium of a Sacrament, and guaranteed by all the teaching of His own divine Life: the fact being, that it cannot be indifferent for man to learn anything which God has been pleased to reveal. It is well that we should pause and consider the force of the term 'Revelation.' It means the drawing back by God of the veil which obscures our knowledge. It is true that He allows men by patient investigation to find out for themselves great truths which affect life; but it is also true, that in certain regions, where human knowledge cannot penetrate, God Himself lifts the veil and shows men so much of the truth as it concerns them to know; and so we shall find that although all Holy Scripture is inspired, not all of it is revelation, which belongs rather to those portions where not only wisdom and inerrancy are guaranteed to the writer, but where he is made the medium of, or records, the enunciation of some truth which patient investigation by itself had not succeeded, perhaps never could succeed, in reaching. This knowledge we should ever seek to make living to ourselves, in every way in our power, and carefully to follow out the indications minutely traced by God. To fail in this is not only to lose, as far as we ourselves are concerned, it is also in a certain degree to depreciate the missionary value of the Church. We think that we are going to win those that are without by a simplified Christianity, or we settle for ourselves, on eclectic principles of our own making, what is of importance and what is not, in the scheme which God has proclaimed for the salvation of the world. We think we are meeting opponents half-way, and do not see that we are failing all the time to attract by an abstract Personality which is but a slight advance on Deism; or that the Being we put forward in the simplest guise which we deem palatable is no compensation to the Atheist for the initial difficulty of belief; or that the mutilated presentment which we give to the Agnostic affords him no point of knowable contact. What a hazy indistinct thing is Religion to the average man! What an indescribable influence it is as presented to the ordinary Christian! We see it of course in its acutest form in circumstances where Christianity should be largely on the defensive and at its best; where a Christian community is living beside or in the midst of a heathen population, as in India, Africa, or elsewhere. Here the contrast should be obvious and decided, and Christianity appear in its most appealing form, as the true religion for man; whereas too often, while the ordinary observer can trace the strong influence and binding force of his religious observances on the heathen, it is difficult to discover in the Christian community any distinctly religious influence whatever, as apart from civilisation.

Or again, how hopelessly ill-equipped is the ordinary Christian in presence of an unbeliever! How little is he able to give an account of the faith that is in him! And while the one who does not profess to believe thinks himself the more bound, it may be, to exhibit the consistency of a moral life, the believer uses his faith as a mere label attached to his life, by which, and not by his actions, men may know that he belongs to Christ.

To their own great harm, and to the detriment of the fair fame of Christianity, men have taken such parts only as they deemed suitable of the Christian faith, and have ignored the rest; and so have relegated what may very easily be shown to be some of the very fundamental truths of Christianity to the regions of esoteric doctrines, there to be pondered by those who like to dabble in theology, as the only thing they are fit for, while they leave the really intelligent man, who does the work of the world, to govern his actions on a general scheme of right and wrong, to be respectable in his own actions and just towards his neighbours; to address prayers sometimes to a Supreme Being, and to read such portions of the Bible as minister to an upright life—such as 'the actual state of public opinion on the subject' decides to minister to edification; to do good in his generation, and in the end to die; then, if he has done well, to go to Heaven, if he has not, well —not.

To such an estimate the intense earnestness of the General Councils of the Church, the subtle distinctions of doctrine which divide Eastern and Western Christendom, or such a doctrine as the revelation of the Holy Trinity, must seem the wildest folly, or at the best 'a murderous tenacity of trifles.' Let us teach people, it is said, to be better men, not about such mysteries as the Holy Trinity; let us remedy social evils instead of plunging into theological subtleties; let us get them to believe in a God of any kind, instead of minutely distinguishing the tenets of rigid orthodoxy. This is the attitude widely adopted, or at least assumed, in dealing with religious questions. Our blessed Lord's command, which S. Matthew has recorded for us, would carry to them no urgency of appeal: 'Go ye therefore and teach all nations if you like, but by all means avoid metaphysical subtleties or theological distinctions, and rather teach them broadly to believe in God.'

Why cannot we accept this as an adequate statement of the case? Why do we believe it to be inaccurate and wrong? In an attempt to answer this will lie the main consideration which forms the subject of this chapter, viz. the practical importance of dogmatic distinctions in religion, or, in one word, the absolute necessity of orthodoxy.

A large number of people object to dogmatic distinctions on the simple ground that they are unimportant. This contention has been prominently put forward in the controversy, which now for some time has been raging, on the subject of religious education in our schools. It seems so easy and so sensible a thing to say, 'Why perplex children's minds about subtle doctrines such as the Incarnation, the Holy Trinity, and the sanctification of the Holy Spirit? It is surely enough for them to know that there is a Supreme Being around them and about them! "Thou God seest me" is quite sufficient as a creed for a child at school!'

And it is but one step on to say further that it is sufficient for the ordinary man of the world, and only one step further still to say that theological distinctions altogether should be left to those who have the time and skill to investigate them. And so those who look on from the outside find little difficulty in saying that modern Christianity is after all only a civilised heathenism; that Christianity as it came from its great Founder was one thing, as it is carried out in practical life among us it is another. Whereas this would seem to be undeniable, that the same people who allow themselves to form this estimate would be the first to recognise in the ordinary arts and sciences of life the extreme importance of exact precision in those who undertook to practise them. A young artist, for instance, who hoped to arrive at the perfection of art by despising the ordinary drudgery of the academy and the study of the laws of colour and anatomy, would be told that something more was necessary than a mere natural taste for drawing. The very men who are loudest in their call for a simplified Christianity would be the first to laugh at the ignorance of one who despised the nice distinctions of chemistry with its careful formulæ, and proposed to proceed guided by a general sense of fitness and proportion, because he had a taste for analysis; they would tell him that he could not even play a game, nor draw a straight line, nor sing a song, without paying attention to the minute and subtle distinctions which mark off the professional from the amateur. If this be so, it surely does not make great demands on a man's sense of the fitness of things to be asked to believe that in a matter which concerns the sum and apex of all science, in a region where every inch of the field covered by human knowledge has been scientifically measured, in a class of subjects which concerns the welfare of millions, and the inmost life and wellbeing of every man, that here at all events there is no room for vapouring about idealism, no margin for unimportant truths, where moreover God Himself is assumed to have spoken, and that so seldom, and in such few words.

It is intelligible to deny that God has spoken at all; but if He is believed to have spoken, we must feel that every word is important. And accordingly we find that the common charge against Christians, and against the tendency of Christianity itself, is inconsistency. That is to say, there is something wanting in the average type of life which it produces. Men and women are good up to a certain point, and then fail miserably and utterly elsewhere. If the accusation be true, surely it would tend to show that men and women are working too often with only half Christianity, and so produce only half results. How often in other things do we encounter the same cause of failure in men, who have left out what they considered to be an unimportant detail which was found to carry with it the gravest issues, and to be fraught with the most serious consequences! Perhaps it is not too much to say that the inconsistency which is the prevailing characteristic of pseudo-Christianity is the product of a Christianity in which many simple yet important elements have been omitted as being of no consequence. As the child grows up from whom the full knowledge of God has been withheld, to whom wilfully and presumptuously his teachers have presented only the Fatherhood of God, a time will come when the sense of sin will demand a Saviour of whom he knows nothing, when his own inherent weakness will need the bracing of sanctifying grace, the knowledge of which has been kept from him; and an inconsistent life will represent a rule of conduct which is the natural development of a mutilated Christianity.

It is of the very last importance that we should receive such a thing as the revelation of God exactly as it has been given to us. Every one can see that a passionless first cause, who sits like the god of the Epicurean poet at the end of a long series of cause and effect, enjoying an unruffled immortality, without a thought or a care for man, a desire to help, or a wish to know—every one can see that such an idea of God can only end in a paralysing fatalism. An empty throne, towards which we mechanically bow in passing, labelled 'Nature' or 'Providence,' may represent a constitutional theory in the order of the universe, it can never have any practical control over the legislation of our life.

In like manner, if we arbitrarily elect to present God as the Universal Father and nothing more; even if we confine ourselves to an appeal to Him as a Saviour, as many religious people seem to do, while they ignore the Supreme Majesty of the Father, or the Personality of the Holy Spirit Who has been revealed to us—refusing, in fact, to acknowledge all distinctions of Persons in the Godhead whatsoever,—we do it to our own great loss. Dogmatic distinctions in Theology may be supposed to represent certain registered observations of laws and forces which have a direct bearing on life. And much more those dogmatic distinctions which have been revealed to us by God Himself never can be supposed to represent certain manifestations given to satisfy curiosity, or as mere unimportant decorations of a difficult truth. Whenever God has spoken about Himself it has been in measured terms, and in carefully prepared crises of history. We have already seen how the development of the idea of His absolute power is followed by that of His eternal existence and gradually, by the lips of Christ Himself, the Unity in Trinity, and the Trinity in Unity, is revealed as the life and spiritual atmosphere of the Christian. And so, whether we regard the world outside, or our own inmost life, we can never hope for anything but inconsistency from a tampering with the completeness of the truth revealed to us. Unless we ourselves are in active vital union with each of the Three Persons of the blessed Trinity, we can hope for only a maimed and mutilated presentment of Christianity. We are living in a world of fierce currents and tortuous eddies. The forces which are arrayed against evil are too nicely calculated to allow us to deal in unimportant doctrines, or dabble in half-truths. If the world is to become Christian it must know the fulness of Christianity. If we are to be considered Christians, we must aim at its completeness. A half-Christianity has no vital attractiveness. Religion has nothing to show to an amateur who despises scientific data as something unimportant, who is an honorary member of all forms of religious speculation, and believes consistently in none.

But this objection, which is more an attitude than an utterance, is also formulated in the mouths of those who deprecate the tyranny of dogma as a hindrance to religious liberty and a bar to freedom of thought. 'Dogma' and 'Dogmatic' belong to the number of those cant terms which by an adventitious significance imparted into them are able to damage and frighten and blind people's eyes to the true significance and value of the truths which they were designed to indicate.

There are enemies ranged against a dogmatic expression of faith, reaching from the lowest religious or political partisan, who is jealous of the authority which a definite statement seems to confer on the Church which makes it, up to the hazy practical unbeliever, who does not care to be reminded of how very little faith actually remains to him by the constant friction of a barrier which seems to menace and press upon him.

In so far as the objection is a sincere one, it ought not to be hard to show that dogmatic distinctions, while they appear to curtail freedom, really give it a larger development. What is dogma? It has been defined in the field of Religion as 'essential Christian truth thrown by authority into a form which admits of its permanently passing into the understanding, and being treasured by the hearts of the people';[1] or, once more, in a wider field, 'as a statement set forth, either by an individual teacher or by some teaching body, to be taken for true, while confessedly not susceptible of logical demonstration.'[2]

And here we recognise at once that Religion is not the only region in which dogma reigns. The very children in the schools from which dogmatic Religion is scouted, are yet indoctrinated with sciences which depend to a certain extent on, or at least deal in, dogma. No teacher looks askance, *e.g.*, at Geometry because it makes use of dogma under the name of 'the postulate.' To quote again from the same writer:

[1] Liddon *University Sermons* First Series p. 78.
[2] Huntingdon *'Peace of the Church'* p. 100.

'Nevertheless Geometry as a rule is shy of dogma, and deals for the most part with what is directly provable. Not so Biology and the mixed sciences in general; here dogma abounds, commonly veiled under the name of "the working hypothesis." The so-called "law" of natural selection is an instance in point. No one alleges that natural selection has been demonstrated, or is demonstrable; nevertheless it is taught, and taught with much positiveness, by those who hold it. In fact, to question this particular working hypothesis brings down upon the questioner in some quarters censure as sharp, if not as heavy, as that which in old times fell to the lot of those who disparaged the dogmas of the Church.'[1]

In fact, the entrance to every science and profession in the ordinary everyday life of us all, is surrounded by dogma to this extent, that it is propped up on the records of experience gathered into law, demonstrable no doubt by those who have the learning and the intellectual power to appreciate the demonstration, but to the ordinary layman as much dogma as any decree of the Church in matters non-demonstrable. And these we habitually act upon. We do not think it necessary, for instance, to demonstrate to ourselves the law of gravitation before we hesitate to jump from a height to the ground; or to explain to ourselves in an intelligible manner the laws which affect tides before we take an expedition along the coast swept by the sea. And yet no one can complain of these laws and dogmatic truths as fettering freedom; on the contrary, they save a great deal of time and labour, in that they bring to the investigator of truth in a handy form the labours

[1] Huntingdon *'Peace of the Church'* p. 100.

and recorded observations of the past, so that the worker can start for himself in a field circumscribed in one sense, but in reality more accurately defined for his labour.

A man does not complain of a fetter on his freedom, if, when searching for a place to pitch his tent in a country unknown to him, he finds that large regions have been declared barren by previous explorers, and is directed to turn his footsteps into regions where former travellers have found water. He may be limited thereby in the extent of his observations, but enriched in their intensity. Whatever may be our feelings as regards vivisection, in the case of experiments made on the lower animals in the interests of science, at least we all join in protesting against the infliction of needless pain, to demonstrate a truth which has been already won by experiment. We feel that experiment should be barred by mercy in that direction, as it is barred virtually by the acquired knowledge. In all these cases the point to be emphasised being this, that dogmatic or experimental precision, which has taken the place of dogmatic truth, does not hamper and restrain, but rather sets free energies, which otherwise would either have been wasted in barren fields, or else would have been squandered in a fruitless re-opening of past fields of discovery, from which the treasures had already been gathered, and stored up for the use of those who should come after.

When we come to Religion the same thing holds good. Here, of course, we face the real difficulty; where men will trust the men of science, even to the extent of not verifying their experiments, when they make those assertions susceptible of demonstration which form the postulates, and in a real sense the dogmas of their science, yet what are they to say to Revelation, to the message, as it professes to be, from an unknown quarter, transmitted through fallible men, exposed to all the accidents which await a manuscript committed to parchment in ancient times, and exposed very often to the subtler dangers still of pious frauds, and alterations either of addition or omission made in the supposed interests of truth? Then, further, there are all the doubtful advantages which have arisen from the patronage of the Church, which has not hesitated, it has been asserted, to make large developments amounting to a new faith altogether? Ought we not to receive with care a dogmatic system which comes to us vitiated by these defects, and which would seem to be incidental to the origin from which it is derived?

Of course, if the objection is of this kind, and very often at bottom it is so—for men believe in a divine morality, in thoughts inspired from without, while they do not believe in Revelation of truth imparted by God, which cannot, however, be strictly demonstrated,—if the objection is of this kind, then the controversy must be taken higher up, and the battle fought under the walls of Revelation. Can God speak to man? Has He so spoken? And if He has, is not a message from God such as this, one of those matters which concern the individual experience, and not to be hardened and crystallised into dogma? This is a controversy which cannot be entered into here, and is in the end fruitless from want of a starting-point. But supposing that God has spoken, supposing that we may use the Scriptures for purposes of demonstration, can it be maintained that here dogmatic distinctions paralyse freedom? Was the ancient world any freer when it felt about after God in Pantheism, in Idolatry, in all the strange philosophic groping after a first cause, than we are, when the Church says these fields of inquiry are for all purposes of practical usefulness barred? They are barren of what you seek. God is One, God is Personal, God is Spirit. But in the unity of the Godhead He has told us that there are three distinctions, known as Persons for lack of a better denomination, each of Whom acts upon us in a special way.[1]

Here again, we ask, what has God revealed? If He has revealed truths like this they cannot be unimportant, on the one hand, neither is the revelation of them, on the other, in any sense restrictive. Where the Spirit of the Lord is, there is liberty.

III

But there is a deeper objection to dogmatic distinction in religion, which is undoubtedly felt in some cases. The old grievance lies very deep in human nature: 'Master, thus saying Thou reproachest us also.' The doctrine that a right faith is necessary to salvation is extremely unpalatable to human nature, more especially in its present moods. True, explanations may be accepted which will mitigate the apparent severity of the saying. The way of salvation is, on any showing, extremely difficult to find, and hard to keep when found, and those who have neglected all ordinary precautions have little chance of finding it. Still, he who would preach these fine distinctions as in any way

---

[1] See Wilberforce *The Doctrine of the Incarnation* chap. x p. 236.

necessities of faith, is narrowing the entrance to the
Kingdom of Heaven, and straitening still further the
gate. It was a startling reminder to some of the distance to which we had drifted in this direction, when,
in a recent controversy, an objection was made to put
the word 'Christian' before 'Religious teaching,' in
denoting the character of the instruction to be given
in the State Elementary Schools. Again and again
we find this same objection, now tacitly assumed, now
openly expressed, now masked under the cloak of
Christian courtesy, which leads men in spite of themselves to water down distinctive Christian doctrines,
lest they should be unpalatable to their neighbours,
while they seek to erect on the general dogmatic flux
the flimsy structure of a religion common to all professions, and distinctive of no sect or denomination,
—without foundation, crazy, useless, and despicable: a
Religion, indeed, which no one objects to, because it
has no sufficient character of its own to make it worth
opposing. In old days controversialists used to burn
each other on account of religious differences, now the
tendency is to burn anything, however sacred, which
may raise controversy. Certainly, if we say, 'I believe
in one Lord Jesus Christ, God of God, Light of Light,
very God of very God,' we proclaim that we think
them to be in error who deny the Divinity of our
Lord. If we say, 'I believe in the Holy Ghost,' and
assert it as part and parcel of essential belief, we proclaim that we think them to be in error who do not
hold that belief. If we say with the Church Catechism,
that some Sacraments are necessary to salvation, it may
sound harsh to those who disbelieve in any Sacrament
whatsoever; but we have yet to learn that it is the

duty of the Church to suppress all doctrine which may be unpalatable to any set of persons, and to confine herself to the watery residuum which even a Mohammedan could accept. It was not so when the Truth Himself proclaimed His revelation on earth. More than once He seemed on the point of being left quite alone. On one occasion His own disciples seemed disposed to go away and walk no more with Him. But He did not on that account lower His standard of truth, nor the absolute character of its promulgation. The rich young ruler may go away, like Naaman before him, sorrowful and rich, but the Saviour of the world cannot alter His proclamation or lower His terms of surrender.

Dean Hickes has pointed out, in a narrower controversy than this, 'that no strict doctrines are to be rejected for the severity of their consequences upon men who will not believe them, or if they believe them will not practise them.'[1] People seem to think that the Catholic Faith is a series of propositions, which have gradually been growing on avalanche principles, to be slowly diminished by an advancing civilisation, and the growth of liberal ideas, under the imperious demands of reason. So that any one who insists obstinately on dogmatic truth is as one who would add fresh subjects in a competitive examination, or insist stiffly on old ones. He is narrowing the terms of admission, he is frightening back candidates, he is making that close which ought to be open. Whereas the act of faith is one. It is one great submission to a Person, not an assent to a diminishing series of propositions, which we will accept only at its shallowest point.

[1] Hickes *Two Treatises on Christian Priesthood* Anglo-Cath. Lib. vol. i p. 270.

An objection will occur at once: Why is it that ordinary men are able to get on so well without any speculative or practical knowledge of those dogmatic distinctions which are the stock in trade of the theological mind? Further: Why are such subjects so dry, abstract, and unintelligible, that the average Christian is repelled rather than attracted by them?

As regards the first part of the objection, no doubt Natural Religion and a pure morality are high and beautiful things, in which a man can obtain proficiency without resort to theological distinctions. But Christianity and Christian morality are higher still, and where the higher is possible, a man is to be blamed who feels safe with the lower. We see it, *e.g.*, in the ordinary development of the science of war, how one type of battle-ship is rendered obsolete by the discovery of another of more approved design; how electricity or some new power will revolutionise all that has been in practice before; and so, when altogether a new type of life and fresh developments of his power have been made possible for man, it is idle to say that he may rest satisfied with a lower. Neither in view of the world-progress around him, which carries with it increased temptation, as well as increased opportunity, will he find the problems of life remain stationary, or that he is able to fight the battles which gather to a head in Christianity, with the weapons, however intellectual or delicate, of a higher heathenism. But as regards the second of these objections, it must be remembered, for the right understanding of the things of God, it is necessary to develop a spiritual capacity. The natural, the animal man, *i.e.* the man who views things on that side of his incorporeal nature which is turned towards the world and the flesh, receives not, rejects, the things of the Spirit of God, and he cannot know them, because they are spiritually judged of. But the spiritual man judges of all things by their true standard.[1] We are face to face with a great truth, that for the reception of religious truth a moral perception is necessary. This is no hard saying invented by religious people that they may strut in an assumed superiority, dwelling on a height which is above demonstration, and triumphing over Logic while they sweep the plain with damnatory propositions, and curse all who cannot see with the same eye as themselves.

It has been pointed out that even an ordinary truth of sensation, although the process may be unconscious to us, demands the co-operation of all our personality; that in scientific knowledge, and the knowledge of a person, mental indolence on the one hand, which allows men to acquiesce in premature conclusions, the idolising or the under-estimating of a person on the other, which hinder our knowledge, must both be discarded.[2]

In an eclipse of the sun, visible only in far distant regions, it would be idle for the common reporter of a London newspaper to sit at his door and make observations on a matter which interests a good many of his fellow-citizens. He would first have to study the preliminary requisites for right observation; to train his powers of sight and contemplation; to make long study of scientific Bibles, in which the exact knowledge of long years of observation is stored up; and then to take a tedious journey to Norway, or Japan, or Australia, and there await the manifestation of a moment,

[1] 1 Cor. ii 14 15.
[2] Illingworth *Personality Human and Divine* Lecture v.

with every help which scientific apparatus and the latest improvements of astronomical research could provide, and then patiently to submit to disappointment, or such partial unveiling of the mysteries of Nature as might be revealed to him. Spiritual observations, in like manner, make great demands on the observer, and can only be made under spiritual conditions. How can a man who only reads his daily newspaper, or devotes himself entirely to art or science or business, be expected to appreciate nice theological distinctions? How can a man, that is, who contemptuously ignores all that previous study and revelation has stored up for him, ignorant of the limitations or field of inquiry, be expected to attain to a practical knowledge in a very difficult department? He needs special training and spiritual aptitude, in both of which he is deficient. There are traces of this truth to be found both in the Bible and in daily practice. S. John Baptist emerges from his distant home, untaught in the schools, unversed in dialectic, to proclaim the mystery, 'Behold the Lamb of God, Which taketh away the sin of the world,' which was hid from the more learned Rabbis and Pharisaical disputants. Our blessed Lord thanks His heavenly Father that He has 'hid these things from the wise and prudent, and revealed them unto babes.' The apostle whom Jesus loves is the apostle of the profoundest mysteries. Bishop Lightfoot has said: 'Gifted with the eye of the Spirit, I say, for in vain the heavens are riven asunder, and the glory streams forth, and all things are flooded with light, if the capacity of vision be absent. God be thanked, the most absolute childlike faith has not unfrequently been found united with the highest scientific intellect. We in this place [Cambridge] have never yet lacked bright examples of such a union, and God grant we never may. But what right have we to expect it as a matter of course? What claim do the most brilliant mathematical faculties or the keenest scholarly instincts give to a man to speak with authority on the things of the Spirit? Are we not told, on an authority before which we bow, that a special faculty is needed for this special knowledge? that eye hath not seen, and ear hath not heard, that only the Spirit of God, the Spirit which He vouchsafed to His Son, knoweth the things of God? Believe it, this spiritual faculty is an infinitely subtle and delicate mechanism; you cannot trifle with it, cannot roughly handle it, cannot neglect and suffer it to rust from disuse, without infinite peril to yourselves. Nothing, not the highest intellectual gains, can compensate you for its injury or its loss.'[1] Accordingly, he who hopes to read Holy Scripture aright must first place himself in the spiritual atmosphere by prayer; an adult, before he is admitted to Holy Baptism, must take a far journey away from the disturbing element of his sins, and prepare, if he is to profit by the gift aright. So with Holy Communion, so with all spiritual gifts, the recipient must place himself first in a spiritual attitude of acceptance. So that when the ordinary man states that spiritual phenomena are invisible to him, he is stating a simple fact. When he goes on to say that they are the hallucinations of those who read fancies into facts, he is guilty of an unscientific disparagement of a class of phenomena which he has disqualified himself from registering. When he calls upon all sensible men to join in this disparagement, it is

[1] Lightfoot *Cambridge Sermons* pp. 305 307.

as if the unartistic mind were bidding us employ a universal drab, or the unmusical ear were bidding us renounce Beethoven and Mozart in favour of the strains of a drum-and-fife band. It is the mathematician denouncing poetry, the poet deriding the man of figures. Spiritual phenomena, if they had been seen only by a few carefully accredited witnesses, would have been far too valuable for us to dismiss them as unattainable; but when there is the rich heritage of those who have lived and died, and benefited richly their race, in the full contemplation of spiritual truth, then the power and truth of spiritual phenomena witnessed by the spiritual man remain as a fact and a possession which we can neither disbelieve nor affect to treat as an unimportant detail appertaining only to a select and highly trained few. In view of the great truths of God, in view of the importance of the issues at stake, and the numerous obstacles that come between us and their realisation, we shall find that orthodoxy, so called, is no higher form of self-opinionated obstinacy, but the careful obedience of one who has marked well the warning, 'Take heed therefore how ye hear,' and has shrunk from the presumption which tampers with authority, and the despair which waits upon wilful error.

CHAPTER III

MORALITY

'When once the obedience, if required, is certain, the child should be very early put for periods of practice in complete command of itself; set on the bare-backed horse of its own will, and left to break it by its own strength.'

In a practical age, and among practical people, the first requisite in Religion to the average man is that he should be able to find in it something to do him good. There is perhaps hardly any couplet which so concisely expresses the popular opinion as to the real region in which true Religion can be tested than those well-known, if somewhat shallow, lines of Pope:

' For modes of faith let priests and bigots fight,
He can't be wrong whose life is in the right.'

And in the same way many will regard the upright life of an unbaptized person as an unanswerable argument against the validity of Baptism, and the integrity of an infidel as destructive of the obligation of a creed —forgetting that the strong man who can dispense all his life with medical aid does not thereby prove the worthlessness of all medical science; nor that the man who never complains outwardly of ill-health necessarily shows that he was free from inward pains and complications from which medicine might have relieved him.

Still the great underlying truth remains, that there must be something wrong about a Religion which does not help a man to be better in his moral life; that a pure and upright life does bear witness to a religious influence of one kind or another; and, further, that one main aim of Religion is to help a man to steer safely through the almost overwhelming difficulties which surround his life from his cradle to his grave, and to make him something more than one who pronounces shibboleth with an ecclesiastical accent; a conscientious, honest, and upright member of society.

This must be one main aim of Religion, as we shall endeavour to show presently, but at the same time it is not the only one. There is one side of Religion which finds its chief expression in worship and praise which has to do with God. Worship is an idea not easily to be reduced to its underlying principles:—why God should require from men the constant expression of their sense of His worthiness; why God should need the praise as part of His perfection, while He teaches us to repudiate it in ourselves as ministering to our imperfection! Still, as we know, this forms a large part of Religion, simply setting forth the praises of God without any regard in the first place to the fact that it is good and beneficial to ourselves so to do. All things as they live and move unconsciously carry out God's will. 'The heavens declare the glory of God: and the firmament sheweth His handy-work.' Wind and storm fulfil His word. And so man, who has the gift of free-will, and can consciously withhold and proffer his service, must needs send up to God his sense of his acquiescence in the perfection, his joy in the beauty, his wonder in the completeness, of God's great design.

I

It is necessary to recognise this aspect of Religion, first, as the expression of a relation due from man to God; but having made this recognition, we return at once to that which common consent demands from Religion, the presence of which indicates its power, the absence of which deprives it of its most vital claims, that Religion must be 'the power of God unto salvation,' that it must help a man to be morally good, and to resist those powers which without its aid would prove too much for human strength. It is one of the saddest spectacles on which the eye of the educated man can rest, to see the magnificent array of moral systems, model republics, Utopias—the ideal conduct of ideal men reposing in the lumber-room of unpractical beliefs: broken in their delicate springs, twisted out of shape by the hard road of prosaic life, and the clumsiness of human nature, unable to handle without breaking a machinery too refined for its rough usage. Not a new carriage was wanted, but a new driver. Not fresh machinery, but a force to make supple these stubborn fingers, which seemed only able to break and twist it before. God had revealed this in measure to His ancient people the Jews; He had at least shown them the moral flaw which weakened all their efforts after better things; while with the dawn of Christianity we see the deliberate effort made to supply the deficiency, not merely in a fresh scheme of moral excellence, however elaborately drawn, but in the development of the power of the will,—in forces to prevent it from being warped by passion, in strength to help it to carry out into active experience those requirements of life which hitherto the majority of men had allowed to lie unused on the shelf, as unpractical and beyond their powers. Those who come to the religion of Jesus Christ hoping to find in it a power to make them good will not come in vain. The Gospel is to them 'good news,' as presenting a practical scheme of active morality; and the point and aim of all its efficacy will be found to be centred in the development of the human will. So S. Paul speaks of 'the power that worketh in us.'[1] Or again he says: 'I can do all things through Christ which strengtheneth me.'[2] Or again: 'It is God which worketh in you both to will and to do of His good pleasure.'[3] So again S. Peter tells us that 'divine power hath given unto us all things that pertain unto life and godliness.'[4] And here we see how Holy Scripture seems to speak out of the very heart of a country which had hitherto been the object of much speculation and research, but which expedition after expedition of trained moralists had failed to penetrate. Even now there are found many who doubt these conclusions and question these discoveries, as the claim is put forward under the name of divine inspiration, to indicate the secret whereby a man can be that which he desires to be, and attain to moral excellence as a fact, instead of admiring it simply as a beautiful ideal. The secret is opened up in a right understanding of the geography of human nature; we

---

[1] Eph. iii 20.
[2] Phil. iv 13.
[3] Phil. ii 13.
[4] 2 S. Pet. i 3.

are shown the region called the spirit, distinct obviously from the body, and distinguishable also from the soul with its provinces and departments. We trace the great river of man's personality, and the historical consequences which have resulted in human action from the formation of the land, as the soul is swayed hither and thither by its position of contiguity to the Flesh on the one hand, and to the Spirit on the other. Here we trace the agony of conflict in man regenerate and in a state of grace, but still brought face to face with concupiscence, temptation, and irresolute action. And when these conditions have been indicated, we are better able to see the reason of man's tragic history. A region so vast, so broken up, which lends itself to so many enemies that war against the soul, can never be maintained in its integrity without a strong government, assisted by helps which in itself it would be powerless to produce. And so God Almighty has provided this central power in the will, which can be indefinitely strengthened, or else hopelessly degraded; which even when most threatened and oppressed can always count on all the reinforcement of Heaven, but, on the other hand, may be degraded to be the tool of passion, and be driven to sanction as a slave that which as a king it was bound to control. We shall find in the will the very seat and centre of all religious energy, and that Religion does not play us false in this particular, but really helps us to be good, by placing firmly on its throne the imperial will, and giving it a power to rule over all those important headstrong and sometimes turbulent feudatories which go to make up the completeness of a man's self.

This is the chieftain whom Religion is bound to win over; and until that has been done, all systems of morals, however beautiful, are liable to fail, simply from the difficulty they have in finding for themselves a home in a region where there is little respect for law and order.

It needs no great power of introspection to see what a difficult combination of forces is marshalled under the authority of the will, which are of the utmost importance to Religion if they can be utilised, but a deadly weight of opposition should they prove to be antagonistic.

There is the spirit, delicate and sensitive, capable of the most exquisite pleasure, and responsive to the slightest touch of Heaven, yet capable in its degradation of deluding a man to his fall, leading him on through pride and presumption, until, under the guidance of a perverted spirit, he can go conscientiously wrong, and while steering by the compass strike upon the submerged rock, unaware of an imperceptible deflection in what he trusted as a heaven-sent guide. Or there is the lower part of our incorporeal nature called the soul, the region of self-consciousness, poised between the seen and the unseen worlds. Seated here, the personality casts its eyes over the untold resources of mind, or listens to memory, as it comes like a troubadour of romance to the open gate to sing its lays of olden time, or turns to watch imagination engaged in painting its pictures, or stops to drink in the beauty of sentiment as it floats in upon the senses in every form of excitement and delicious joy. The mere rapture of being alive is enough to rouse a sense of restless exultation, such as we see in the quick vitality of a child, with whom to live is to move and to move is to live.

> 'A simple child
> That lightly draws its breath,
> And feels its life in every limb—
> What should it know of death?'

Or in such a power of vitality as comes to a man when life has been restored to him after some serious illness, and although shattered and weak he feels himself to be alive, the sceptre once more in his hand, and the resources of existence open to him to follow up some intellectual triumph, or perform some physical feat, or simply bask in the light and joy of the sun. Certainly as we gaze at these forces, which march under the banner of the soul to place themselves at the service of their feudal lord, we feel what a moment it was when God paused, and God deliberated, and God breathed, and man became a living soul.

And there is all that motley troop marching under the badge of what is loosely known as the body, excellent servants, but somewhat turbulent and unruly, ready to break out as private marauders, and turn a crusade into a foray, ready to clamour down reason and defy the spirit until the will itself trembles on the throne, and is at last driven to sanction that which it seemed powerless to avert.

It is a bitter experience when Phaethon begins to find the horses which he started to drive gradually slipping out of his control. No one likes to be run away with, to lose power or the ability to stop or to alter his course. There are certain periods in life, shorter or longer, which we look back upon, when we had the reins in our hands, and we were our own masters, and acquired a momentum for good or evil. Some have to look back to a catastrophe as the violent and merciful check to a downward course. But the formation of character for all of us has had to do with the power of the will to regulate and govern; experience has helped or injured, in so far as the will has listened to, or neglected, wise counsellors and the inner light of conscience. Goodness has grown into holiness in proportion as Religion has given strength and purpose to this power within to curb the passions, to choose advisers, to arm the executive, to proclaim a policy, in all the power of a life, in which a man not only knows what is right, but is able faithfully to carry it out.

II

If it be true then that Religion produces right action by influencing and strengthening the will, this means that our energetic co-operation is required, or, in Scriptural language, that we must 'work out our own salvation.' Religion, as it has been revealed to us, is no dreamy sentiment, in which a man languidly acquiesces, as he drifts down the stream of life. Life will not go on automatically, we cannot trust things to fall into their place naturally, the spirit, such as we have described it, to remain unclouded, and faithfully transmit to the will the warning of the coming storm, or the light-giving sunshine, or the bracing air. We cannot trust to the soul simply to push its way, throwing off evil by its vigorous vitality, and shedding from its stunted growth the blight, mildew, and decay which fasten on it. We cannot trust to the senses simply to do their duty and go, to the appetites to discharge their functions according to right reason and retire, to the impulses to take up what is good, and drop what is bad, and this simply because we are living in a fallen world, and that the Fall has jarred the whole mechanism of life. The will has a flaw in its spring which impairs its vigour; it has been played with so often that it is weak. The spirit is subject to cloud and fog. Merely to drift along, trusting to common sense, or to prudence, or to ethical maxims, is to be shattered on the rocks. Neither can we draw in the motive force that we need from a carefully prepared environment. We have not secured an unruffled progress, if we have laid down a smooth road stored with stimulating energy. There are break-downs in the path where everything has been made easy, in the many-roomed house, the carefully selected surroundings, the refined atmosphere, as well as in the rough road, the scanty opportunities, the squalid surroundings, and the presence of moral ugliness. In the environment of Eli's house, Hophni and Phinehas topple down to scandal and shame, and the child Samuel rises through goodness and purity to be the prophet of the Lord. There are saints in Cæsar's household, and a devil in the Apostolic College. We cannot drift, trusting to the current of life to take us straight. A man without principles is sure to go wrong. He has nothing on which Religion can fasten, nothing whereby God can attach Himself to the life, which is tottering to its fall without Him. Religion fails because men and women are so wanting in seriousness, because they seem so little able to appreciate the immense importance of life. They seem to be like a tourist who is driven round to see sights for an hour, just to look at things in which he takes no real interest, and which will have no bearing on his better life to-morrow. Men skim about as the whim takes them, or join in the large field of amusements opened to them, or dabble in books, and bend all their lives towards some miserably inadequate purpose, and then they are gone. Life has its hours, which never come again, its opportunities, which are all too easily ruined, its many diverging roads, which it was incumbent on them to distinguish with deliberate choice, and which they may have to find out again by a shaping of circumstances very like necessity. It requires no little effort of the will to assimilate what is good, and reject what is bad : to feel the responsibility of self-government, and the importance of principle. Want of seriousness, want of vigour, want of a robust development of mind, may load men for life with a burden which they would fain be rid of; may tax their tributary powers to the verge of rebellion, so that they cannot do the things that they would. If the will loses control, other powers will seize the reins of government; we commence by drifting, we end by finding ourselves in the merciless arms of a strong current. We began by going with the stream, we end by being sucked into the whirlpool. Tito Milemma, it has been said, is the type of the average man. He begins by shrinking from doing a disagreeable thing, his naturally soft, easy nature falls back aghast at the mere semblance of giving pain to any one. To refuse to do what he feels to be wrong may mean a cruel unkindness or a disappointment to a friend. His will is warped, it gives way, it is bent and made unreliable for future action. The next time a greater concession is made against his inclination, until power passes out of his hands, and he finds himself doing cruel actions, mean actions, despicable actions, criminal actions, when at first he only shrank from the pain of doing an unpleasant thing. It would be well for every one if he realised how much depends on the action of the will. There it stands plied with suggestions and besieged with importunity; it must decide, it cannot shift the responsibility. Christ stands before the judgment-seat of Pilate; Pilate may wash his hands as much as he pleases, he may cause the innocent One to be scourged, he may send Him to Herod, he may stop to listen to the warnings of his wife, still the moment must come when all this temporising has fatally weakened the supreme authority within the man, while he has whetted the eagerness of those who marked the gradual sapping of resolution. It must come. Listen to the lame conclusion! He is innocent, but crucify Him! Listen to the merciless verdict of every unthinking Christian child, who in spite of the washing and the protests, and the visible longing for the higher course, pitilessly says, 'Suffered under Pontius Pilate'—it began with timidity, it went on with irresolution, it was consummated in an unworthy concession, the authority of the will is gone, and I have given up Christ to His enemies, when I thought I could drift past the corner, and admire Him and conciliate His enemies at the same time. We must beware of drifting, there are corners in every life, which require careful steering. If we have not studied our course beforehand, or tested the vessel's power, and seen how she answers the helm, we shall not do it when the angry spray of ridicule is blinding our eyes, and the shock of the waves of opposition makes us stagger. It is the voice of Religion which speaks out of the heart of the well-known collect, 'Stir up, we beseech Thee, O Lord, the wills of Thy faithful people,' for only the well-governed life can hope to weather the angry sea of this troublesome world.

In like manner, if we may not drift along, trusting to a blind chance, and to an automatic salvation, we become conscious of another danger which threatens us, the danger of acquiescing in a divided authority. There is a tendency which must be resolutely met, towards a dismemberment of the empire of our own personality, thereby putting whole tracts outside the government of the will: of reproducing, within the little limits of our own life, that 'fatal divorce which was known to exist in the ancient world between the various departments of life, the public and the private, the moral and the religious, the intellectual and the sensual.'

The apostle has emphasised this point when he says, 'Whether therefore ye eat, or drink, or whatsoever ye do, do all to the glory of God.'[1] It cannot be allowed for one moment by a Christian that any one department of his life, any one of his manifold activities, should stand outside the dominion of the will. It is not only that thereby God is robbed of His rights to our whole being; it is not only that a double empire is set up in our life, but also the mere fact that we have lost power, or do not exercise moral control, over any one part of our life, is in itself a source of danger. When our old pirate ancestors had done the work for which they were summoned, they were allowed then to settle off the coast of Kent; but they soon found that

[1] 1 Cor. x 31.

there were riches to plunder on the mainland, that the dividing stream was narrow, and the opposition weak, and in the end they became masters of that territory from which it was vainly desired to exclude them. So it is a source of danger to our spiritual life to allow rude passions to remain passive but unconquered. It is not wise to allow our will to be tampered with even in little matters. The animal within must always know its master, the world without must always feel the administration of government extending to the very edge of the empire pitted against it. The devil must not be allowed a foothold in the domain of life. And hence the importance to every one of rule, of a definite mode and system of life, out of which he will not allow himself to be driven. Is there any one point in which I allow my will to be beaten? It matters not whether it be in a great or little matter, if I allow myself to be beaten in it, as regards self-discipline. Sloth, for instance, is a deadly sin, from which a Christian man would naturally shrink. Does he feel and know that his will is insensibly warped in that direction every time that he allows himself to be overcome, against his will, even by a venial indolence? Lust is a deadly sin, from which he shrinks with loathing and with dread. Does he know that his will is being insensibly warped towards surrender every time he surrenders his imagination against the pleadings of conscience, or allows himself under specious pretences to dip into the degrading literature which mistakes indecency for boldness, and a nasty realism for a strength of delineation? Anger is a deadly sin. Does he know that he is drifting towards it when he allows himself in bursts of uncontrolled temper? Gluttony is a deadly sin.

Does he know that he is preparing chains for his neck when he allows his will to be warped towards extravagance and costly living, which are rendering him incapable of enduring the hardness which belongs to the good soldier of Jesus Christ? Envy is a deadly sin. Does he know, once more, that he is allowing his will to be warped towards it, when he gives way to ungenerous rivalry and unworthy jealousy of the power of an antagonist? Pride is a deadly sin, towards which vanity, which feeds on self without being satisfied, and a conceit which self-love deems to be pardonable, may only too surely drag him. Avarice is a deadly sin, towards which unchecked greediness and selfishness may lure him on. We cannot keep the will only to be let out on great occasions to reinforce some other determining power, too weak to act without it. If passion or caprice take the reins, the will must always just be asked, even if its consent appear to be a grave formality. And hence the importance of seeing to it that life does not go on unchecked, moved by agents who treat the will with only scant respect. In great things and in little, the will must be set firmly on the throne, and the passions and impulses made to feel its power. It is recorded in the Life of Charles Kingsley, that he would delight to go up to a dog, tearing at his chain, chafing, and savage, and impatient, and force him to go back to his kennel by the sheer power of his will. He liked, as it were, to feel his will, to feel the power which it gave him over creatures. And the resolute will is a power which in the end carries everything before it. It can surmount obstacles, triumph over ill-health, survive defeat, outlive temptation, never know when it is beaten. Macaulay describes the power of will which can surmount obstacles apparently fatal to success. 'At Landen,' he says, 'two poor sickly beings, who in a rude state of society would have been regarded as too puny to bear any part in combats, were the souls of two great armies. In some heathen countries they would have been exposed while infants. In Christendom they would, six hundred years earlier, have been sent to some quiet cloister. But their lot had fallen at a time when men had discovered that the strength of the muscles is far inferior in value to the strength of the mind. It is probable that, among the hundred and twenty thousand soldiers who were marshalled round Neerwinden, under all the standards of Western Europe, the two feeblest in body were the hunchback dwarf who urged forward the fiery onset of France, and the asthmatic skeleton who covered the slow retreat of England.'[1] In more modern times, we may hear Sheil, with his voice like 'a tin kettle, battered about from place' to place, commanding the House of Commons with innate eloquence, triumphing over obstacles.[2] Or we may see S. Paul made an example of patience, S. Peter of bravery, a Magdalene of purity, by the power of consecrated will. But it is a power which we must not tamper with. Here too it is true, that he that is faithful in that which is least, is faithful also in much. It is in the daily struggle with indolence, self-indulgence, evil suggestion, and low ideals, in the daily victory over self, under the daily imposed bridle of rule and principle, that we prepare for the great actions of life, and make possible its noblest victories. While, on the other hand, a will which has

---

[1] Macaulay *History of England* chap. xx vol. vii pp. 32 33.
[2] Justin M'Carthy *History of our own Times* vol. i p. 34.

been disobeyed over and over again in some one of those many outlying departments which it ought to govern, gives its orders in vain to passions which have learned their own power, to wishes which have gained their own way, to faculties which have learned the fatal lesson of disobedience, and to listen to the call of inclination before the command of duty.

III

It is in strengthening this empire of the will that we shall trace the most characteristic exercise of Religion. Any form of moral integrity for some, and the highest form of morality for all, are only possible through Religion. Religion, if once accepted and practised, will tend to minimise that distressing gulf between the good which a man knows that he ought to do, and the actual good which he does. And this is not effected by any mutilation or suppression, except in cases where actual spiritual disease may have made the treatment imperative. A man by long indulgence in vicious courses, and persistent degradation of the will, may have brought himself to such a state that his salvation depends on his cutting off his right foot or plucking out his right eye. But the normal action of Religion is to help a man, in the truest sense of the phrase, to be himself. He need suppress no faculty, or allow any part of his rich endowment to become useless through neglect. It would be comparatively easy to carry on life under these conditions, without the aid of special grace, by means of a strong will and firm resolution, as the Stoics were able to do in the state of insensibility to strong emotions to which they were able to reduce themselves in the midst of the pains and pleasures of life. Religion would seem to set itself not so much toward suppressing the body, or blindly submitting the intelligence to a higher authority, or placing the man in an artificial environment, as towards rendering the man, born as he is, placed as he is, tempted as he is, perfect; so that while maintaining each part of his composite nature complete and entire, all may be brought in their working under the power of the will, with the ultimate aim of bringing into captivity every thought to the obedience of Christ.

The aim of Religion, then, once more, is to arm the executive within a man, to set up unimpaired the dominion of the will over the component parts and passions of his composite being. And its first function in this respect will be to show the will its own power. From time to time, and from various quarters, attempts are made to persuade the will that after all it is not free to order or capable of commanding, that in this sense or in that it is a slave, must do as it is bidden, and not prepare for itself the inevitable mortification which is bound to follow in one who gives orders which are never obeyed, and never can be obeyed.

The will, we are told, is hopelessly bound, at least in one direction, by what is known as heredity—a man, that is, is born with certain tendencies inherited from his parents; these have filtered down into his nature certain traits and characteristics as definitely marked as those outward peculiarities which are known under the head of 'family likeness'; that the sins of the fathers are, on the highest authority, visited on the children; and that society when punishing a murderer would with much more justice punish a murderer's ancestors, from whom this homicidal tendency has been inherited; or that Religion is engaged in ploughing the sand, when it is trying to persuade a person to be pure who never can be pure, by reason of hereditary taint; to be temperate, when he has inherited a craving for strong drink from a drunken mother; to be honest, when for generations his ancestors have lived on plunder; to be believing, when the intellect had received a strong sceptical bias from an atheist father. The will is in no sense free in this direction: it is bound down by the dead hand of an ancestry long laid in the grave; moral responsibility, religious effort, spiritual possibilities, must all be judged in the light of this well-known fact, or else pay the penalty in dismal failure and hopeless disappointment.

'I was born bad, I have lived bad, and I shall die bad, in all human probability,' is the melancholy epitaph which a soul writes over the grave of his free-will, which has been pressed out of life by the misuse of the doctrine of heredity. Temperament as a predisposing cause to sin and of various kinds of moral impotence, is a milder form of the same doctrine. The doctrine of divine gifts, even, is pressed into the service, so that a man will justify himself in doing his work badly because, as he says, he has no gift for it; or in not doing a thing at all because he cannot do it well. The large number of men who are diligently engaged in burying the one talent which God gave them are examples of this; because it is one talent they bury it; if it had been five or ten they would have done their best to develop them.

'Temperament,' no doubt, in itself, like heredity, is a fact which we cannot deny, and plays a large part in the formation of character. Different individuals are sent into the world with a different mingling of tendencies, feelings, and aims, known as temperament. In some there is a tendency to ease and light-heartedness; in some to moroseness; in some to anger; in some to gratification of the appetites; in some to indolence. Like as we are to one another superficially, we differ in reality as much as the leaves differ from one another, although they hang on the same tree. We differ according to our temperament, according to the mingling of qualities in our character, so that a man may even allege temperament as an excuse for what he calls his natural faults, while the will is warned in no uncertain tones, that any attempt to dictate, alter, or amend in this direction will be met with decided opposition, and must end in failure. Perfection, such as it is, must in such a case be the best that can be done with a man ill-tempered, indolent, or otherwise morally deficient. The city of God within the soul must be allowed to have its Alsatia in which the King's writ does not run.

Besides these inner barriers raised against the empire of the will, a large place must be allowed, we are told, for the strong power of environment. A man may follow the guidance of his enlightened will so long as he is not otherwise drawn by his environment. A man, after all, is very much what circumstances make him. There are loadstone rocks which no ship can pass without being dashed to pieces. There are sirens whose voice will lure any mariner, however careful, to throw himself into the waves, if fate leads him to navigate these seas. Virtue depends largely on the healthy surroundings and the wide elbow-room, while vice is the natural product of the crowded attic and the filthy alley. Chameleon-like, a man will take his colour from his surroundings, and no power of the will, however firmly wielded, will make a child pure who has grown up in squalor, or honest who has been surrounded from his earliest years with vice. While, on the other hand, honesty is easy to one who is never in want; truthfulness to one who is never put in fear by his companions; modesty to one who is brought up in sheltered refinement.

Religion must do something more than strengthen the will; it must set itself to make environment. For on that, more than on deliberate choice, will depend, at least for a large number, the issues of life.

With others, once more, the will is represented as being suspended by God Almighty Himself. At some period in life a sudden turn to God has come, after which moment any further fall into sin is impossible. From the first this soul had been irresistibly predestined to eternal life. In spite of itself, salvation was designed for it, and now the grace received is indefectible. The helm is fast tied down towards the harbour of righteousness; no gale can alter its course, no menace of opposing force can deflect it, no indolence of pilot, no voice of the sirens, no weariness in welldoing, can possibly affect it. The will has ceased to be free, salvation is forced upon it by a deliberate choice or by a divine election, and life is henceforth drawn along, it does not move of itself. The captain is not helped and instructed by the pilot, he is superseded by him; and God has suspended in His creature the exercise of free-will.

As against each and all of these several perversions of several truths, Religion sets itself first of all to maintain the freedom and responsibility of the will. As against self, with all its awful drag and tendency, Religion, recognising what has to be recognised, says to the will, Not only are you free, but you are supreme. As regards this outside environment, Religion says once more, Not only are you free, but the environment, whatever it is, is the environment out of which your perfection will be wrought. While as to God Himself, Religion bows the head in reverence, and says that the same God who will not condemn me without myself, will also not save me without myself, and adores Him for that love which respects in us that image of His own divine Nature, our own free-will.

> 'Our wills are ours, we know not how,
> Our wills are ours, to make them Thine.'

Let us examine this a little more in detail. As to heredity, of course it would be idle to deny the underlying facts, which are palpable and open to everybody. A whole stock of temptations crowds upon one man, which are quite absent from another. One will do without effort what another can scarcely attain to, even when he is held in tight by bit and bridle. These are the obvious and obtrusive indications of inherited predisposition to vice, which is the despair and puzzle of all moralists. But we know that heredity with all its mysterious power was known to Him Who has promulgated the highest and most perfect code of morality which has been given to the world, Who reversed the estimate of ages in pronouncing poverty to be blessed, Who ran counter to the feelings and the experience of mankind in refusing to regard mourning and sorrow as a curse, Who plunged into the circle staked off as vice, and came back triumphantly bearing 'humility,' which He had rescued from its cruel covering of little-mindedness, and displayed it as a virtue; Who spoke of purity of heart, of the unspeakable blessing of tenderness, yielding submission, and patience as regards others. He knew the centuries of selfishness, of mutiny and slavery, which lay behind those passions which He was trying to mould into conformity with the Christian life. He knew the grand schemes of morality, whose barriers against the sea of vice had been torn and swept away, and tossed as straw before the wind, as the inflowing tide of passion leapt upon the wall.

'Video meliora proboque
Deteriora sequor'

floated mournfully in the breeze over the wreckage of life, as a melancholy tribute to the irresistible power of heredity. And knowing this, He instituted at the very forefront of this scheme the Sacrament of Baptism. Baptism, we may almost say, owes its existence to heredity; it presupposes it, deals with it. Baptism is the initial force which is brought to bear on a soul by nature born in sin. It is the recognition that unassisted human nature is incapable of the higher forms of Christian morality, in some cases of even its most elementary forms. It recognises that to attempt to dispense with it is but labouring to construct a rope of sand, or carve a statue out of crumbling stone. A man by nature born in sin requires to be made capable of perfecting the highest Christian virtues. Neither must we suppose that in the system of Christ there is any attempt to ignore heredity. Before Baptism and after Baptism alike, different men are differently disposed to different blemishes, defects, and sins. One has to wrestle with a fierce irritation, another with a corrupting sensuality, another with a deadly sloth, another with congenital dishonesty. Only in Holy Baptism these tendencies emerge transformed into capacities for good. Irritation passes into judicial anger or resentment; sensuality into a healthy development of body, entirely controlled by the will; sloth into peace and patience; a desire to attain dishonestly into a desire to profit in accordance with the will of God. By Baptism a man is enabled to be himself.

So with the kindred difficulty of temperament. Temperament may not only be resisted, it may be utilised for good. Jacob the supplanter, always seeking to push out other living things, and seize all the soil for his own roots, the sky and air for his own health, all the room on each side of him for his own growth, who buys birthrights from hungry men, and snatches blessings from blinded old age, he may, if he will, become Israel, the prince who has power with God and with men, and may prevail in many a generous conflict. He Who made us, Who so mixed our natures, has also redeemed us, has given us a power stronger than nature; and He has brought that Redemption home to us by Sacraments through the power of the Holy Spirit. We cannot alter our nature, but we can utilise it. The long ridges of shifting sand along the low coast-line may seem but a flimsy defence against the waves which threaten to submerge the country. The sand flying before the wind may seem to scatter sterility over the pastures and to damage the crops. But a few tufts of grass here, and trees there, bind this shifting barrier into nature's own bulwark. We cannot change our nature, but we can spiritualise it, and energetically refuse to cower before the boasting tyranny of temperament. Environment also no less must give way before the power of Religion. God, as if to show His omnipotence, brings saints out of Cæsar's household, and gathers together a flock amidst the abominations of Corinth, the corruption of Antioch, and the privileged sin of Ephesus. Still, if we look we can see the New Jerusalem coming down from heaven as a bride adorned for her husband. It settles down on the squalid district of the city, where the long rows of featureless houses have swallowed up the green fields and the outward signs of God's presence, and there with its material fabric speaks dimly yet plainly of King's courts, with its bell rejoicing with them that do rejoice, and weeping with them that weep; with its Sacraments of strength, its refinement, its beauties, its patriotism, its corporate life. Here is an environment within an environment. 'He maketh Him families like a flock.' Or if it be some poor struggling life surrounded by evil, with sights of shame and sounds of horror, where the very atmosphere is tainted by moral death,—to him, too, descends the heavenly city, the New Jerusalem, in the power of prayer. God in the environment of His Holy Church, within whose influence we can place ourselves at will, has supplied us with a power which can countervail the forces of evil. There are other influences besides good rooms, good books, good drainage, good water, good exercise—all of them, it is true, excellent things where they can be had, but which will not of themselves make the foul clean, nor elevate the victims of passion, nor purify the morally base. There is a wider and deeper environment known unto God, in which He wraps the son whom He loves. 'Thou shalt hide them privily by Thine own presence from the provoking of all men: Thou shalt keep them secretly in Thy tabernacle from the strife of tongues.'[1] Still we may pray for the timid, struggling soul, 'Lord, I pray Thee, open his eyes, that he may see';[2] and the mountain will be full of horses and fire and chariots of fire that wait upon the servant of God. In an age of panacea and experiment, we work away at some new device, and start a company, as it were, to float it. We run a union to exploit some new scheme. We form a guild to prop up some new remedy. One plan treads fast upon the heels of another. We burn what we adored, and we adore what we burned with startling rapidity. And then we find those evils which so disturb us had already been foreseen and provided for in the comprehensive scheme of Christ's goodness. Obedience would carry us further than we think. Authority would save us from many disappointing

[1] Psalm xxxi 22.   [2] 2 Kings vi 17.

shoals which have swallowed up whole ship-loads of fair-sounding schemes. Human nature is a complex and difficult thing. We see its course mapped out in history, we trace it in ourselves, and as it passes us in the moving panorama of life. But there are strands of rope concealed from us, mechanisms and motive powers which we do not always calculate upon. Human depravity, divine Sanctification, Predestination on the part of God, Free-will on the part of man, Justification, the Atonement, the pleading of Sacrifice: these may be only names to us, or labels of barren theological discussion, when suddenly we find them alive with hidden force, where we least expected it. Powers which we did not calculate upon upset our conclusions; barriers which we had not foreseen intercept our purpose. And God triumphs at our cost, and succeeds where we have failed.

The problem which Religion has to face is not the problem of life in the abstract, but of life menaced with danger, beset by sin, and confronted with death. Men are being driven away, some by their passions, some by false ideals, many more by the mirage which plays upon their path and lures them to destruction. Our safety consists in setting on a firm basis the sovereignty of the will: in living a life formed on principle, and well regulated in its aims; which insists that there shall be no divided allegiance within, but that every part of our composite nature, in its varied functions and activities, shall render feudal service to its sovereign lord. And as we remember that once in the history of the world a perfect Man lived a perfect life, and called upon all who love Him to do the same, we shall feel, amidst all the perplexities of the path, and the uncertainty of conflicting duties, that we may ask in confident expectation of an answer, and in some hope of succour, not only, 'What would Jesus Christ have done?' but, 'What will Jesus Christ now help us to do?'

CHAPTER IV

THE HIGHER LIFE

> 'It is comparatively easy to train any one to make the best of himself; it is a much more difficult matter to induce him to make that self better.'

CHRISTIANITY, as taught to the world by Jesus Christ, is, we instinctively feel, a great deal more than a new system of morality. It is not a new lesson to be learned, it is rather a new life to be lived.

The function of Morality, as we were considering in the last chapter, is to help a man to move without risk, and to live without disaster in a world stored with valuable yet highly dangerous materials. It teaches him in his childish eagerness that he must master the elementary lesson of how not to touch; or he must learn how to temper in the right proportions that which either in excess or defect may very easily pass into a serious blemish on his character. He must learn to bring everything up to the standard of duty instead of the whim of inclination, and so to get all that is good out of this life and throw off what is bad, and develop a rightly adjusted character.

Christianity, it is true, traverses the same ground, strengthening at the same time the motive of duty, by the further motive of obedience to a voice and devotion to a Person, while the individual is enabled with power from on high to deal with the disturbing, overmastering passions, which mocked the call of duty, and forced him to choose the worse course, even while his higher self confidently approved the better.

But having sought to make this basis sure, Christianity lifts a man higher. It is absolutely necessary that there should be this elevation into the purer atmosphere, where no smoke and dust darken the air, where no earth-born clouds confuse the vision and stupefy the senses. But then beyond this, by reason of a strong morality, there is a fresh departure and a new life, only possible to those who have made the ascent. Now, instead of the restraint of morality, there is freedom: freedom to do things which are only possible in that bright air. If before he has learned not to touch, here he has to learn how to reach out all round him with the most complete freedom. If there below he had to temper, measure, and adjust, here he has to widen more and more his capacity for that which is waiting to overflow his whole being with a stream which knows no intermittence.

And yet it would be a mistake to think that a Christian, provided that he is moral, may lose himself in a wide field of rapturous ecstasy. Below there are the fires of energy, vigorously fed, carefully restrained, according to the Christianised law of duty; but the brilliant light above which is generated thereby has also its laws and principles of development. There are three prominent virtues in this sphere, which Christian men are expected to produce, which open up and give access to those peculiar treasures of God about which his powers must be exercised. Where in the region of morality self-restraint said 'Touch not,' here Faith says, ' Reach out further and further into an ocean which never can be exhausted, where all is good and all is hopeful, where the eye is not satisfied with seeing nor the ear with hearing.' And the good we seek is no delicate flower placed in the midst of a quaking morass of evil, but one continuous uninterrupted fulness of blessing opened up by this Faith. Where Temperance, once more, helped us to walk with confidence, while we laboured rightly to mingle and adjust without the danger of excess or the failure of defect, here, in the higher regions of Christianity, the strong virtue of Hope leads us ever on and on to greater efforts and greater confidence, the Hope which maketh not ashamed; while Love has wrapped round duty in the life which is no longer held in by the bit and bridle of rule, but is guided by the eye of personal devotion. The hedges are there, the restrictions are there, but the Christian walks evenly between them, with his eye fixed on Jesus, the author and finisher of his faith—leading on to the union of the soul with God, so that a Christian may walk with God, as a man walketh with his friend.

Let us examine then the higher region which Christianity opens up to us, along the paths of Faith, Hope, and Charity, and see whether we have done more than reach the fulness of moral restraint which Christianity makes possible, whether we have added to this the new virtues of the new life which reaches up to God.

When the apostle S. Paul speaks of these virtues, he speaks of them as 'abiding,' as if they were three necessary virtues, which could not be removed without removing Christianity itself. Some of these, it is true, may seem to disappear in another state, not because they are abolished, but because they are carried on into a higher development; just as the Law of Moses, although in one sense abrogated, was in another sense carried up into the law of Christ. Here, he would say, are three fundamental virtues, without which a man cannot be a Christian, and his Religion becomes only a flimsy mass of ill-assorted materials, vague opinions, and half-matured plans, which are doomed to vanish like the fleecy cloud-castles which we spin in youth.

I

Faith—what an ill-used word it is! It has been so hurled about in controversy that we have almost learned to dread the very sound of it, as if it were a dangerous and inflammatory irritant. It has been so emptied of all practical common-sense that we have almost begun to suspect it, as coined in the interests of antinomianism. We have long credited it with being at the bottom of every sort of silly superstition which a sane man most earnestly shrinks from, while the sermons, treatises, and lectures which deal with it seem to have as little bearing on the anxious problems of life as the fiddling of the mountebank Nero when Rome was in flames. And yet, if we are to believe the Apostle, it is a master virtue, a virtue which, whatever else we may strip away, must remain if we would be Christian.

Faith is the realisation of things hoped for, the proving, the bringing into sight, things not seen.[1] And

[1] Heb. xi 1.

the attitude of Faith consists in a giving up of the self to God. It is not an assent to a series of propositions, in which we jealously keep watch over an ever increasing pile of exacting demands upon our reason. We do not timidly put out our foot on these propositions one by one, while with the other we retain our hold on firm ground. Faith rather resembles the plunge which S. Peter made when he threw himself into the water to go to Jesus. It is the first step which counts. The reproof which reached his sinking agony was this: 'O thou of little faith, wherefore didst thou doubt?'[1] And so it is of little importance whether the water is comparatively shallow or deep, if we cannot touch the bottom, and walk as we have been accustomed to do on dry land. If we demand that the Holy Scriptures shall be expurgated and made easy to our faith, still, if we are to lay hold of this great virtue, the time comes sooner or later when we must plunge; and the man who hesitated to believe in some historical statement made by our blessed Lord, because demonstration seemed to fail him, finds that he has to make a deeper plunge to reach the essential truth of the Incarnation.

Faith is an attitude of the soul towards God, in which we repose trustfully in what we believe Him to have said, in what we believe Him to have promised, in the course of action which we believe Him to be pursuing at the present moment in the world, and in the guidance which He bestows upon our lives.[2]

And without this belief in God as a real Person, whatever else we may be, we are not Christians.

[1] S. Matt. xiv 31.
[2] See T. B. Strong *Christian Ethics* p. 90.

There is a commandment of God, which we often hear read from the altar, which tells us, 'Thou shalt have none other gods, but Me.' And we ask God's grace to keep this law of His ordaining, while perhaps all the time our real danger consists, not in having too many gods, more gods than one, but in having no God at all. It is easy for a man to test himself in this respect. Suppose it were decided, on testimony which could not be denied, that there was no God in heaven, that all which purported to be a revelation of Him was a pure invention, that the Bible was only a collection of ancient oriental literature, that the Sacraments were picturesque shams, and that everything went on in the world in a merciless chain of fated necessity, which Prayer could not touch, simply because there was no one who could possibly be said to listen to it: suppose all this, and more, to be proved, what change would thereby be made in life? Perhaps some would omit having Family Prayers, or cease to go to church on Sunday morning, or to pay the homage which irreligion pays to devotion. Yet, if the apostle S. Paul is true in his estimate of Faith as a foundation virtue, the whole prop and stay of life would be removed by such a discovery, and when God had been taken out of it all would fall to pieces. The end of life would then be gone. I should at once become a hopeless enigma to myself. I could neither tell why I came here, nor whither I was going. I should be like a wheel that has dropped out of gear, aimlessly going round in space without contributing anything to the general efficiency or welfare of life. Then I should feel that a barrier between me and sin had been removed; that when next the storm of temptation came rioting in before the gale of passion, its white-crested waves must overwhelm me, because that which I had hitherto placed between temptation and my soul, the precious merits and death of Christ, His atoning Blood and life-giving Sacraments, were a sham; and that henceforth a weak will must be left to cope with strong passions. I should feel that the life which helped me to assimilate what was good in the world, and throw off what was bad, had fled, and that the sun of happiness which had cheered me and ministered to my growth, and the bright air of pleasure which had braced me, might at any moment minister to my decay and hasten corruption.

Faith, where it exists, is such a real thing that all life is propped and supported on it; to withdraw it would mean nothing short of complete disintegration. But, on the other hand, a spurious Faith is only a worthless ornament, which is but a concession to propriety, and contributes nothing to the stability of life. What can be more worthless to a man than to utter prayers which he does not feel to a God in Whom he has ceased to believe? to read a Sacred Book which he distrusts, and to attend religious services which are meaningless to him, and wearisome? Faith has its revenge; if we banish it, if we cease to cherish it, if we omit to keep it bright, it carries with it in its departure some of the fairest and purest of our joys, and leaves Religion, which we are afraid to relinquish altogether, as a dreary incubus, which fetters our freedom and dulls our happiness. And so it comes to pass that while Faith to many is a glory which irradiates all their life, others there will be who have ceased to look for even a struggling beam of light through the dense and heavy mass of conventionality, hypocrisy, and propriety, which to them represents Religion, and which makes Sunday, the day of typical religious observance, the dullest and the most dreaded in all the week.

It may be useful to notice that the apostle S. Paul, who speaks to us of the theological virtue known as Faith, if in his own person he was never wholly destitute of some form of faith, yet knew what it was to see religious things through a perverted medium. He was a man who had his own ideas about Religion strongly developed, and energetically carried them out, but who nevertheless was fatally in the wrong. He would never forget the time when he left Jerusalem as a religious enthusiast, and found himself in the end in conflict with Christ. But also there was apparently only one view which he would allow himself to take of those years: he looked upon them as a disastrous and terrible failure in his life. When he is speaking of himself, and of God's mercies to him, he says, 'And last of all He was seen of me also, as of one born out of due time.'[1] He could only regard himself as an untimely birth, a misshapen child of God's providence. All those years which might have been so helpful, years in which he might have met Jesus Christ and have become His disciple, had been wasted. There had been no careful training for him, no speaking to him the truth as he was able to hear it; no explanation of parable, no emphasis of miracle, no mystic Eucharist of Maundy Thursday, no station by the Cross, no memories of Easter and the Ascension. He had fallen to the earth in the throes of a conversion, and he was

[1] 1 Cor. xv 8.

an untimely birth (he could call himself nothing else), with a large gap in his life, and a period to which, as a Christian, he could not look back with piety nor regard with affection. It is a serious break in the continuity of life if a man loses his faith for any considerable period, if he fails to develop it, or holds it as a loose and worthless thing, if he is only lightly attached to Christianity as a national religion, or as, on the whole, the most enlightened form of so-called belief.

There is a tendency to carry further than the great poet meant the sentiment of those well-known lines:

> 'There lives more faith in honest doubt,
> Believe me, than in half the creeds';

to think that a man is the better for a little dash of scepticism, and a stronger man if he does not carry his convictions too far, or commit himself too deeply; if he displays wisdom in not burning his ships, in case he should have to retreat from positions won by the onslaughts of destructive criticism. There is a disposition to regard Faith as a musical instrument which will not admit of being perfectly tuned, if we are to elicit from it its sweetest tones; or as a spirit too volatile to exist in the atmosphere of the world without some form of adulteration. And yet all the time a loss is going on. Life is too short to spend days and years in academical discussions about the relative probabilities of conflicting forms of truth. The battle is too fierce that we should spend the time in the rival merits of various sorts of weapons when the foe is upon us. Christ would lead man from faith to faith by a graduated scale of ever increasing strength. To have missed, to have failed to put out the foot at a critical moment, or to reach out the hand towards proffered help, may determine life to the very end of its career. And then, when at the hour of death a man must act as if all were true, if he is to have any help from without, he finds that he has to leap over a space, where he might have ascended by a graduated approach, and make the great plunge of Faith at last.

> ' Have mercy, Lord, on hearts grown cold,
> On sheep that long have left Thy fold ;
> On hearts once full of eyes within,
> Now blinded through deceit of sin :
> On hearts Thine own in early youth,
> Now coldly asking, " What is truth ? "
> Who leave the path their fathers trod,
> Forgo their faith, and lose their God.'

And yet there is no doubt that Faith has to win its way in spite of many obstacles. There is, for instance, such a thing as spiritual blindness, or at least shortsightedness, to which Faith makes appeal in vain. Why is it that people who are shrewd enough in everything else, bring themselves to believe that Religion is a thing which any one can take up without study and without effort? It is not only that people think that theologians are born and not made, and that saints are people who have failed in everything else, and have taken up Religion as the only thing they are fit for; there is, besides this, a certain Philistine contempt for Religion, which prevents it from having a fair chance and full development in the minds of men who are fair enough in other things. And further, Religion has to deal with difficult and delicate questions, questions which will no more yield their treasure to contemptuous impatience than the heavens will reveal their mysteries to one who ostentatiously despises all that is known as astronomical research. And further, the spiritual vision is more exposed than any other to fatigue, disease, disabling injuries, error, misuse of all sorts and kinds. The beauty of heaven and of heavenly things may be obscured by an intercepting line of sin, or blotted out by an earth-born cloud, or marred by impatience, or made invisible by a refusal to accept the conditions of investigation.

Blindness is a very real and a very serious difficulty with which Faith has to contend. That there is this blindness few will care to dispute, and many of us are affected by it more than we care to believe, or would be ready to acknowledge. When God appeals to us, and asks for our Faith, He has to meet with a great deal of unwillingness and dislike on our part, barely expressed, barely conscious, but still there. We can readily understand how much the Law of Moses, as inculcated by God, demanded in the way of Faith from those who came beneath its sway. It penetrated into every action of life, it governed the food, the dress, the habits, the political status, of those who submitted to it. When people cease to feel a pride in being the peculiar people of the Lord, they may very easily go on to chafe under the singularity of a position which tends to make them appear ridiculous. And if Religion does not seem to make such demands now as it did from the Jew of old, its requirements are still sufficiently onerous, if we once begin to discharge our duties as a tax, instead of offering them as a present. Religion makes a claim to all our powers and to all our faculties; it claims a tithe of our time, it makes a definite demand on our money, it controls our appetites and restrains our words, and puts before us duties which sometimes seem to make us the peculiar people, in the same way as the Jews were made peculiar by their elaborate system of sacrifice and religious service. And we can see how people chafe under this at the present day, and are always trying to throw it off. We are familiar with the cry which is so intensely popular, 'Give us a simple Christianity. Let us get behind the Christ of the Epistles, and go to the simple Christ of the Gospels. Let us penetrate beneath the different peculiarities of varying religions, and get at the strong underlying *residuum* which will constitute a common Christianity, or even a universal Religion.' But suppose, in another sphere of our necessities, we were to seek, under pressure of ill-health, the advice of some famous physician, and were to return armed with some medical prescription which he assured us would without fail ease our complaint, and restore us to our wonted health. What would be said of our earnestness, or indeed our intelligence, if we compared this prescription with others given by other physicians for other and various maladies, and by omitting some elements which we disliked, and others which we regarded as poisonous, while we substituted some which took our fancy, we were to attempt to cure ourselves with a harmless *residuum*, which represented our idea of the medical basis of all cures? Should we not be told that a great deal of the medical skill expended on our case, and more than half its virtue, depended on the carefully weighed adjustment, the accurate tempering of many and conflicting elements for the purpose of a cure? And so when the Great Physician says to His Church, 'Go ye therefore, and make disciples of all the nations, baptizing them into the Name of the Father and of the Son and of the Holy Ghost: teaching them to observe all things whatsoever I commanded you : and lo, I am with you alway, even unto the end of the world,'[1]—who are we that we should presume to alter this great precept, or talk of a necessary *residuum*? Let us say we dislike it in itself, if we will, and fear its far-reaching claims. There is at least something intelligible in trying to ignore it; it is the height of folly to presume to better it.

And yet the most serious form of spiritual blindness may be traceable in some way or another to sin. 'They could not believe' is a statement whose meaning it is not always pleasant to dwell upon. Balaam, under the influence of Balak's bribe, seems to have betaken himself to tortuous policy, and to have lost the fineness of his sense of spiritual appreciation. Judas, under the influence of his covetousness, has become irresponsive and unsympathetic in the presence of the great truths which are opening out before him. And when for us the light seems to die out of Holy Scripture, and the last sceptical book is eagerly welcomed, is it sometimes that sin is lurking behind, which, almost unconsciously to ourselves, has blinded the keenness of perception? Why is controversy welcomed, and an eager longing developed to hear all that may be said on the other side—where before religious observance was welcomed and honoured, the altar loved, God's Holy Word respected, and His presence cherished as a source of health and peace? It may be that there is that buried beneath the floor

---

[1] S. Matt. xxviii 19 20.

of the tent which checks all progress, the Babylonish garment and the wedge of gold, which damps all enthusiasm. The eye no longer sees distances, nor reaches out after the unseen. If this be so, a greater obligation is laid on Christian men carefully to guard the spiritual eyesight against all that may thus disable it. Faith is a delicate, subtle thing, and our true welfare must largely depend on it. The world without it is a poor narrow place; without its clear and open gaze we are like stones when the sun is shining, or birds where men are opening treasures of wisdom. To lose Faith is to lose our bright and open horizon; it is to be imprisoned in materialism, and to forget the breezy expanse which opens out around our cage, while we beat ourselves against its gilded wires.

II

It is easy to conceive of Faith as a theological virtue; it accords well with the other-worldliness which is the puzzle and the scandal of religion to so many. But when we come to think of Hope, it seems more like a luxury of temperament, useful where it can be found, depending largely on constitutional qualities, but hardly of the nature of a fundamental virtue.

And yet it has been selected by S. Paul in a well-known Epistle[1] as one of the three essentially permanent virtues; that is, one of the three virtues which bind the soul to God. And if we look around us, we see how very largely Hope, under other names and in various dress, enters into the main elements of success in different departments of life. In Education, for instance, it is

[1] 1 Cor. xiii 13.

an ungracious task merely to teach a boy so much reading, so much writing, so many branches of learning, if he takes no interest in anything that is set before him, if he is permanently indifferent as to whether he rises or falls in the little world of school; or if in a larger field, he has no ambition, no aim in life, no vision of a future, to attain which he is willing to stake the idle gratification of the present hour. Without Hope in the guise of emulation or a higher ambition, his education becomes a useless cram and a monotonous treadmill of unproductive work. So when he becomes a man, if he is not to be always a mere drudge, if he is not merely to become a local preacher of the gospel of discontent, if he is not to be dragged downwards by an 'inverted hope' which is something very like despair, which whispers in his ear that his every action is doomed to failure, and the blighting effect of unjust conditions—again he must have the stimulus of hope in the shape of emulation. It may be only a sordid desire to excel others; it may be only a wish for a mercantile reputation which can be converted into hard cash; but it may be a striving after perfection, a desire to do good work, and ever better work, simply because it is good work.

There is a great and wide difference between the workman who will throw down his tools because it is past the stipulated hour of work, and who refuses to work a minute longer, even to stop an impending danger, and the great engineer of the Brooklyn Bridge at New York, who, succeeding to his father, who died in the early stages of its construction, himself crippled with an accident, was able only from a couch in a chamber hard by to superintend the completion of that great engineering feat, which a nature less indomitable would have believed to be impossible to him.

If we search the records of engineering skill and military and naval prowess, if we study the records of inventive and philosophical enterprise, we shall see in them all how large a part Hope plays in these things. And in matters which affect our health and bodily life, many a doctor will tell us that when the patient gives up hope he loses the most valuable co-operation towards producing a recovery. It is so in other regions as well. Hope will be found a most valuable instrument in the daily ordering and developing of life's resources.

Now inasmuch as Christianity would seem always to employ the whole man, using imagination, memory, intellect, bodily capacity, and even bodily pain, so Hope, the power of leaning on the future, or, at least, on a power without from which the present can borrow what it would not otherwise possess, is a permanent and structural virtue. It is one of those virtues which adjust the grand self-sufficiency of ancient morality by its proper counterpoise. By all means let us aim at self-sufficiency, if we remember that 'our sufficiency is of God,' Whom Faith brings near to us, Whom Hope makes actively present, Whom Love receives as the joy and peace of the soul.

When we are bidden, then, to cultivate this theological virtue of Hope, we are bidden first of all to shape our life by a purpose towards a goal.

This purpose and aim stands out wonderfully in the lives of the patriarchs, whose faith men are sometimes disposed to regard with contemptuous pity. They were men whose lives were shaped by a promise. It stands out all through their history. God had promised them something, and He would perform it. This was dearer to them than home. 'By faith Abraham, when he was called to go out into a place which he should after receive for an inheritance, obeyed; and he went out, not knowing whither he went.' 'These all died in faith, not having received the promises, but having seen them afar off, and embraced them.'[1] 'Your father Abraham,' says our blessed Lord, 'rejoiced to see My day: and he saw it, and was glad.'[2] This was dearer to him than ease, comfort, and fatherland, dearer than an only son. The promise stood sure, even if death seemed to bar the way. More wonderful still, the impatience for the realisation of the promise coloured some of the darkest sins which stain their personal history. What God had promised was a reality to them. He was able to, He would, perform it, even when everything seemed saddest and most black. If death came, still they died in faith that the promise was true, and that they would some day see it. Surely it is a hasty judgment which pronounces that the ancient Jew had no, or only an imperfect, expectation of a future state. Is it not rather true that the apparent silence as to a future state, which men think they discern in their writings, a silence by no means unbroken by explicit statements, arose 'not from a want of religious belief, but from excess of it'? The future life was not denied or contradicted, but it was sometimes overlooked, set aside, overshadowed, by the consciousness of the living, active presence of the living God Himself. It arose from the fact that they lived with God here in this world much more completely than we do. Life itself, each day's

---

[1] Heb. xi 9 13.   [2] S. John viii 56.

life, and death when it came, were each of them only one step onward with God. The rewards and punishments of conduct which men look forward to as future were present realities to them. Heaven had begun here; and sometimes to them to die seemed only to be removed from the more active and sensible presence of God in life, and hence they shrank from it.

Still they never swerved; however gloomy was the outlook, however dark seemed the nether world, their confident hope always rested on this: 'they judged Him faithful Who had promised.' This was their neverfailing support through death and through failure: the promise will come, it cannot fail, because God cannot deceive us. All their lives were coloured by it, their actions shaped by it. And their expectation has been fulfilled: the Child of Promise has come, although a strange and judicial blindness has happened to Israel in part. Blessed are our eyes, for they see, and our ears, for they hear; prophets and kings have desired it long, and died without the sight. And the promise which cheered them has been handed on to us in another form. 'That I may know Him, and the power of His resurrection, and the fellowship of His sufferings, being made conformable unto His death.'[1]—This is the hope and object of the Christian.

There are certain roads and channels, as it were, along which He has promised to meet us. In the dry path of duty we are sure to find God. If we have strength to persevere, through ill-health, failure, or loss, we shall find God at the end of it. Religion itself is another path in which we may always find God; difficult it may seem and stern, but always yielding to

[1] Phil. iii 10.

Hope. It should be the constant endeavour of the Christian to lift himself up out of the well-worn rut of formalism, to endeavour to realise, and to hope for, all that Religion promises to give; dry, and stern, and repelling as she is without Hope, full of beauty and blessing to those who will lay firm hold of her promises; while in the background there is the promise of our lives—that which God leads us to expect, that towards which He is ever drawing us. How wonderfully it has all been planned out! We can often for ourselves trace indications of the design. It is a melancholy statement which is sometimes made in estimating a man's career,—'he is throwing himself away.' The mere fact that we have been born at all; the labour bestowed on our education; those talents, great or small, which He has laid up with us; the hopes and efforts of parents and friends; the prophecies which went before on us; all the generous anticipations which they have formed of our life and character; —all these have, as it were, a promise attached to them, which ought to shape our lives. When a man thinks of the promises which lie all around him, it is a sad thing if he has to acknowledge that he has shrunk away from a great responsibility, and despised God's purpose. There are promises from which our life seems to shrink with every wave of the ebbing tide, until we see tracts once covered with a rippling flow of joy and brightness now bare and gaunt, long reaches of forsaken flats, relieved with shallow pools of stagnant water. The promise of childhood and the expectation of youth too often have to be searched for as a region touched with a high-flood mark which has long ago receded.

If, by God's mercy, the better world is reached, among its new-found blessings and glorious prizes one of the greatest will be this, that then 'I shall begin to be myself,' to answer to God's will concerning me, to correspond to His gracious purpose, to answer to the predestinating love of His good Providence, which for His own righteous purposes caused me to be.

If Hope, this grand theological virtue, as we are led to regard it, gives a purpose to our life, it also shows us a purpose and an issue for the world around us. It has been described as the most desperate of all fears, ' that God has given over the world to pursue its own course, and that there is no rational and orderly climax to the course of human things.' We all of us should repudiate with energy the idea that we are fatalists, and yet how often men act as if large parts of their life lay outside the beneficent control of God! Men act as if life were a game of chance, which depends largely on a lucky deal, and on shifts and turns over which they have but little control. Men neglect to leave a place in the schemes of what they call ' Providence ' for the beneficent action of sickness, misfortune, pain, and trouble. They do not in the least practically believe that ' whom the Lord loveth He chasteneth,' but hasten in every way to avoid the least danger of personal trouble, and pursue the quest of an unruffled life up to the very jaws of suicide. Rather would they be without life at all than have to bear a life streaked with trouble. But Hope opens out a better aspect of things than this. It is the temptation of mental indolence to refuse to look beyond things as they appear to be, and strike the imagination, to what they really are. It is a distinct sin against society to despair of the State. It is a distinct failure in duty for a Christian to acquiesce in evil as inevitable and necessary, and to cease to strive to improve society. Surely it is a form of fatalism when good people fold their hands and say that things are as they are, and we must not expect to find them otherwise. How easily, for instance, a bad practice wins its way to a recognised position, from which it is very difficult to oust it. There are two things especially, of which religious people in England have made their boast. The one is the observance of Sunday, and the other is great reverence for the Bible. And yet, without being able to trace the steps of the process, or to accurately gauge the causes which have brought it about, there is a marked loosening of the affection, a marked relaxation of the reverential estimation, in which both of these religious traditions are held. It is very easy for a man to fold his hands and say that the study of ecclesiastical history shows us the marked distinction which has always existed between the Jewish Sabbath and the Christian Sunday. The wider spread of intercourse with the Continent makes it inevitable that our insular manners should be somewhat corrected by a common-sense treatment of questions of this kind. People will not be coerced or controlled in what they are pleased or not pleased to follow in the way of religious observance. But at the same time, if a man is quite sure himself, that, whatever history or custom may say, the distinguishing characteristic of Sunday is that it is emphatically the Lord's Day, and not a day for self or selfish pleasure, ought he as a Christian to acquiesce in a lower standard, as if nothing could be done? Surely to do so is to lose hope in the ultimate triumph of good and the greater power of what is right and true, as compared with what is false and fleeting. It is equally possible to set a good fashion, as to acquiesce in a bad one. Christianity has beat up against opposition all through the ages. Is it to be overcome by a passing sentiment?

And in like manner, if we part with our traditional reverence for God's Holy Word, we shall lose a great deal with it. Already we are beginning to see a turn in the tide, and New Testament literary scepticism pronounced immature and out of court. While scientific men wrangle, and literary empirics advance their hypotheses, it will be a sad thing if we consent to throw away an influence which is easily lost, and not so easily recovered. If we manfully refuse ever to despair of the State, let us also be careful never to regard the Bible as a testimony that has been largely discredited, or as an instrument of spiritual advancement which may well be viewed with suspicion and treated with contempt. Let us rather hope that a wider outlook will cause a return to a fuller acceptance of its divine truth. Surely this magnificent virtue of Hope will never allow us to acquiesce in what is wrong, or less than right, in face of the eternal promises of God.

There are many things which Christian people deplore in the world around them, but it is no use to deplore and yet to follow. To deplore is to take steps to amend, because the stream of good has never quite turned, if only we would listen to Hope. 'What cannot be endured must be cured' is the true rendering of the old proverb in the mouth of a Christian. It is sad to see literature debased into a frivolous nastiness, simply because a certain number of people have not the courage to say that what is wrong never can be right, what is ugly never can be beautiful, what is false never can be true, what is deadly never can be healthy. Evil will always be strong, evil will always be at work to subvert society. But it is a serious thing when good people cease to strive against evil, because this means that the natural protectors of society have lost hope. Sometimes, in history, the resistance seems to have been confined almost to single individuals, one here, and another there; men who, like 'the little black Bishop' in the days of the Stuarts, were prepared to resist evil even in high quarters, at the risk of deprivation, degradation, and even death. Never to despair of the State, never to lose hope for society, never to acquiesce in a disruption of principles, never to consent to a lowering of the standard in quarters where our authority can reach—this is a duty which we owe to society, this is to have firm hold of the great virtue of Hope. However sickly, however degraded, public opinion may become, at least we can uplift the standard of apostolic purity, which shall be a rallying-point for the children of God: 'Whatsoever things are true, whatsoever things are honest, whatsoever things are just, whatsoever things are pure, whatsoever things are lovely, whatsoever things are of good report; if there be any virtue, and if there be any praise, think on these things.'[1]

And the same virtue which forbids us to despair of society will forbid us to despair of ourselves. The struggle with self is a long and difficult one, full of disappointment and full of failure; oftentimes we are driven to the verge of impatient acquiescence in defeat. We commence with a resolution, perhaps, to do the thing which we know ought to be done, but the will gives

[1] Phil. iv 8.

orders only to mute slaves and passive instruments of disobedience. Or we resolve to give up a habit which is evil, but the obstinate persistence of its deadly influence serves only to show us the powerlessness of our efforts and the absolute irresolution of our strongest determination. Or there is an imperfect virtue which needs development, or a system of devotion which requires perfecting, or a method of almsgiving to be made more worthy of divine acceptance, or a rule of fasting to be brought more into accordance with the mind of the Church; and our very efforts seem only to plunge us deeper in the mire, while resolutions which fail in their accomplishment serve only to weaken the snap and spring of the will.

Here comes in with its vigour and helpfulness the theological virtue of Hope, which refuses to despair of victory for ourselves in the inner circle of our own lives. It is the main work of him whose name is 'the Accuser' to cast this impotence in our teeth, and tell us that victory is impossible. It is one great work of God, by the 'patience and comfort of the Scriptures,' to give us Hope. This is a fact that every Christian should firmly grasp, that whatever strength of evil may be struggling within us, grace is stronger than nature; that the victories which we can trace in the characters of Moses, S. Peter, the Magdalene, S. Paul, S. Augustine, and many another, are being repeated every day in the lives of the followers of the Crucified. The miracles of grace are not to be denied, and the miracles of grace may be renewed in us at any moment, if we will only be workers together with God, instead of onlookers. The key of the position, as we have already seen, is the will. No doubt, if we are for ever making resolutions which we never even attempt to keep, we are thereby weakening its energy and its spring. If a man resolves in himself that he will do a thing, whether it be great or small, it ought to be done, otherwise the spring of the will is to that extent impaired. The weakening of our will is the danger we most need to dread, coupled as it too often is with a ridiculous under-estimating of the forces brought against us. As well might we hope to meet with bows and arrows a modern army equipped with weapons of precision as to meet the scientific onslaught of our spiritual foes with a mere wish to turn, or a resolution generally to lead a new life. Habit is, of course, one of the strongest forces in nature. Look, for example, at the trees with their head of foliage violently twisted and turned in one direction by the force of the wind, which sets off the sea and has been forming them for years in one shape; so habit has been turning us with a steady force into one groove, unchecked and undeflected; it is not to be altered from its course by a half-formed resolution. If we examine all the means of grace provided for us in the Church, we shall see that in every case an effort is presupposed on the part of those that use them in co-operating with Him Who is the 'strong Son of God.'

The difficulty of the struggle must never make us despair, but it ought to make us more thoroughly in earnest. Grace must meet human effort, strength co-operate with weakness. But the devil trades on despair; he sets up scruples which aggravate our natural sinfulness, and persuades us that everything we do is wrong. He keeps us from the means of grace by all manner of devices. He makes us trust in ourselves, and then dashes all our finest resolutions to the ground.

Hope, if we persevere to its attainment, will give a new interest to life, and lift us out of the rut of fashion. It will enable us to renew our strength. Only let us remember that we have not unlimited stores of hope. The Hope which animates penitence may become the Despair which points remorse; while at length, if we refuse to receive her gentle pleading, she may 'fold her wings reproachfully, and looking backwards become regret.'

CHAPTER V

THE HIGHER LIFE—*continued*

'Love is of God'

I

OF the three theological virtues possible in the higher region of Christianity, S. Paul tells us that the greater is Love,—greater, that is, because it contains in itself the root of the other two. For we believe where we love, and we hope also where we love.

The language indeed of the New Testament is persistent on this point. When our blessed Lord was asked which was the great commandment of the Law, He showed us how the whole Law was summed up in Love—Love to God, and Love to our neighbour. S. James calls this Love 'the royal law,' and S. Paul himself speaks of Love as 'the fulfilling of the Law.'

And yet we feel at once that here at all events is something which must be rescued from clouds of unreality and false sentiment. When we pursue a virtue into what seems ominously like the region of the feelings, we are conscious that we must establish its position on something higher than like and dislike, sentiment and imagination. As the great Christian virtue of Humility suffers from unworthy counterfeits, so Love no less is dimmed by unreality,—as if to put

Love on this pinnacle were to assert that the solid foundation of all Religion consists in emotion. But one glance will show us that Love is a virtue which cuts at the root of mere isolated action, or selfishness. This is emphasised by all that God has told us, all that He puts before us. It is clearly laid upon us for our earnest consideration, that we are not men and women acting alone, but living wheels in a living machine, which acts not by a fated mechanism but by loving co-operation. Here is my life, with all its wonderful equipment of powers, passions, impulses, and the like; and selfishness calls aloud to me to work it entirely in the interest of my own gratification. It bids me bend all the subtle powers of life towards self as a centre. 'You were turned in upon life,' says this narrowing voice, 'when you were born, you will be broken off from it when you die. You were not wanted in the world when you entered it, you will not be missed when you leave it. It is a rich inexhaustible stream. Take what you like, and enjoy it while you can. No one will be permanently the better, and no one will be permanently the worse. All the good you can do is soon wiped out, and all the harm you can do is soon forgotten. Nature is a prolific mother of individuals, whose wisdom is to seize as much as they can.' But Love will intervene in this false estimate, and her intervention is of the utmost moment. Love points to all the correspondences of life, which by their very existence show that this selfish estimate was wrong. Love opens up the view of the presence and purpose of God, and shows to the man that life has a definite aim and issue, and that he himself is included in that aim. It is thus that he wakes up to a new interest such as selfish gratification never could produce ; and he will find that instead of being a selfish parasite on Nature, he is an integral part of her great purpose, and that he is not even a fated wheel in a necessitated machine, but that he is a free agent consulted and honoured by God, the great Artificer ; that the plan of God's making, or as much of it as is sufficient for him to know, has been displayed to him in Revelation ; that he is invested with all the honour, all the interest, and, more than this, with all the power of one who is allowed to work together with God, a great Power Whom he must respect, and above all a great Being Whom he may love. And if he thus looks around on his fellow-men, he will find that they have ceased to be rivals, or greedy competitors for the same prize : henceforth they are fellow-workers in the same cause. Love reaching out to our neighbour in sympathy, sacrifice, and thoughtfulness, returns to us laden with blessings which a selfish life would have been powerless to discover, and we find that the many points of contact which exist all around us are also points of enrichment. And hence it is that Love stands out as the greatest of all virtues, because it gives life its only true meaning, because it helps it to attain its only proper end, and because it binds the world together in a unity of purpose within the strong influence of the love of God.

II

If we try to examine this in detail we may see, first of all, how Love is the master virtue in our dealings with God. It is not needful to say, indeed it is painfully obvious, that it is easy to live without the consciousness of God. But at the same time there is a terrible blank when first this conscious love of God has been felt to drop out of life. Travellers tell us of the morose irritability which settles down over people who are enveloped in the long night of the arctic winter: its gloom affects the spirits, and sours the temper, and damps all enthusiasm. So when the love of God has vanished there must needs be a great blank in life which is keenly felt. It is an experience which may not uncommonly be met with, that restlessness and spiritual irritability settle down on the soul which has just abandoned Prayer, or Holy Communion, or the offices of Religion. Prayerlessness deprives the soul of its proper rest, and makes it fretful and unsettled. And this is even more markedly the case in matters which concern the object and purpose of life. It is very hard to carry out God's will; it is harder still sometimes to see that God's will is the best. A stoical indifference may succeed in passing unruffled through life by shutting off a large part of its sympathetic machinery. A spirit of resignation may help a man to a grumbling acquiescence in the inevitable. But the love of God would carry him higher,—to rejoice in His will, not to wish it otherwise, and to accept it as absolutely the best course. We can see what the prophet Jonah would have been spared if only he could have brought his obstinate self-will into joyful acquiescence with the will of God. S. Peter would have avoided the most dreadful episode of his life had he accepted at once God's will concerning him: 'Thou canst not follow Me now.' A man cannot attain to any great height of virtue who is rebellious, discontented, jealous, anxious, and distrustful. Love of God strikes a blow at the petty larceny of murmuring and the indolent rebellion of discontent. To be in love with God's purpose is to have given life its true orientation, which is of the very last importance in determining our actions; while to us, to whom has been revealed the manifestation of God in the Incarnation, this love should be all the easier. We read that when our blessed Lord had healed the soul and body of the paralytic, the multitudes glorified God, Who had given such power unto men. The Incarnation has brought God near to us. True, to have loved God before this manifestation would have prevented a man from seeking to supplant Him, or put any other god in His place. To love God would have safeguarded His worship from the profanation of idolatry, His Name from the irreverence of a false familiarity or treacherous betrayal, and His holy days from neglect and profanation. But now as God has appeared in human flesh it is easier to love Him, and to acquiesce in His guidance for our soul's good. When we are tempted, we know that our God experienced the force and bitterness of temptation; when we suffer, we can look to the divine Sufferer on the cross; when we faint and fail we can appeal to His sympathy, Who agonised in Gethsemane. It is the personal love of a personal God which we must seek to develop, not admiration for the beneficent working of an inexorable first cause. It is of vital importance to a man's religious life that he should attain to this love of a personal God. Love should ever be gradually supplanting the mere sense of duty in his dealings with Him. To take a homely example, there is a great difference in religious value between coming to worship in church because we ought so to come, and coming because it is our delight so to do. There is all the difference in the world between the cold propriety of a service mechanically performed and a service in which the devout worshipper catches sight of God. There is a great difference between a Sacrament which is the memorial of an absent Lord, and a Sacrament which is the present pledge of His personal presence. There is a vast difference between a book of antiquarian interest written in exquisite phrases, of commanding importance, and the same book in which we detect the voice of God Himself. So in dealing with sin: in the awful conflict which is ever raging round its battle-fields, if we believe that sin is not merely sinful because God forbids it, but that He forbids it because it is sinful, we shall find it easier to resist. Supposing that sin could be declared an open matter to-morrow, and the barrier which separated us from it were removed, still the Christian who loves God could not sin, because he has learned to love the true, the beautiful, and the good, and having so learned could find no pleasure in wickedness.

Surely the love of God would more than anything else serve to purify the air and shed a healthier atmosphere around us. God would not then be separated off, as it were, in a consecrated temple outside the ordinary influences of our lives, but His felt presence would pervade it all: whether we ate or drank, or whatsoever we did, we should do all to the glory of God. And our life would be spent in His presence, and sanctified by the sense of His love and fear.

'Thou shalt love the Lord thy God with all thy

heart, and with all thy soul, and with all thy mind'; [1] if we once have grasped this we have the sanction of all Morality, we have the foundation of all Faith, we have the earnest and impulse of all Hope.

III

But Love not only reaches upwards, it reaches out all around us in relation to our neighbour. Selfishness lies at the bottom of all sin; if there were no selfishness children would not need to be told to honour their parents; they would recognise a right, which only a prejudice for self had usurped. There would be no need, were it not for selfishness, to forbid murder; lust would flee away ashamed; theft would be abolished; calumny would hide its head; and covetousness would find no market for its wares. But the battle with selfishness is a long and a difficult one; it begins with childhood, and does not cease with old age; it rages round the body, the soul, the very spirit. The desire to gratify appetite, the love of comfort, the wish to turn all the aims and objects of life into a scheme for self-gratification, and the very powers of spiritual life into a scheme of self-preservation—these form one long record of selfishness. When we say, therefore, that Love is the fulfilling of the Law, we mean at the same time that selfishness is at the bottom of all sin.

Now selfishness, like all the sins which spring from it, takes two forms: a negative and a positive. It takes the form of neglect of what is right, or else of active perpetration of what is wrong. The most common and the most dangerous form of selfishness consists perhaps in the utter negation of all feeling

[1] S. Matt. xxii 37.

of responsibility towards our neighbours. Cain expressed this in forcible language when he exclaimed, 'Am I my brother's keeper?' All through our life there has been much to show us that we are not the isolated individuals we believed ourselves to be, but members one of another. We are born into the family. We find ourselves members of a community, sons and daughters of a nation, and members of a great body called the Church; and we shall be judged not only for what we individually are, but for what we have done for the good of the community. This sense of responsibility ought to make itself felt in many ways. There is the simplest case of the individual in his family life. How many a home is being made wretched because one or two or more members think themselves entitled to live in utter independence and disregard of the comforts and interests of the rest! There is the selfishness which will not take the trouble to curb an irritation of temper which takes all the sunshine out of family life, from which childhood, which was meant to brighten and cheer, shrinks away chilled and disheartened, and only gloom and discomfort mark the path of a selfish want of control. Or there is the man of business, the shrewd man of the world, who has been working hard all day, who has met his friends at the club on his way home, and has satisfied his keen mind with all the interests and excitements of the hour,—has he nothing but coldness and silence and evident weariness for those who await him at home? has he no thought for the interests there, which claim some of his time, for the duties which demand some of his attention? When the valets and private secretaries do write the biographies of their masters, they sometimes convey a very different impression of the man who dazzled society by his wit and cheered the world by his brilliancy.

Are there no responsibilities, again, from master to servants? Is the rift to become wider and wider, and the relationship to be purely a commercial one between them? Can a master say that no responsibility rests on him if his servants never go to church, when his arrangements have actively prevented it? Can he say that it is no fault of his if they lapse into gay or vicious ways? If his example is always all that it might be, must he not also ask himself whether he has done all in his power for their welfare? There are many young lives brought up to town from good country homes, and good church ways, which are being chilled and damped into the paths of sin by the want of thought and want of sympathy which mistakes a freedom to do wrong for the liberty with which Christ makes the servant free. Further, if we take a wider outlook in the same direction, while every one mourns the corruption of society, how many are taking the trouble to recognise their responsibility for its improvement! We may mourn the tendency of literature, but literature follows, like other things, the law of supply and demand. We may make what we call society the whipping-boy of our faults, but society is after all the aggregate of individual lives, or the influence which is thrown off from them. 'Let your light so shine before men, that they may see your good works,' said our blessed Lord. We have not fulfilled this obligation if we put a screen of shame, which is not necessarily the same thing as modesty, before the good works which we do, and use the light which was meant to illumine the street simply as the entrance-lamp for our own door-step.

Or, to take a wider outlook still in the same direction; in the face of the great stress which is being laid on social claims, whatever construction we choose to put on the formula, 'My own,' we must feel that property can only be defended before God, in so far as it is a trust held for Him. We cannot think that we have drawn our respective fortunes out of a lucky-bag in which some have gained prizes and some have only drawn blanks. We cannot think that it is for any desert or favour in ourselves, that where others are starving we have a competency, or even wealth. No; there is a priesthood of wealth as well as a priesthood of religious grace, and that means responsibility. Indeed, we can easily see how, if this were recognised and acted upon, a beneficent scheme for carrying on the world would have been inaugurated. The block and the frequent catastrophes arise, as they are bound to arise, where men have forgotten their responsibility; where those who have received large deposits on account of the famine fund to distribute, spend it instead upon themselves. The responsibility for the possession of money is immense; and it is this responsibility which points the blame which we all bestow on the wrong use of it. Money is too serious a thing to be spent on unworthy and trifling uses; it is a part of God's endowment which we could no more waste with reverence, remembering its purchasing power, than we could cast loaves of bread into the river, unblamed before the face of a starving multitude, because we were pleased to call them our own, and liked to hear them splash.

Even further still will this sense of responsibility take us. It will open out into that love which forbids us to think of anything human as foreign to us. Our interests are apt to get cramped: selfishness winds itself round our very religion, so that as long as a man enjoys the means of grace, and has his seat in church, with a good choir to conduct the services, at times convenient to himself, and this with all the organisation of a good parish, well arranged and supported—all outside may perish as far as he is concerned. How much we have to learn in this way from the old Jews! Let us only listen to the intense patriotism which breaks out in the Psalms. Often and often must the Wedding Psalm sound as a reproof when its joyful cadences break over the heads of the happy bridal party now ascending to the altar for the final blessing from on high. There they stand, with all the joys of a new and untried life thick upon them. Blessing after blessing pours down upon them from Heaven: 'Blessed are all they that fear the Lord: and walk in His ways. For thou shalt eat the labours of thine hands: O well is thee, and happy shalt thou be. Thy wife shall be as the fruitful vine: upon the walls of thine house. Thy children like the olive-branches: round about thy table. Lo, thus shall the man be blessed that feareth the Lord.' And then to crown it all, as if this were a blessing without which no Israelite could rejoice or be at rest: 'The Lord from out of Sion shall so bless thee: that thou shalt see Jerusalem in prosperity all thy life long. Yea, that thou shalt see thy children's children: and peace upon Israel.'[1]

[1] Psalm cxxviii.

Here is no isolated unit founding a home for self-gratification. It is an Israelite alive with the patriotism of a great nation. It is a home which opens out into the kingdom of Messiah itself, in a love which loses personal happiness in national prosperity.

But if there is a negative selfishness which merges responsibility, much more is there a positive selfishness which subsidises sin. It is appalling to think of a sin which ruins another's soul simply to gratify self. Nathan's parable to David has lost none of its pathos, and, alas! none of its meaning.

There are no more fearful words in Holy Scripture than those sentences of stern denunciation against 'offences' uttered by our blessed Lord. 'It were better for him that a millstone were hanged about his neck, and he were drowned in the depths of the sea, than that he should offend one of these little ones.'[1] Surely there can be no consideration more agonising in its impotent despair than the thought of souls spinning down the abyss of sin, who were first launched there by a selfishness which had only thought of self-gratification, and had forgotten the reverence due to the delicate handiwork of God, so splendidly constituted, so easily set on the path which leads to destruction. He, the betrayer into the paths of sin, may have been led by God's great mercy to see the sinfulness of his action, and to mourn and amend his evil ways, but they who shared his sin, whither are they gone? They have been whirled away out of his reach; and they may have gone only to taunt him with the last curse of a despairing soul: 'I should not have perished but for thee.'

[1] S. Matt. xviii 6; S. Luke xvii 2.

We trace this evil beginning in the selfish boy at school, who is ashamed of standing alone in his baseness; he is become the active missionary of Satan in destroying the innocent lives of others. Now it is the smart writer who wants to sell his book. Now it is the lion greedy of his prey, who feeds on the souls of men. The selfishness of sin is a subject about which everybody seems to know something, and whose very prevalence shows us what a master virtue Love must be, which will seek always and everywhere another's good, and not the advancement of a self bloated by another's fall, elevated on another's dethronement, enriched by the stolen treasures of another's happiness.

Love may be said with truth to be even a wider influence than this, in its countless ramifications and all-pervading beauty. It moves like the gentle Saviour of mankind with a tender tread, in a world loved by God, and cruelly oppressed with evil. Little children lift up their heads at its approach. The suffering and the sad smile out of their tears. The ignorant, the unfortunate, the old, the worn-out, those whom a rough world would brush on one side as useless, are better and brighter for its sympathy. Even Nature herself represses her mute inarticulate wail of failure before the loving touch of those who remember that God once saw the world which He had made, and pronounced it to be very good.

Just as we see the monks of old settling down on the fever-stricken morass and thorn-covered wilderness, tenderly wrestling with its barrenness, and drawing out its innate powers, as yet stifled by failure, and crushed by neglect, until the desert blossomed like a rose, and the beauty of the situation which they rescued is cast in their teeth by a generation who have persistently blackened skies and poisoned streams —so the loving heart is a presence of good wherever it goes. It is at peace with God, and at peace with man. The animals, the plants, the obstinate troubles of the earth, are bettered and softened by its presence. And as of old, in the streets, the afflicted and sorrowful were brought under the healing influence of the apostle as, barely conscious of his own power, he passed along his way; so a man will find that even when he himself is least conscious of any effort, and least anxious to appropriate praise, men in their myriad troubles will be attracted to a life which sheds abroad the spirit of love, and innumerable openings will present themselves of doing good to those who move along life's paths, and who are anxious that at least the shadow of one who loves, as he passes by, should overshadow some of them.

CHAPTER VI

THE GREAT IDEAL

> 'Our first temptation was that we should be like unto God in knowledge, and by that we fell; but being raised by Christ we come to be holy like Him, by knowing Him, as we are known, and by seeing Him as He is.'

WE all know the despair of a man who hopes to gain practical experience merely out of text-books. An artist is not made out of art treatises, nor an engineer by lectures on construction. We need constantly in these matters the living comment, and, if possible, the living exemplar. Goodness, in like manner, is confusing from its very greatness and the complexity of its many details. A life of pure morality is difficult enough amidst all the opposing forces which are waiting to seize up and dissipate our powers. Such refinements as the theological virtues, or the graces inculcated in the Beatitudes, are destroyed by one frosty night of a lapse into sin, or snapped and bruised by repeated gusts of passion. Clearly we need to see some practical exponent of principles so delicate and so difficult as carried out under the average conditions of human life and with the ordinary equipment of human nature. We need some one to show us the way, some one to imitate—in short, an ideal. It seems to be almost a necessity of our nature. Man is the most imitative of all creatures; he is dependent on others for the full exercise of his powers. He is little self-contained, feeble, irresolute, plastic. Now he is cleaving to the dust before the disapprobation of the world; now he is carried up to heaven by its applause; gregarious in his instincts, in his pursuits, his pleasures, and his sins. He must needs have some one to imitate, some one who shall guide his hand, and help him to apply that which theoretically he knows.

In his very dress he is following fashion; in his estimate of things he is being guided by public opinion; in the inner affairs of his business life he needs an adviser: is it to be wondered at, if in the guidance and aim of his whole life he needs an external ideal?

Certainly, whether consciously or unconsciously, he chooses habitually such an ideal, and follows it. The youth, now taking possession of his full stock of responsibility, when the last leading-string is cut away from him, and he is beginning to reign over his powers, sends either, like Rehoboam, for the old advisers of matured experience, or for the young abettors of his craving instincts, and follows, or at least sets out with the purpose of following, an ideal, when as yet he has not begun to drift before the wind.

And it is not hard to see that a very great deal depends on that choice. It is no slight responsibility which devolves on parents and teachers to educate the taste and guide the choice of those who are in these matters dependent on them. There was a time, we are only just emerging from it, when children were held down by parental authority to a line of choice, which might or might not commend itself to their aspirations, when even such a sacred thing as Holy Orders was enterprised in obedience to a father's command, whose authority might not be questioned. The pendulum has swung back now very much in the contrary direction. Now we have new panaceas, of unbiassed choice, of absolute freedom, of nature not to be constrained. But it is not yet clear that the change has been one of unmixed advantage. When the Church resigns the child into the hands of the god-parents at the font, it is with the distinct understanding that he shall be prejudiced towards good, brought under the influence of strong and definite teaching, under the yoke of Jesus Christ, under the power of Religion. 'Ye must remember,' says the Church, 'that it is your parts and duties to see that this infant be taught, so soon as he shall be able to learn, what a solemn vow, promise, and profession, he hath here made by you. And that he may know these things the better, ye shall call upon him to hear Sermons; and chiefly ye shall provide, that he may learn the Creed, the Lord's Prayer, and the Ten Commandments, in the vulgar tongue, and all other things which a Christian ought to know and believe to his soul's health.'[1] Has a parent or a guardian performed these obligations if he says, 'My child, there are many ideals in the world, choose which you like. You do not like going to church? You shall not go. You prefer modern investigations to the Bible? You need not study it. You like a life in the open air? You shall go and drive horses in the Colonies. I do not seek to prejudice your mind. You shall judge for yourself.' But in the meantime history has begun to

[1] *Book of Common Prayer:* The Ministration of Public Baptism of Infants.

prejudice his mind. Passion has no such scruples, it openly solicits it. Friends and companions are instructing him, as by diagrams displayed before his mimetic mind, prejudicing him towards a certain course, and an outlay of moral strength which may or may not be desirable. Among the many shams of an age which seems to be the sport of formulæ, stands out conspicuous the figment of an absolutely unprejudiced choice. There is no such thing; there never can be: a man follows the strongest attraction, the most impressive ideal, and needs to be educated in his choice as much as in everything else.

Coleridge's 'botanical garden' is well known to readers of his works. 'Thelwall,' he says, 'thought it very unfair to influence a child's mind by inculcating any opinions before it should come to years of discretion, and be able to choose for itself. I showed him,' said Coleridge, ' my garden, and told him it was my botanical garden. "How so?" said he; "it is covered with weeds." "Oh!" I replied, "that is only because it has not yet come to years of discretion and choice. The weeds you see have taken the liberty to grow, and I thought it unfair in me to prejudice the soil towards roses and strawberries."'

No; the Church has no hesitation about the matter. Day by day, throughout the Christian year, she does not hesitate to set before a man, from his cradle to his grave, Jesus Christ as the Exemplar, the Ideal of his life —no mere character in a dead history speaking faintly across the ages, with a voice muffled by opposing cries, and stifled by the crash of dynasties and the ceaseless march of humanity, but as a living Person, a living Master, Who takes note of our efforts, softens our mistakes, and guides our energies as we try to assimilate our imperfect lives to the matchless Model before us.

Here, without doubt, is the Ideal for man. Here is One Who, once in the world's history, worked to the full bent of its power all the equipments of human life, Who at the beginning of His earthly existence could offer it all to God, and say, 'Lo, I come—that I should fulfil Thy will, O My God,'[1] Who at the end could say, 'It is finished.'[2] Here is the Model which has been the guiding influence of the great company of the saints, who have striven, however imperfectly, and with whatever falls, still to be faithful to the great call, 'Follow Me.'

But before the will contentedly resigns itself to follow this Ideal, less brilliant than other figures which flit across the world with dazzling flash—stern from its very greatness, inaccessible from its very completeness,—it demands and expects an answer to certain questions.

'Are you sure,' it says, 'are you quite certain, that Jesus Christ was very man? That Godhead in reserve—did it not make all the difference? That real "conversation in heaven,"[3] which to me is such a figure of speech, and so hard to realise, was it not always a present reality to Him? Was His weariness real, and not dramatic? Was His hunger natural, and not symbolical? Were not His sufferings, after all, merged and absorbed in the conscious fulfilment of a great mission?' The pendulum of controversy would seem at the present moment to have swung rather the other way. There has been an apparent desire to minimise at least one part of the influence of the divine nature on the human nature of our blessed Lord, and to assume,

---

[1] Psalm xl 9 10. [2] S. John xix 30. [3] Phil. iii 20.

as a necessary result of His perfect humanity, the existence of a real nescience on His part in the region of His human nature : that there were some things which He did not know; that about others He made mistakes; that in ordinary matters of experimental research and scientific truth He was not ahead of the ordinary knowledge of His time;[1] that He increased in wisdom and stature like any other boy; that, by His own confession, He was ignorant of the date of the Day of Judgment. He was intensely human, perfect man ; if He were not so, He could not really help us. But let us take care. The will, while wishing to find a closer point of contact in the perfect humanity, can very easily damage its ideal, and find only a distorted image and an imperfect character. While acknowledging that Jesus Christ was perfect man, let us take off our shoes from our feet, for the place whereon we stand is holy ground. Let us acknowledge that we are in a region where it is only too easy to make mistakes, and let us jealously guard the lustre and the glory which differentiates this image from all others, viz., that if Jesus Christ was perfect man, He was at the same time perfect God. And let us carefully recognise one or two primary truths to which we must constantly refer while making our estimate, by which we must correct every theory and plumb every hypothesis.

Let us remember, then, first of all, that we are dealing with only one Person, Jesus Christ, but that Person has two natures. That is, He possesses in His own Person two spheres of being, a higher and a lower, and it is

---

[1] 'He was not beyond the level of His age, inasmuch as He speaks as though salt could lose its savour, which we know it cannot do.' See Bishop Reichel *Cathedral and University Sermons* p. 131.

through the lower that He habitually, yet not always, manifests Himself to this world. And let us note, in the second place, that when our blessed Lord became man He did not cease to be God: and therefore, in His own Person, He knew all things.[1] It is impossible to limit knowledge in this way. I, in what is understood by the term 'I,' either know a thing or I do not. I cannot, if I do know it, by any known faculty *not* know it. But approaching us as He did, generally through His human nature, it may well be that there were some things which to the very end could not be translated, as it were, into the human sphere, but nevertheless 'as God He knew, in its Divine form, all history and all science, and He could at any moment make this infinite Divine knowledge available in the human sphere by simply translating it into human form.'[1] But nevertheless this would not have always been possible. As an infant, there would not have been the capacity for receiving in the human sphere what was afterwards possible to it when it grew into manhood. And so, all through the natural growth of the human nature, He gave to each stage of His growth that measure of human knowledge and wisdom which was appropriate to it, and of which it was capable. So He was the perfect infant, the perfect boy, the perfect man; but still at the end there may yet remain some things of which the perfect man even is not capable of receiving the translation; such, it may be, is the knowledge of the Day of Judgment— not a mere date which has to be kept profoundly secret from every human being, but a marvellous gathering up

---

[1] See a series of remarkable articles in the *Church Quarterly Review*, and especially, Our Lord's Knowledge as Man,' in the number of that periodical for October 1891.

of causes and effects, a bringing together of lines which seem rigidly parallel as they pass in front of human understanding, such as Predestination and Free-will. It is not that He is ignorant of the date of the Day of Judgment: He does not withhold knowledge so that it shall not pass from one of His natures to the other. But while we eagerly recognise the perfect Humanity, let us be very careful not to sacrifice the Divinity, nor listen to the desperate endeavour to damage a witness who cannot be got rid of. It is incredible that our blessed Lord could have made mistakes, or be ignorant, or be associated with error, or make accommodation. Yet for all this we say triumphantly to the will, 'Follow Him, imitate Him, He is a perfect Man. For the first time you see the human outfit undeflected by error, unstirred by passion, moving in perfect harmony and subservient energy, and in submission to the divine will.'

He suffered, He was weary, He was faint, He was hungry, He died; but He never made a mistake. He never was associated with error. He never was in doubt; yet Man, perfect Man, because perfect God.

But, in saying this, have we at all touched on the one point of sympathy in which the will most needs help? Could this divine Man sin? And if He could not sin, how could He be tempted in any but a purely academic and to us unreal sense? Most assuredly Christ could not sin, because He could not will to sin; and when we affirm that He could not will to sin, we do not merely mean that we cannot conceive of such an inflexible, firm, heaven-illuminated will consenting to sin. We mean more. We mean that it would be impossible in the nature of things for Him to will to sin, inasmuch as it would involve a contradiction, because the Person of our blessed Lord is divine. The person directs the will; and if by any hypothesis it were conceivably possible that He could sin, then we should be involved in the contradiction which belongs to the affirmation that God can sin. Shall we say, then, that God is not free, that He is less free than man to choose or not to choose, to take or not to take? No; man himself is not free beyond the limits of his nature. He does not complain because he cannot ignore natural obstacles, like a spirit. He is not less free because he cannot fly like a bird, or exist in the water like a fish. So, with the utmost reverence be it said, God is not free beyond the limits of His divine nature. He cannot deny Himself, He cannot lie, He cannot alter eternal truth, *e.g.* the truths of mathematics; He cannot make parallel straight lines meet, or two straight lines enclose a space; and yet we do not hesitate to say that God is absolutely free. And so, in the case of God Incarnate, there are some things which we cannot predicate of the Manhood alone, or the Godhead alone. We cannot speak of the Manhood being omnipotent, nor of the Godhead as suffering or as dying, although we can speak of God dying, and of Jesus Christ being eternal. But there are also some things which we can never predicate of the divine Person, where Humanity meets Godhead; and such are error, falsehood, and sin. To do so would involve the contradiction that God the Eternal Truth is fallible, God the Eternal Justice can deceive, God the Eternal Holiness can sin.

How then, it may be said, can Jesus Christ be my ideal? In this consists the most cruel, the most galling part of my trial. Here the will is caught up helpless by the inrolling tide, and tossed by the billows of temptation, and hurled out of its path, and twisted like plastic clay or snapped like a twig. And I look to Jesus Christ, and His humanity seems to bear a charmed existence. No wave can submerge Him, no eddying current deflect Him. How can He be my example? How can He feel what I feel? If I were God as well as man, then to me too temptation would be a very different thing to what it is.

But this is not the case. Although Jesus Christ was God, although He therefore could not sin, we yet feel that the author of the Epistle to the Hebrews was right when he said of Him, 'He was in all points tempted like as we are, yet without sin.'[1] It may be that He even suffered more keenly the fierce onslaught and the bitter horror of that poisonous breath.

For what, after all, is the pain of temptation? Surely a great deal more than the mere fear of falling, the possibility of falling into sin. A beleaguered outpost, which has no doubt about the issue, and is within hail of reinforcements, has to endure the full brunt of the conflict, and fire, it may be, its last shot. It knows more of the bitterness of the conflict than the detachment which gives in at the first onslaught. Many a man knows what it is to be tempted, where yet he never had any thought of giving in. Temptation in itself is a real pain and difficulty, a contest which has to be fought out over and over again before the fortress of the will. Our blessed Lord is no mere potentate from another state, making a dramatic visit to the scene of our woe. He 'was in all points tempted like as we are,

[1] Heb. iv 15.

yet without sin,' and we may take Him as our pattern under the blows of suffering, the buffets of misunderstanding, and the onslaught of temptation. He had a human will, in union with the divine Will, and hence He is able to show us how perfectly the will should rule within the compass of a man's nature. And if we look closely at the Ideal which we thus wish to follow, we shall find out some of the salient points which He offers for our imitation. First of all, there stands out clear the unbroken continued union with God, of which we have a certain image, as it were, in Religion. The will is powerless before its enemies; they find their way in through weak and undefended places, through moral, intellectual, or spiritual failures, unless we maintain intact this union with God. The abiding sense of God's presence, the strengthening of all the approaches which lead to God, the quickening of the divine side of our life, will more than anything else help us in our endeavour to conform to our great Example. For to man is offered an extension of the Incarnation. 'Christ in you.'[1] 'Nevertheless I live,' said S. Paul, 'yet not I, but Christ liveth in me.'[2] These are not rhetorical expressions, but realities. In our measure and in our way, the words we speak, the thoughts we think, the actions we do, may be the action of God within. This is the true enthusiasm, the sense of the indwelling presence of the divine Life. Assuredly this is our hope in temptation, that the more we become fulfilled with God, the more temptation will become external to us, and it will be true of us to say, he 'doth not commit sin; for His seed remaineth in him: and he cannot sin, because he is born of God.'[3]

[1] Col. i 27.   [2] Gal. ii 20.   [3] 1 S. John iii 9.

But still, in our endeavours to be like Christ, if the poor weak will eagerly asks what it can seize upon, how it shall begin its study, we must remember the one great point which distinguishes this ideal from all others is this: He was perfect. There is no note of sin in His character; if we interrogate history, if we ask His accusers, if we ask the witnesses who spoke against Him, the judge who condemned Him, and the centurion who witnessed His execution, if we ask Himself, the witness is one: He is innocent, He is sinless. And in copying this faultless character we must not aim at less; to do that were to run the risk of losing all. Life is either good or bad morally; you cannot talk of a fairly fresh egg. If the taint of sin is wilfully admitted anywhere, the verdict of Holy Scripture is merciless in its judgment: 'Whosoever shall keep the whole law, and yet offend in one point, he is guilty of all.'[1] And God never hesitates to put this ideal before us as attainable. He does not say, 'Be as good as you can; get most of your figures right in the sum of life.' What He does say is, 'Be ye therefore perfect, even as your Father Which is in Heaven is perfect.'[2] And to have grasped this great truth means an unsparing warfare against weak points and privileged sins. It means that life itself depends in some instances on plucking out the right eye and cutting off the right foot; that we cannot read a degrading work of fiction simply because it deals in striking situations, or mix up worldliness and Religion because so many other people seem to do so. 'I, at least, have a weak eye, a diseased foot; I cannot read, I cannot go: it means death to me.' And in doing this

[1] S. James ii 10.   S. Matt. v 48.

we learn something of the ideal at which we are aiming. In following after the perfect, I cannot tolerate a fault which a little resolution will remove.

And further, our Ideal is nailed to the cross. To follow it means unpopularity, and a running counter to public opinion. It means shame, it means a long struggle. It is one of the most perplexing things to find how goodness contrives to elude our grasp. In former years we used to say that the cause of this was to be found in the low state of Church-life, in the meagre worship and neglect of sacramental truth. Now we have restored our churches and revived sacramental life, yet sin and worldliness go on merrily as before, while even our immediate predecessors in the Faith seem to leave behind in their memories tints of beauty, delicacies of form, and beauties of character which seem to show that they caught—what, alas! we so often seem to miss—just the lines, the curves, the lights and shadows, which give the likeness to Jesus Christ.

There is no short road to goodness. Restored churches, choral services, uncompromising orthodoxy, will only be valuable to us in so far as they are stamped with the stigmata of the Crucified. The will must submit to Christ, and the will must rule over the passions, over everything which is not of God; while the secret of a good life is a close conformity to the divine Model, the motto of which is the happy boast of the Psalmist, 'I have set God always before me,'[1] or, as we should say, in the timid language of our daily life, 'What would Jesus Christ have done?'

[1] Psalm xvi 9.

CHAPTER VII

THE OBSTACLES TO RELIGION—EXTERNAL

'About the river of human life there is a wintry wind, though a Heavenly sunshine; the iris colours its agitation, the frost fixes upon its repose. Let us beware that our rest become not the rest of stones, which so long as they are torrent-tossed and thunder-stricken maintain their majesty, but when the stream is silent, and the storm passed, suffer the grass to cover them, and the lichen to feed on them, and are ploughed down into dust.'

WHAT a beautiful thing Religion appears to be, as we discuss it with our friends, or study its fair proportions in a theological treatise! We could extend indefinitely out of our fuller knowledge the utilitarian proverb, and assert that not only 'Honesty is the best policy,' but that Religion itself is obviously the highest good for man, and the secret of all happiness. It deals with simple things, and great aims, and pious aspirations. Just a good resolution, a few prayers, and ordinary perseverance, and the thing is done. But as soon as we pass out of the region of books or sympathetic friendship, how violent and startling is the contrast! This affair of sentiment, resolution, good desire, turns out to be a matter of most astounding difficulty. 'It is a real work to be good.' The obstacles that have to be surmounted, the opposition which has to be faced, and, stranger still, the real struggle which has to be gone through in order to carry out its simplest requirements, are at first sight perplexing, and wellnigh disheartening. If a man of ordinary education has determined with himself to carry out a certain course of action, or relinquish a lifelong pursuit, he finds that he has the necessary energy to carry it through, and the proper determination to make the alteration which he had decided upon. Why, therefore, when he has settled to do such a simple thing as say a prayer, does he find it so astonishingly difficult? Why, when he wishes to relinquish some habit which he believes to be contrary to moral perfection, does he find himself baffled by an almost sensible opposition? He sees the advantage and the beauty of a consistent morality; he sees the transcendent excellences of the higher virtues, and the supreme loveliness of the divine ideal put before him in the Gospel, and yet he is met by an opposition and by difficulties such as he encounters in no other sphere of effort. He is like Moses bringing Israel out of Egypt: he is thwarted by a Pharaoh at every turn, who knows not the Lord, neither will let Israel go. He is confronted by a set of ideas in which beauty, and excellence, and moral aspiration seem to melt away, and leave only the broken framework of a wrecked resolution.

God in His divine Revelation has supplied the answer, an answer which is justified of all His children, who have taken Him at His word, and are pressing anxiously onward along the strait and narrow way that leadeth unto life. And the answer is this: that these difficulties, so strange, and complicated, and persistent in their nature, are traceable to the fact that we cannot make a step in the direction of spiritual excellence without encountering a fierce current of opposition from three distinct classes of foes, which have been distinguished and classified, and scientifically studied, and may be recognised by their titles, at once distinctive and descriptive, as the Devil, the World, and the Flesh. Twice over, at very solemn crises of his life, the Christian is brought into violent conflict with these foes, that he may recognise them and renounce them, namely, at his Baptism and, in the Church of England, at his Confirmation; and all through life he is warned of their nearness, their malignity, and their determination. Any attempt therefore to deal adequately with the subject of Religion would be incomplete if it did not take account of the active opposition which every Christian man must expect to encounter from these ancient foes of the human race.

I

These foes may be divided into two groups: those which are external, which await him in the outside world, and those which come from within. The first we know under the familiar titles of the Devil and the World, the second is comprised in the designation known as the Flesh. With each and all of these Religion is actively concerned. They may mean its utter failure and destruction; they may mean, on the other hand, its fuller development and perfection through the temptations which they bring. It would be well therefore carefully to consider each of these antagonistic groups as they affect the Christian in his endeavour to reach out to the fulness of Religion in its moral and spiritual excellence. If we take first of all the group of external enemies, it will be well carefully to examine the nature of that being whom Holy Scripture, at all events, consistently puts before us as our chief foe,—the Devil. Certainly, whenever we attempt to consider sin, in its bearing on human life, we are struck at once by its extreme malignity. It would seem to be so much more than a mere blemish on nature, a mere privation of goodness, a branch which fails to be productive, or a mechanism which is hampered in its working, a state of being which fails of the highest. The disorder is too active, the hindrance is too positive, to allow us so to regard it. Looking at the extreme malignity of evil, its sometimes apparent causelessness, to the utter degradation brought about by it, in which man of all creatures has an unhappy pre-eminence, we can count on the acquiescence of a large and thoughtful body of experience, when we point from evil to an evil agent, from sin to a personal tempter, from disaster to one who evidently with consummate skill has marshalled his allurements, and prepared his traps, baited with pleasure and barbed with death.

It is the fashion to dismiss on *a priori* grounds the belief in a personal devil, and to substitute in its place an impalpable principle of evil, which floats in the moral atmosphere with poisonous germs, or which, more probably still, merely represents the uncontrolled desires of human nature, dressed up in a picturesque garb, and personified with a concrete existence outside the individual from whose inner consciousness it takes its rise.

This might be a perfectly reasonable explanation of a widespread belief, were it not for the fact, that on no showing can it be maintained that our blessed Lord, in the pages of the Gospels, ever spoke and acted on any other idea than this, that He indorsed the popular Jewish belief on this subject prevalent in His day, and evidently acted as One Who, more than once, and notably at a great spiritual crisis in His earthly life, had conflicts with a personal agent of evil known as the Devil. There can be no doubt on this point; and therefore to trace up the Jewish belief on this matter would be idle, or to attempt to sift or minimise the unquestionable earnestness of their conviction. It is, as we have said, indorsed, and, more than this, expanded, by our blessed Lord, almost to the extent of a revelation on the subject. So that it becomes to a Christian a simple case of accepting this belief on His testimony, or else of launching out into the shoal-water of a limited knowledge in His humanity, or even of a perilous economy of truth, by which, in seeking to save the divine wisdom, we come terribly near a shattering of the divine truthfulness.

With the opening chapters of S. Matthew's Gospel we are brought face to face with this being, described as if already well known under the title of Devil, a title which, it will be noticed, had already appeared in the Septuagint version of the Scriptures as the Greek equivalent of Satan, the adversary, namely, in 1 Chron. xxi 1; Job i 6, ii 1; in Zechariah iii 1 2; and in Wisdom ii 24. And under the plain teaching of Christ and His apostles, there stands out a clear conception of a potentate of evil, who appears in the first book of Holy Scripture as well as in the last; now

I

described by this significant designation, now by that; of whom we learn, that while of great power, he is in no sense of a co-ordinate power with God, neither omnipotent, omniscient, nor omnipresent, but yet with a terrible facility of turning to evil and ultimate destruction those who are heirs of salvation. We learn that no one, not even our blessed Lord Himself, is exempted from his attacks; but that on resistance he is powerless to harm, and is never allowed to wield a temptation too great for human endurance. We learn, further, that, exercising as he does a mysterious dominion in this world, his power has been curbed and practically crushed, by the atoning death of Christ on the cross, to those who will avail themselves of it; and that the whole Christian system is charged with strength to those who have to fight the battle against him, and those powers which are allied with him.

All the titles given to him in Holy Scripture are significant, and well worthy of our spiritual study. But in examining the two especially by which we usually designate him, we shall best see the nature of the obstacles which he interposes between us and the realisation of our religious ideal. To speak of an evil spirit opens up a general view of his nature; to call that evil spirit by the unusual names of Devil or Satan, shows us that our attention is thereby invited to particular aspects of his assaults, for which we must be prepared, and against which we must arm ourselves.

In the first place, then, God in His Revelation of the spiritual field of combat would have us know that we must expect to encounter one whose systematic action may best be described as a prolonged slander.

The particular malice against which we have to guard is the malice which comes from a clever, unscrupulous, and very plausible slanderer. And a moment's reflection will show us what a powerful weapon misrepresentation will be, in giving a wrong orientation to our life. We believe ourselves to be beings of considerable importance, associated with other human beings to whom we can do good, and who will do good to us, by a Supreme Being, Whose one aim is to promote our welfare and happiness. A terrible doubt crosses our minds that we are mistaken on all these points. Revelation shows us the cause of the suspicion in the person of a malignant slanderer, who is sapping the principles of life and action by deadly doubt, and a most potent suggestion of evil. Clearly if Religion be a personal relation with a Personal God, as we have tried to prove it to be, the effect of evil would notoriously be directed towards impairing that relation, and so we find that the devil is busily engaged in slandering God to men. It is easy to see his tactics manifested when he persuades the sinner, as he persuaded Eve, that death is not the penalty of disobedience, but only a scare to frighten away from the fuller enjoyment of life: that fall, if fall there be, will be a fall upwards, and that an increase of knowledge and resource forms the best answer to a petty restriction. It is not so easy to see the dark figure which stands in the front of every vocation to turn aside those to whom life appeals with its seriousness, or the direct call of God with its commanding importance. It is not so easy to detect a malignant influence behind the zeal for God's honour which affects even to distrust His condescension, and to deprecate His special providence, or His minute care for our personal needs. It is astonishing to see how many are inquiring what God ought to have said, and how few what He has said; how many are anxious to have God on their side, and how few are anxious to be on the side of God. Among the sad incidents of religious controversy, surely one of the saddest is to notice how quickly God is denied the freedom of action, and His right to give orders. 'Yea, hath God said?' seems to be a call to criticism, and a challenge to rebellion, and that which makes these attitudes to be possible is a *pheme* which has been subtly spread abroad, that either God is not what He is supposed to be, or that the command has been strangely perverted in the delivery of it.

A slander as regards the world of our fellow-men is no less potent as an instrument of evil. We have read the sigh of the libertine for a life in some region of the globe 'where the best is like the worst,' and where the obligation to obey the code of the Ten Commandments is not recognised. It is a sad thing when Satan appeals, under the high pretexts of morality, to the bad lives of some who have failed to live answerably to their profession. The falls of good men, besides the pitiable damage which is thereby done to their own lives, have this particular malignity, that they tend in the devil's hands to sap public confidence in the existence of goodness, and to foster a belief that good people are hypocrites who have not been found out. Hypocrisy, even if it be the homage which vice pays to virtue, stabs it in its most vital part, in the very act of the most profound protestation of respect. A belief in the universal corruption of men, and in the insincerity of all religious profession, and in the impossibility of being good, is the most damaging of all convictions. It is the inversion of the powerful appeal which a good example affords to the soul. It is like the failure of instances on which we relied for our proof, and becomes a potent agent of despair in the depression which shrinks back from a struggle doomed to failure, on the testimony of those witnesses on which we relied to prove the contrary.

The slanderer of mankind has done a clever stroke of work when he persuades Elijah, whose energy he most fears, and whose success is most disquieting, that he is alone and unsupported, that all have gone out of the way, all have become altogether abominable, and that Israel has answered his passionate summons by an unanimous and total apostasy to Baal. We have advanced many steps towards the belief that holiness is impossible, when we have listened to the slander that all holy men are hypocrites, and all heroes undetected impostors.

And there is a further development of his malice still, even more damaging, if possible, to the spiritual life, in which the slanderer slanders us to ourselves. 'Fret not thyself, else shalt thou be moved to do evil,'[1] says the Psalmist more than once. Depression, gloom, unhappiness, a rooted sense of spiritual impotency, are a fruitful seed-bed from which under his influence issues a whole crop of disfiguring weeds. There are some people whom the devil is damaging by pride, making them think of themselves more highly than they ought to think; but there are many others whom he is damaging by depression. Surely it is one of the most malignant aspects of temptation that by a subtle process which

[1] Psalm xxxvii 8.

he wots of, the inducement to sin may be made to take the form of sin itself, and the heart be prepared for a deadly fall, because it had believed for a long time that the dark cloud of temptation had been self-produced, and was the exhalation of a heart given to evil. How terribly hindering, again, is the taunt which imputes wrong motives to good actions! There are some who have even given up the reverent expression of a religious faith, because they have been taunted within by an accusation of hypocrisy. There are some who have brought themselves to believe that any form of good works is the most dangerous kind of sin ; or who have been led to believe that even the barest satisfaction in doing a good action is of so dangerous a nature, that the action, though good, had better not be repeated, lest it should set up the feeling which may only too possibly be sinful. In the legends of the saints, it is recorded that a holy man was taunted while saying his prayers by the evil suggestion, that all these prayers and acts of devotion were dictated by a spirit of display, and ministered to pride, whereupon he replied to the tempter, 'I did not begin to say my prayers because of thee, and I shall not leave off because of thee.' No one in the ordinary experience of life would give up doing his simple duty because a bystander taunted him with display. And it must be regarded as an unerring sign of defeat, when a man allows himself to be depressed into a lower life, or frightened out of doing good actions by an unworthy sense of his own unworthiness; while of all difficult obstacles to overcome scruples remain the most difficult, —just the pebble put in the shoe to take all pleasure out of progress, and to make the Christian limp instead of run in the way of God's commandments with a heart which has been set at liberty. There are some people, it has been said, who think that 'pretending everything that they had done was sinful, is a sign of holiness.' And the unreal and unnatural state of mind thereby set up is a distinct and dangerous hindrance. A man is bound to be as business-like with his own spiritual life as he is with every other department of his nature. He will know, when he has done all, that he is still an unprofitable servant. He will know that he is but a child daubing with the materials of an artist, or just roughing out the imperfect outline, which is all that he is able to achieve; but still faithfulness, effort, earnestness of purpose, honest labour, are terms which have their meaning even in the elementary strivings of a child after a perfection which eludes him; whereas an indolent refusal to do the best possible because it will be inadequate, an unworthy waiting for some one else, not to finish or correct, but to initiate and undertake, indicates a temper of mind not to be praised for its diffidence, but blamed and punished for culpable neglect. More and more evident become the signs of the gigantic slander which represses honest effort in any part of man's composite nature, under the sense of a crushing powerlessness, and an indolent acquiescence in it. Each generation starts afresh with the glorious enthusiasm which God inspires, and each generation sinks back in the utter depression of having been deluded, or of having miscalculated the opposition, or underrated the difficulty. God inspires in His children the generous longing to undergo hardships, and to patiently undertake great things. The breath of slander too often sweeps across with its scorching blast, and leaves behind it a shrunken heap of lifeless faith, blighted hope, and shrivelled enthusiasm.

'The slanderer' is clearly a title which comes to us from those spiritual regions, where the force of evil is more subtly distinguished than we are able to distinguish for ourselves. But the common title of Satan, or the Adversary, which Holy Scripture also gives to the agent of evil, is an indication of his nature which more directly appeals to us. Every one who has tried to serve God has known what it is to feel the shock of a rude and determined opposition. The difficulty of goodness we have already discussed, and it is in itself sufficiently remarkable; but a closer study will reveal the fact that this difficulty is largely brought about by direct opposition on the part of a spiritual foe. We are allowed to study, in the pages of the Evangelists, the Pattern-Man encountering the opposition which was designed to stop Him from entering on His ministry in the full strength of an unsullied humanity. Satan fell back from that impregnable citadel baffled at every point; but he is not always so unsuccessful with those whom he encounters and seeks to damage for the purposes of their mission. We note that every portion of man's composite being is attacked, and the effort is made to set up in each department, as it were, a disabling hindrance which shall ruin the main purpose of life. First and most easy to be attacked are what may be called the low-lying parts of human nature,—the body, with its craving senses and delicate susceptibilities. Solomon, the wisest of men, was seduced through these to the condition of an undignified sensualist, and the builder of the temple was turned into the undenomitional idolater. David, whose heart had been responsive to every ripple of the divine breath, lapsed through these into a dull and timid time-server; he lost his delicacy of spiritual insight and his straightforward earnestness of purpose. Long lines of captive youth, of degraded heroes, dead to all sense of mission, lost to all sense of dignity, exhibit, in all ages and in all countries, the sudden arrest of life, under the withering blight of passion.

It is to this region that the adversary first directed his attack in the temptation of our Lord and Master. He comes to Him as if the first thought in His mind must be dictated by the cravings of hunger. 'Turn the stones of the desert into bread, and abandon an unnatural fast.' He could hardly have expected to succeed with any temptation of gross allurement, but many men who have conquered sensuality in its worst form are keenly exposed to the hindrance which comes in under the guise of a search after comfort. Samson in the arms of a Delilah is an extreme case, but the young nobleman who misses his vocation because he has great riches is by no means an uncommon instance in which a life full of sap and vigour, which promises great things, is perverted and blasted by the sudden arrest caused by a suggestion in which the love of comfort is allowed to thrust back the purposes of a higher life. Satan, the adversary, has no need to go further, in the great majority of cases, than the region of the body, with its senses and desires. But to the man who has escaped, and ascended the mountain-top of ambition, he equally knows how to accommodate himself. If he fails in the region of appetite, he can almost certainly succeed in the higher region of the soul, where from the council-chamber of the will issue forth the imperial projects and the designs of the vigorous mind reaching out after power. How subtly the adversary shifts for his victims the focus of vision! 'Not Jerusalem, with the Cross and Passion; look towards Greece, with its sun of intellectual splendour still tinging the clouds of its night; look towards the region of beauty, warm life, and ever-widening development; look towards the stern granite rocks of Roman vigour and commanding imperialism!' Satan stands behind many a young man as he looks out over his vocation from the hill-top which he has won by his youthful successes, and delicately shifts the field of his vision, from the stern outline of duty to the beckoning distances of cloudland, whose castles mount up in terraces of brilliant promise in the air, as yet unruffled by the storm. Satan makes havoc of vocations in the region of the soul; while, if he fails here, he knows that he can find a place for the sole of the foot on the very pinnacle of the temple, in the region of the spirit—when the choice has been made, and the sacrifice of all has been enterprised, and the life of spiritual energy has been chosen. Here, too, we can see the success of the adversary in the sullen hatred breathing through religious controversy; in the strange fantastic pride, which is ever seeking exemption, to be treated as a personal friend of God, with a private chariot of angels always at hand, instead of the monotonous stair of graduated grace.

In one region or another of our being, perhaps in all, we are sure to encounter this enemy of our life. Can we wonder then that Religion is hard? that we succeed so indifferently when we have to encounter opposition such as this? Is there not reason and prudence in the oft-repeated warnings which we receive as to the hatred of this foe? Can there be any course more fatal than to listen to the last and clever device in which our enemy, while feigning to be dead, induces the sons of God to believe that they are showing their superior wisdom and knowledge by refusing to believe in his existence at all?

II

Besides this enemy, known as the Devil and Satan, we are warned that we must expect opposition and hindrance from another enemy whom it is less easy to detect, and whom it is much more difficult to describe. Over the infant life, barely conscious of any part of its environment, is breathed a challenge in his name, returnable to him when his time for conflict has come, against an impalpable foe called 'the World.' Again, as the paths of life open out at his feet, along all or any of which he may hear the jingling bridle and the clatter of steel which herald the approach of his adversary, once more he challenges the World, and before many days are over he finds himself immersed in the heat of conflict, a conflict which never leaves him until he sinks to rest after the long fever of life. What then is this adversary known as 'the World'? How often we are warned against it! how often we protest against it! How afraid we are of what it will say! how zealously we watch its moods! Now we are eagerly welcoming its approach, and putting out our hand to take the prizes which it brings. 'The Great World.' It is a queen of beauty which presides over the tournament of life. Now we are chiding it and shrinking from it: 'the heartless World' we call it, which has stabbed and crushed us, and has given its cruel blow without a word. Now we appeal to it in triumph: 'Every one says so, therefore it must be right; it is the verdict of the World.' Now we protest that it must be wrong and unbecoming a Christian, because it is 'an unworthy common-place, a mere vulgar maxim of the World.' What is it—this power which we alternately welcome and avoid, denounce and coax, love and hate? Who is this enemy who moves about holding our infant challenge and our boyish gage, which he means to answer and acknowledge? What is the device upon his shield, the war-cry of his onslaught, the signal of his approach? If it is difficult to grasp the personality of Satan, the other enemy whom we were just now considering, it is still more difficult to realise a foe in 'the World,' for here, at all events, there has never been any conflict of opinion; no one has ever pretended that 'the World' is a person to be scientifically studied and appraised, or carefully watched like a beast of prey now ready to spring. What is it then? Is it 'a nickname for everything that the Church hates,' a name which we give to something outside ourselves which fascinates us, as a child will speak to trees and bushes and flowers, as if they were kings and queens and giants? Or is it merely a peevish impersonation of something which has failed to please, help, and gladden us in life as we see it around us?

It is difficult to grasp what we mean by 'the World'—still, it is a real foe for all that; not indeed as a person, but as an influence. When we talk of 'the World,' it is needless to say that we do not mean the beautiful scene in which God Almighty has placed us. It does not mean, it could not mean, that this world, so fair and so exquisitely planned, is after all only a gilded cloak of lead which presses down the soul, and that we must resolutely put away its influence as we value our soul's welfare. Neither do we mean the society of our fellow-men, from which we must withdraw like the hermits and pillar saints, useful as such lives may have been as a protest, that those who lived in the world must make it a place where a Christian could exist without fear of contamination.

> We need not bid, for cloister'd cell,
> Our neighbour and our work farewell,
> Nor strive to wind ourselves too high
> For sinful man beneath the sky.

Whatever may have been the state of the case in the semi-Paganism of the first ten centuries, there is no uncertainty on this point now. It may be, it is true, a 'World' which comes out of these surroundings, but not to be confused with them,—a 'World' wholly and entirely evil, which can only be met by a Christian in one attitude, which is summed up in that vigorous and comprehensive word, 'renounce.'

It is possible that before now we may have ascended some eminence which commands a large outlook, and have gazed down on some city lying at our feet, with its acres of houses, its teeming ant-heaps of swarming humanity, and its large industrial machinery busily at work. And we notice, as we gaze, the smoke from the many thousand chimneys pouring forth their black wreaths of vapour into the air. We see it sailing before the wind, now in this direction, now in that. We see it hanging like a pall over the city, to descend in sooty showers, or, in certain states of the atmosphere, to envelop the inhabitants in the Egyptian darkness of a fog, which wraps the city in gloom, while a few miles away there is sunshine and sweetness. Something like this surely in the moral region is 'the World.' Hundreds and hundreds of lives are being lived, and have been lived, by human beings—bad lives, careless or indifferent. Some are like the tall chimneys beneath us, lives wholly of worldly business. Some are like the chimneys of places of amusement, lives wholly given up to pleasure. Some are like the clustered chimney-pots of the foul rookeries and squalid dens of vice, lives wholly noxious and bad. Out of all these lives ascends, as it were, a thin smoke-like vapour which we describe as public opinion, the spirit of the age, or by some equivalent term. There are fires which have never been put out, all down the centuries, the fumes of which are issuing sometimes blacker and more poisonous as fresh materials are piled on. As the machinery of life becomes more complicated, more chimneys spring up, and more smoke blows up to add its density to the great cloud of materialism which sways in the wind, black and poisonous, light and subtle. There it is, where it has been all through these ages, that influence called 'the World.' Sometimes there is a fog, and the historian chronicles an outbreak of revolutionary violence, or of immorality, or atheism, or contempt of life, or a general eruption of evil. Sometimes it is only hazy, dull and poisonous, and delicate lives languish, and beautiful objects are tarnished, and flowers wither and die. We say then it is an unhealthy atmosphere. Such is 'the World'— an influence subtler and more deadly in some places than in others; but everywhere it penetrates the houses of the great and of the humble, the church, the study, the very cloister. It is a question which is asked of every child without distinction, at his Baptism and at his Confirmation—'Dost thou renounce the World?' And the answer put into his mouth is short and decisive—'I do.'

It becomes then a serious question for any one who is aiming after true Religion, how he is to meet this foe, so ubiquitous and so subtle. Ample room as there still is for the life of consecrated devotion withdrawn within the cloister, yet, on the other hand, there are 'those wonderful and unexpected openings for a true service of God, those unthought-of possibilities of character and goodness which have been shown to men in states of life, where of old such service seemed impossible.' The perfection of the great majority of men has to be wrought out not only in spite of, but to a certain extent by means of, contact with the world. It is Mr. Ruskin who tells us of the Alpine flower which he first saw growing in a fat pasture, and only noticed it because it was new to him, but failed to see its noble function and order of glory until he had found it alone among the rack of the higher clouds, piercing through the edge of avalanche, poor and feeble, and seemingly exhausted with its efforts, but there fulfilling its ideal character.[1] It is true that in this respect we may miserably deceive ourselves, and think that all dinner-parties are going to be to us like the marriage-feast at Cana, so many opportunities for manifesting forth God's glory; that a reputation for coming eating and drinking may make us like Christ,

[1] Ruskin *Mod. Painters* vol. ii p. 115 new edition 1897.

while to be abstemious and ascetic may saddle upon us the contemptuous charge brought against S. John Baptist, 'he hath a devil.' We may think that a knowledge of the World and its maxims is as necessary as a knowledge of Heaven and its maxims—still the road to victory, and the road to our perfection, leads across the plain which is scoured by the onslaughts of 'the World,' a foe which may also injure the most retired and sheltered life. 'I pray not,' said our blessed Lord, 'that Thou shouldest take them out of the world, but that Thou shouldest keep them from the evil.'[1] Whether we like it or not, we must encounter the onslaught of a subtle and dangerous foe, who fights under the cognisance of 'the World.' But true it is, here as everywhere else, ὅπου δ' ἀγῶνες ἐκεῖ καὶ στέφανοι.

There are many forms in which the subtle influence of 'the World' makes itself felt. The World, for instance, has a form of religion, peculiar to itself, which is in sharp contrast with the Religion of the Crucified. There is Religion as we know it, so grand, so beautiful in its exquisite proportion. Even natural Religion, as it is called, incites mankind to worship and fall down and kneel before the great Maker of the World, Whose glory leaps out behind the sunrise and the sunset, and throbs in the spring flowers, and lingers in the notes of birds, and the wondrous order of the universe. 'Let him see the glory of our God,' said the Patriarch of Constantinople to the envoys of Vladimir, seeking for the true Religion; and the beauty of the Liturgy, the magnificence of the Service of the Sanctuary, sent them back impressed as with a heavenly visitation. Still the pure precepts of the Sermon on

[1] S. John xvii 15.

the Mount, the exquisite refinement of Christian virtues, rare and imperfectly manifested as they may be, extract an involuntary homage from those who witness them. Over Religion is traced the legend, 'Thine eyes shall see the King in His beauty, they shall behold the land of far distances,'—distances where Nature melts into God, the veil of the Sacrament into a visible Presence, the beauty of the Christ-like character into Christ Himself,—distance behind distance in the Communion of Saints; distance behind distance in the supernatural Church; distance behind distance in the possibilities of saintliness. But the World-fog obliterates distances, it settles down pitilessly on all, and brings with it everywhere the stamp of a brown formalism. It is astonishing to note how the distances die away under its depressing influence. Hard and vigorous, scarred with martyrdoms and maimed with persecution, emerged the Church of the Catacombs, yet strong in a strength not of this world, vigorous with the vigour of a life hid with Christ in God. Toleration and court-favour soon stifled it. The distances died away, men supposed that godliness was a way of gain, they had the form without the power. And gradually there sprung up the idea that the world was a place in which piety could not live, and the desert was filled with its refugees, who fled, too often carrying with them the ghost which they wished to escape from.

Religious phraseology with the Puritans lost its distance and became cant. Religious observances with Catholics lost their distance and became mechanical duties. The World knows how to read its Bible, but it is expurgated; the World knows how to go to church, but it is a mechanical routine ; the World knows how to fast, but it is with the refinements of carefully arranged dishes, and a Lent cookery-book. It would make sackcloth becoming, and ashes which at least would not blacken. Worse than this, the World makes its Communion without the hand of faith to receive, or the preparation of the heart to welcome. It makes confession without sorrow, and does penance without amendment. The religion of the World stands outside life, and affects it only in so far as it stills a craving, and stops a gap, or hinders a too abrupt breaking with the piety which binds us to a religious past, or from the shock to propriety which would serve to rouse us to our real state. Surely this is a foe which every religious man needs to watch. When Prayer opens out no distance, when Holy Communion lifts no veil, when Confession leaves us unmoved by sorrow, and Sunday is only another day in a round of pleasures, on which, as in a musical box, the same mechanism is set to play another tune with another set of barrels—then we must anxiously ask ourselves, Is not this the World ? Is not this the spirit which turned golden priests with chalices of wood into wooden priests with chalices of gold ? Is this the spirit which made Bible-phraseology ridiculous in the mouths of hypocrites, and made Church rites a mockery in the inconsistent surroundings of a careless life ?

At such times, when we sit at home like the reckless king, and cut out the pages of God's message which speak to us of His wrath ; when Religion has become a routine, in which heart and interest refuse to follow ; when there is a startling and ironical discrepancy between our profession and our practice : then it behoves us to take care; already we are enveloped in that cold clinging vapour which obliterates distance. We cannot join in the cry of victory which sounded from the lips of our Lord and Saviour, 'Be of good cheer; I have overcome the World.'[1] The testimony is more true which says of us, 'They are of the World: therefore speak they of the World, and the World heareth them.'[2]

And it is not only in its estimate of Religion that the World is so dangerous. It has also its pernicious estimate of sin, which is full of peril to those who allow themselves to be taken in by it. The worldly estimate of sin is of such a character that it obliterates the familiar warnings placed to keep men from danger, and curls deceitfully over its most treacherous pitfalls. Here the World proves itself to be no unimportant auxiliary to Satan, inasmuch as it brings people nearer to sin than they would otherwise have allowed themselves to come without it. It succeeds only too well in obliterating by a hazy indistinctness the division between right and wrong, while it hides the ill consequences of misdoing, and the certain issue of an act of disobedience. For instance, it would not be easy for Satan to penetrate in open vice into the carefully guarded home of a strict propriety, but it is perfectly easy for him to do so within the cover of a novel, which 'every one is reading, and which has so many striking situations, and is so astonishingly clever.' A deliberate proposal to upset the accepted estimate of modesty would scandalise and shock. *Maxima debetur pueris reverentia* is a maxim which has taken a prominent place in the ethical systems of society. 'But after all,' says the

[1] S. John xvi 33.   [2] 1 S. John iv 5.

World, 'young people must know sooner or later the guilty secrets of this strange life. Is it better that they should snatch them for themselves from the horror-chambers of life with surreptitious tread and stolen key? Is it better that they should be startled by the abrupt and malicious revelation of the serpent, twined in the branches of the tree of knowledge, and learn with the shock of a surprise, that which might have been imparted to them with care and due precaution, and all the forearming which forewarning was meant to give?' Surely here the fog lies very dense, and many people are being led thereby into a terrible and irreparable loss. If there is one beauty in the world for which nothing can compensate, it is that priceless gift of innocence. 'Ye shall not surely die.' 'Ye shall be as God, knowing good and evil.' These are not utterances made for the first time at this period of the world's history. Granted that in some rare cases the knowledge of evil may pass over a soul, and leave not a stain behind; still it is an experience which has made all the difference between that mysterious and wonderful power, which we recognise in a little child, and an older life which just lacks that fearlessness of progress, because it is conscious of a danger, when not conscious of an evil desire.

In a sermon on the rare and beautiful topic of Innocence, speaking of curiosity, the writer says: 'There are forms of it, which for all their intellectual disguises are immediately hurtful to the spiritual life. They creep upon us in the name of culture and humanism, and a liberal acquaintance with all that men have thought or done, and the motto '*Humani nihil alienum*' is the fair pretext under which we sully the imagination, and debase the heart, and dissipate the power of the soul. Now the intuition of innocence sees through all this. No man or woman can preserve that priceless jewel who has not fought the temptation to curiosity in one or more of its many forms, and knows something of the bitter struggle to bring every thought into captivity to the obedience of Christ. . . . While the curious have weakened and degraded their faculties for using the experience they have gained, the innocent possess an imagination which is their servant and not their master, a memory that is a storehouse of knowledge, not a haunted chamber of remorse, a reason that has not been paralysed by straining at impossible tasks, a will that has not lost the power of issuing in action, pure affections that instinctively tend to guide the mind aright; and theirs, and theirs only, in the end, is the vision of the truth that shall make free.'[1] The anatomist does not welcome mechanical experience if it damages his sensitiveness of hand, the pianist does not accept the knowledge of artistic construction as a compensation for the loss of delicacy of touch; neither can the Christian welcome the knowledge of evil, if it cloud over, be it only with a film, the brightness of that vision in which he looks to see God.

Propriety, etiquette, the verdict of society,—these are some of the artificial barriers by which 'the World' hopes to keep out the grossness which would startle the soul to a sense of its position. But true it is of its pitiless justice, that here the transgressor finds

'Though God has mercy, man has none.'

---

[1] See 'Innocence' No. VII of *University and Cathedral Sermons* by Rev. R. Illingworth pp. 107-109.

It is the sense of sin which must be rescued from the obliterating fog of a careless World, which panders to the devil by confusing the issues of life and death.

There is yet another region in which we can trace the dangerous influence of 'the World.' There is a power of evil which succeeds in confusing and distorting the view of life which a man deliberately puts before himself. Under this influence men and women lead an artificial life, and forget its true nobility, mistaking gaslight for the sun, and the heated room for the soft air of heaven, while amusement is substituted for purpose, and recreation made to be the end and object of life. Perhaps one of the most dangerous developments of modern life is to be found in its want of seriousness of purpose, and of a true recognition of our own dignity. There are two remarkable phenomena of the present day. One is the great growth of amusement, ranging from bodily exercise to entertainment and diversion of the mind; and the other is the great and ever-increasing list of luxuries which minister to the needs of our quickened activity. Is the World right when it puts these things before men as the end and object of existence, when all the powers of mind and body are scientifically directed simply to amusement and easy living, when banter does duty for wit, and criticism of others for conversation, where life is a recurring series of pleasures, varied with excitement? Perhaps we hardly realise the damage which is done to our character by simply letting ourselves go without restraint, while we allow life to lose its dignity when it loses its purpose, and to dissipate its happiness by an intoxication of pleasure, which only leaves the heart the colder and the more weary when the spell is over, ready to offer a prize for a new sensation, or reward the discoverer of a novel amusement. Rome was shocked out of her scant propriety when she saw her emperor drive about disguised as a charioteer while the Christians were being tortured to death. Is it less sad to see those to whom God has given the gift of life squandering it only on the passing pleasures of self-gratification, or degrading it by a heartless frivolity, while all around them there is that infinite pathos which only an infinite pity can reach, while there are gigantic evils to be met on all sides, and work which taxes our strength in the quietest home? Activity is Godlike. 'My Father worketh hitherto, and I work.'[1] God, Who placed us in this beautiful world, with its changes of light and form, and surrounded us with flowers, and hung the heavens with clouds, and placed in us the instinct of imagination and the power of humour and mirth, can never be angry with recreation, when it takes its proper place, and ministers to our ultimate good. But it is sad to see a Samson, with his God-given strength, who was sent into the world with a mission to strike a blow for God and deliver Israel, asleep and shorn of his strength in the arms of his Delilah; or, at the best, slaying Philistines to pay a wager. It is time that the victims of 'the World' should realise their thraldom and shake themselves free; free from the slavery of custom, and free to follow each for himself the guidance of his own better self. The slavery of fashion, the tyranny of society, and the chains which men bind about themselves in habits which they will not give up, and in

---

[1] S. John v 17.

modes of life which they say they cannot change,—these are strait and cramping and hinder the development of a better self.

> While the locks are yet brown on thy head,
> While the soul still looks through thine eyes,
> While the heart still pours
> The mantling blood to thy cheek,
> Sink, O youth, in thy soul!
> Yearn to the greatness of nature,
> Rally the good in the depths of thyself!

In 'the World,' at all events, there is a foe worthy of the steel of the tried combatant. If Religion could assert itself, and realise the hopes of those who so nobly strive to set it free from the burdens which keep it down, if restored men and women frequented restored churches, and beautiful altars were thronged by beautiful lives, if the services of the sanctuary were a concert of beautiful sounds, the basis of which was a deep and penetrating penitence, if confession of sins went hand in hand with amendment, or if confession brought amendment with it—then the World-fog would roll away, then men would see more clearly whither they were going, and would walk more warily in these dangerous days, fleeing from those vices for which they know the curse of God to be due,—then men would be less the victims of panic, and not be taken in by bubble-companies of spiritual promise which are going to redeem the world by sanitation, and banish sin by an extension of the franchise. Life must be rescued from the cruel foe which exacts day by day its harsh task, and promises to pay in happiness from coffers long known to be empty, and from resources long proved to be bankrupt.

It is a fascinating cry, which must attract even the most careless, 'Be of good cheer: I have overcome the world.'[1] And we look up, and lo! it is the voice of 'a Man of sorrows, and acquainted with grief.'[2] It is the voice of power from 'the outcast of the people.'[3] It is the royal message from a King Who reigns from the throne of the Cross.

[1] S. John xvi 33. [2] Isaiah liii 3. [3] Psalm xxii 6.

CHAPTER VIII

THE OBSTACLES TO RELIGION—INTERNAL

> 'I peccator carnali,
> Che la ragion sommettono al talento.'

We have hitherto dealt with those difficulties in the way of practical Religion which come to us from without, by the instigation and influence of those two enemies known respectively as the Devil and the World. It remains now that we should consider a third enemy to Religion, in one sense more deadly than those which have hitherto been considered, inasmuch as it is an enemy which attacks us from within, and is therefore armed with all that malignity which proverbially belongs to a civil foe.

Little does the tiny infant realise what is being promised in his name at Holy Baptism; hardly do the boy or girl at Confirmation realise the full force of the question which is put to them, 'Dost thou renounce the Flesh?' to which they so courageously respond, 'I do.'

I

What, then, is the Flesh? Can it be indicated, scientifically marked off, defined, so that we may know it and avoid it? As with 'the World,' so with 'the

Flesh,' perhaps it is easier to describe than define, to indicate rather than delineate, what is, after all, a power for evil only too evident to those who are striving to gain the strait gate of heaven.

In some parts of this world there are large tracts of marshy swamp, whence an evil miasma is ever rising up from the rotting vegetation into an atmosphere made stifling with jungle overgrowth, and heavy from its windless calm. Fever and ague burn and shake those human beings who come under its deadly influence. The only way to resist it is to minimise that influence as much as possible,—not to sleep on the steaming ground, to be careful as to hours, exposure, and fatigue, and, above all, to keep up the general health. The Flesh, in like manner, is a sort of moral fever, a weakness which is thrown off the body, as it were; which affects us because we possess a body. And while we say this, let us remember that Holy Scripture has no quarrel with the body—very much the contrary; but it has a grave quarrel with 'the Flesh.' We shall not find, for instance, in Holy Scripture at least, as a general attitude of expression, any such thoughts as would lead us, with S. Francis of Assisi, to call the body 'the beast,' to be beaten, crushed, and despised. No doubt in its violence and wanton strength it has provoked such treatment, as the only adequate readjustment of its disturbing power; but in the New Testament, although the body must be bruised and kept under, although it is a 'body of humiliation,' still it is capable of being offered as a living sacrifice, holy, acceptable unto God. And so a more careful investigation will discover a double antithesis, in which soul is opposed to body, and spirit is opposed to flesh;

that is, when the perishable part of man is balanced against the imperishable, the antithesis is body as against soul; when it is a question of a lower and a higher principle of life, then the opposition is between flesh and spirit;—as if, when the strong winds of action set off the body, they are called 'the Flesh'; when they set off the soul, the higher region, they are called 'the Spirit.' We need not conjure up a disabling asceticism, which ignores and despises the body, when we gird ourselves against 'the Flesh.' Christianity knows that the body has been for ever dignified by the Incarnation of our Lord Jesus Christ, Who took not on Him the nature of angels to help it and to elevate it, but was made man. The body is far too valuable an agent to be left out of all spiritual calculation; if it cannot help, at least it can terribly hinder. Nay more, when the apostle looks out upon human nature as an Advent offering to the approaching King, he prays for his converts that their 'whole spirit, and soul, and body be preserved blameless unto the coming of our Lord Jesus Christ.'[1] No; let us remember that the body is not 'the Flesh.' 'The Flesh' is a servile rebel seated on the imperial throne, as the result of a victory in a civil rebellion, ruling where it ought to obey, squandering in passion what should have been spent in feeling, lavishing on self what was meant for the common good, dissipating the resources of empire in a selfish debauch and an ignominious voluptuousness. 'The Flesh,' that principle of life in which passion rules, is a very real and dangerous obstacle to Religion. S. Paul just indicates by a stroke of the pen, as it were, in his Epistle to the Galatians, its course. He says its works are manifest;[2]

---

[1] 1 Thess. v 23. [2] Gal. v 19.

they are spread over life like the holes in some valuable material eaten out by the moth. Gross personal sins in the body; tampering with Religion, putting a Religion of form in the place of a Religion of the heart; in the spirit, dabbling in necromancy and spiritualism just to satisfy its cravings; ending up in a selfish disruption of all neighbourly feelings and duties. Selfishness is the little moth which eats outwards further and further into every part of the being, the product of this deadly atmosphere known as 'the Flesh.' Many lives costly and beautiful, with endless possibilities before them, are consumed by it, ready to fall to pieces on their personal, religious, or public side, which have been reduced to a tinder that will break up at the first stroke of temptation, and the beauty and the power will go up as dust, as they crumble away from their very rottenness. The life dictated by 'the Flesh' is one of the most serious exhibitions of selfishness which can be witnessed. It is sad to see a man who has persuaded himself that all this beautiful and exquisite mechanism is merely a toy which he can play with and break as he likes. He shrinks from the labour of open antagonism to God, but he has carefully removed all the sharp angles from religious observances which might interfere with comfort, or run athwart self. He pushes further and further his roots into the soil, regardless of all neighbouring growth, and thrusts up stem and expands leaf at the price of the life and comfort of others, while he battens and thrives on their loss, exhausting the soil of life, and darkening the very beneficence of heaven. There is no doubt that the selfish life, the life dictated by 'the Flesh,' is a terrible curse. It sharpens the wolfish cries of discontent, it hardens the craving eyes of those who resent that others should be full of comfort while they starve. It points those words of bitter scorn: 'They toss us the life of another world, who have robbed us of this; they bid us go to Mass, us the poor *canaille* of the streets, to keep us quiet. But we too out of our starving mouths would swell the cry which mounts up from the sons and daughters of the Flesh: Let us eat and drink, for to-morrow we die.'

The power within us which we look to to deal with the enemy within us, is, as we have already considered in chapter iii, the divinely guided will. The conflict which a religious man must wage with 'the Flesh' is in its essence a conflict between the will, with all the helps which God has given it, and unregulated desire.

II

But it must also be remembered that 'the Flesh' has a narrower and a sterner meaning than this. It is not only that unregulated desire, flushed and excited by the manifold richness of life, may seriously affect our whole attitude, and deflect our most vital actions. As what a man does well is overshadowed by what he does best, so there are achievements in evil, masterpieces of malignity, which the Flesh marshals against religious life, which have caused a partial and peculiar development of this evil to monopolise almost the name, and certainly the terror which hangs about 'the Flesh' in the mind of every earnest Christian man.

It is necessary to think about this particular and secondary development of the Flesh, because, as every practical person knows, a defeat or a weakness here extends sometimes into the very inmost recesses of the religious life. And oftentimes when a man is combating the bitterness of unbelief and the taunts of godless doubt within, if he knew himself at all, he would rather be addressing himself to drive out an enemy whose seat of attack lay within the camp of 'the Flesh.' The widespread prevalence of this awful evil it would be idle to affect to ignore. From time to time the molten streams of burning pollution which are poured down through our schools, our newspapers, the lives and conversations and amusements of men, lap over and burn their mark on the public conscience. It is an old evil, as old as the Fall, this influence of the Flesh which hangs like a miasma over the wrong use of bodily appetite, charged with poison and death. In the interests of man, it has been necessary to deal with it. In ancient systems there seems to have been an oscillation between two methods,—either simply to take 'the Flesh' and make the best of it, deify it as Bacchus or Venus, or else absolutely to crush it in stern stoical repression: to make the best of it as a development of nature to be held in reasonable check, or utterly to repress it as interfering with man's higher and truer self. In Christianity, as we have seen, while the body is honoured and sanctified, a careful distinction is made between it and its corruption. The Christian owes it to the integrity of his nature, as well as to the positive law of God, that he should move through life with a pure mind in a pure body. Certainly, that the enemy should have fixed his seat within the very recesses of life is a masterpiece of evil; that he should have so seized upon the mysteries of life in the interests of sin, that a pure-minded person cannot even dwell upon them, is to have won a tremendous victory. We look back at the description of innocence in the book of Genesis, and see that it was not always so ; we read perhaps some of the outspoken simple facts of the Bible, and thank God for His revelation of awe and mystery, and for the dignity which He wraps round the inner secrets of life. On our knees we approach the Incarnation, with its holy, elevating, purifying influence, or we sit amazed before the dignity and gravity with which medical science deals with these same mysteries of life. And we feel that 'the Flesh' is no mere robber who defrauds life of its health and happiness, but that it is a sacrilegious profaner who desecrates the inner sanctuary of our being.

1. In viewing 'the Flesh' in this its narrower signification, as an enemy to Religion, it will be necessary to glance at some manifestation of its working before we trace it in its subtlest forms of opposition to the Christian life. No collapse is so complete as that which is caused by a defeat in the region of the Flesh. Among the illustrious heroes and mighty men and women whose ashes lie in Westminster Abbey, there lies one over whose grave is written the simple record of a noble achievement, a life spent in the endeavour to mitigate Slavery, which is there described as 'the open sore of the world.' But, alas! in every city, in every town of Europe, while it still calls itself Christian, there is a sore, worse, more terrible still,—the slavery of souls bound fast in deadly and loathsome sin. It is said that in London alone there are eighty thousand of those whose fate is described in that gentle, yet touching word, 'fallen.' There are young lives crushed and

broken, who but lately were innocent children at their mother's knee. There are grey heads bowed down, and shrinking away to die, stricken through and through with a child's shame. There are no creatures in all God's creation so cruelly wronged as those who are the victims of these sins of the Flesh; there is no sin so utterly damning in its cold cruelty as that which injures so shamefully the souls for whom Christ died, who are made in His image and likeness, as well as purchased with His Blood. As we watch the glare on the midnight sky as it hangs over the city, as we listen to the dull inarticulate roar in which that life restlessly expresses itself, no deeper stain flushes the sky, no shriller cry of hopeless pain, than comes from the perverted life of the victims of man's sin. If we look at some poor fallen life, we see in it a captivity such as the captivity of Babylon in Holy Scripture only faintly portrays. We see an utter break-down of some of the grandest terms of life, such as womanhood, motherhood, home, and holy marriage. There used to be a picture exhibited for sale in the shop windows, so infinitely pathetic, so terrible that it would seem impossible to hang it on the walls of a dwelling-room. It is a representation of the Vestal Virgin who had been false to her vows, being pushed down alive into the pit, a helpless spectacle of abject despair, holding in her arms her little baby with those wide-open wondrous eyes, 'that wide-gazing calm which makes us older human beings in our inward turmoil feel a certain awe in the presence of a little child, such as we feel before some great majesty or beauty in the earth or sky.' It is an awful contrast there depicted: crushed, conscious, fallen, abject despair, and the wondering look of the child, who knows no sin and plays with death. We may well be thankful that here and there Christian men and women are waking up to the cruel nature of this evil amongst us. We are afraid to talk of it, and the evil is there; it is the pestilence walking in darkness, striding on with its malignant steps. In the case of some deadly epidemic, sad as it is that youth and health should suffer, and the individual victims die, we know that after all this is only half the mischief. The evil spreads from an infected centre, until the whole region is corrupted. The existence of a great moral evil, practically unchecked, is a menace to Christian society. We hear the cynical sophism, 'Things always have been so,' and we know it only thinly hides the indolence which would shirk the responsibility of finding fault. The philanthropic achievements of the great Lord Shaftesbury are a magnificent witness *per contra* to the success which awaits a good man who patiently acts upon the principle that intolerable evils cannot be tolerated. The wicked lie which would set up the plea of natural impulse which it is impossible to resist, cannot be maintained by those who boast themselves to be the possessors of reason, and the children of God.

Still the difficulty remains. There is no collapse so complete, no defeat so overwhelming, as that which follows an onslaught in the region of 'the Flesh,' and by looking at it in this, its extreme manifestation, we can the better see its danger, and the absolute necessity for the Christian to remove it out of his path. Everything combines to tell us this. If we look into God's Holy Word, we are startled by the phrase in which the beloved apostle speaks of 'a sin unto death,'[1] and we feel instinctively that this is of that nature. There are sins which end in death, which cause God to leave the soul, which force Him to cut off grace, which even induce Him to refuse to punish,— sins where He will not any longer attempt to heal, and where prayer at length fails to reach Him. There are sins, on the other hand, which are in themselves deadly, which eat out the life of the soul, which not only cut off good, but actively induce evil, as with their heavy weight they press out the last spark of life. It was said of the cholera in one of its awful visitations, that 'it began in death.' So it is with the sin of which we are now thinking. Or if we interrogate history we see the same thing. Passing by Sodom in ashes, and Canaan doomed to utter destruction because of this evil, we glance at the history of David. The defeat which swept him down under the heel of passion left him a maimed and altered man. He never recovered the effects of it, or ceased to expiate the malignity of his crime. 'Wash me more and more from my sin,'[2] was his persistent cry. 'The sword shall never depart from thy house,'[3] was the inexorable punishment. Wise Solomon again, whom God visited, whose wisdom was the wonder of his time, passes through sensuality into the gloom of a moral night. While in the page of history which lies open before us at the present day, we may see everything swept away, culture, position, self-respect, affection, health, home-life, and happiness, as the merciless victor exacts more and more of life and liberty from its prostrate foe.

---

[1] 1 S. John v 16.   [2] Psalm li 2.
[3] 2 Sam. xii 10.

Such is 'the Flesh' where it has its terrible way, unbarred by grace, unchecked by spiritual strength. It is idle for the man who allows himself to be beaten in a conflict like this to hope for any progress towards Religion. The way is utterly and completely barred, and penitence, which means a re-conquest of those regions wrested from him, alone can restore him. Over the dread prisons where the Flesh binds his victims is written a sentence more terrible than that which the poet saw inscribed over the portals of hell: 'All ye who enter here forego the vision of God.' The barrier which is set up by the Flesh is absolute and impassable. The sensualist has lost the sight of God.

2. And yet there are few incidents which so startle us, while our heart tells us that it is a true experience, as that recorded for us in the Gospel of S. John, where our Blessed Lord is surrounded by an angry crowd of respectable and religious men, who were menacing with angry threats a poor woman taken in all the degradation of sensual sin. It was a test case, in which all sense of compassion for the sinner was lost in the hope of being able to implicate our Lord either in a weak condonation of sin, or in antagonism to the Law of Moses, or in undue harshness. In a few moments the menacing throng vanished away: one winged sentence from Him had penetrated their consciences, and, convicted in spite of themselves, all had departed, 'beginning at the eldest, even unto the last.' 'He that is without sin among you, let him first cast the stone,'[1] is a word which has lost none of its penetrating effect at the present day. There are those who have escaped from the meshes of this sin, who still find

[1] S. John viii 7.

that it clings and hinders, with a disabling sense of guilt, with shafts of evil out of the past, it may be with painful and serious relapses, from which they recover themselves only bruised and bleeding, with a sense of shame which necessitates humility, with a sense of weakness which throws them upon God. Quite apart from the hardened victims of the Flesh, who seem shut out from all hope of religious life, there are those who are hindered and maimed by the malice of the past, and by recurring falls which injure and retard the soul. A great deal of Religion is taken up with simple repairs, repairs which too often seem to leave the will to that extent weakened, while the integrity and soundness of life seems injured and marred. This need not be so. It has been the case before now that the strengthened weak point, where the wall was always giving way, has become the strong point in the character. Just the one place where the natural defence seemed to be deficient, where the rampart of rock ceased, and there was an easy slope towards sin, long years of repair, and the accumulated débris of past falls, brought together and welded into a rampart, have made stronger than the rest. But at the same time the malice of a fall, where the defences have been sapped by the Flesh, is great and abiding. Nothing so demoralises the soul as the sense of having been beaten by a savage foe; the tradition of life is lowered, confidence in religious methods is weakened, the will is impaired, and above all, that fineness of character and delicacy of Christian virtue is damaged and spoiled. Spiritual doctors will tell us that breakdowns in the region of the Flesh are responsible for many symptoms of a cold faith, a weariness in welldoing, and religious petulance. Certainly a life spent in repairs cannot hope to make any serious progress in the way of Religion.

'Out of the heart of men proceed evil thoughts,'[1] said our blessed Lord, as if He knew well that these were the detachment of the enemy that was the first to come and the last to go. Many years ago a childish curiosity invited them in; now they seem inclined to stay. The old story of the siege of Troy speaks to us, as by a parable, of a similar siege within the region of the spiritual life. Long and weary has the siege been; evil companions have been kept at arm's-length, evil places shunned, evil suggestions repelled with scorn; but life seems hard, the siege is straitening, the road seems barred by armed Greeks in every direction; we pine for greater freedom, and chafe under the trammels of discipline, when one day we wake up to find the Greeks gone, temptation seems to have ceased, the roads to be clear of the enemy, the gates of the senses no longer besieged with menacing attack—only this curious wooden horse visible in a country free even from the glitter of an enemy's spear. If the Greeks are treacherous, still they cannot fly on wings; if they still are bent on subduing the city, still a wooden horse is not an engine of war. Why is it there? what is it? what does it mean? what shall be done with it? Curiosity prevails: the walls are levelled, to the strains of piping, with dancing and with joy. *Dividimus muros et moenia pandimus urbis*, and the wooden horse is dragged into the citadel as an offering to the goddess. In the night, when men slept, a trap-door is opened in the side of the monster, and first there steals out one

[1] S. Mark vii 21.

armed soldier and then another; the gates are opened from within, and Troy is in the hand of the Greeks. It was but a three-volumed novel, which every one was reading, it was but a story which was told in secrecy, it was only a song, or a play, or a conversation, or a divorce case in the newspaper: the citadel was filled with evil thoughts, and there they have been striving to stay ever since. There is no doubt that a garrison such as this, if it is allowed to stay, will effectually bar the road to Religion, and will issue in marauding parties, difficult to control, and full of evil menace to the spiritual life. There are few who are in earnest in their endeavours to attain to Religion who feel any doubt about this.

But it is more difficult to deal with such thoughts as seem to force the barrier, to pass the guard, and beat down the challenge, and strike before the soul is aware of their presence. There is no doubt that 'the Flesh' wins many battles by the sheer annoyance of these skirmishes. There is the very fact of their presence, which seems to indicate either an imperfect defence, or else even an adverse occupation by permission of the will. Many a soul is terrified by the appearance and persistence of thoughts of evil, and is vanquished in the struggle because he believes that his citadel has been already seized. But this is not so, it cannot be so. Sin is a victory which can never be won without a direct challenge to and consent of the will. No one can sin without being conscious of being attacked, no evil thought can occupy the citadel of the soul without being admitted formally by the will. The will must first be either vanquished, or else invite. The Christian soul will again and again rest itself upon this certainty, and rush into battle not in the despondency of a defeat to recover lost ground, but in the confidence of its unbroken will, and in furious indignation at the insolence which simulates victory. The soul which refuses to be terrified by the mere appearances of the enemy, has then time to gather strength from the knowledge of the causes which probably account for their presence. He remembers the fatal day of curiosity; he remembers the day when these intruders came by invitation, and were sought for and welcomed; he remembers the day when he dragged them in, and made his enemies sit at his table, and allowed them to fetter his freedom, and make demands ever more, and more insolent than before; and now he remembers with shame that they know the way to his door and do not understand being turned away. And here he finds an opportunity has come to him, which he must use aright. There is something to be captured from this enemy in hard fight, by which he can in some way recoup himself for past losses and disgrace. A help to humility is always hard to find, and still harder to use. This easy familiarity of the enemy, this insolent confidence, this menacing approach, shall at least leave behind it some advantage, some trophy of the field of battle. Temptation, says the enemy, means defeat. No, says the Christian, it only means humility that I should be capable of being tempted.

More than this, the conviction gathers strength that such a threatening assault of evil can be met and turned back. It has been well said that 'there is perhaps no strength so great and abiding as that which follows from a resisted temptation.' And to have learned by practical experience the vital difference between temptation and sin, between the outside and the inside of the heart, between suggestion and desire, is in itself a great source of strength and a real step to removing a spiritual discomfort which may very speedily pass into a spiritual distress and become a most dangerous hindrance. It may be true, however, if the Christian be in earnest, that he will have to take strong steps to clear the outer defences of his soul. When Nehemiah was purging Jerusalem he did not rest content until he had driven away all the merchants and sellers of all kind of ware, who lodged about the wall. The recurrence of these familiar advances is in itself an insult and a menace to inward peace. It is here that we recognise the intense practical wisdom of the methods prescribed by the Church. An age of comfort is only too ready to listen to the unnecessary suspicion which confounds good and bad in an indiscrimate onslaught on superstition. Fasting is not the childish thing which some people would have us believe it to be. It is true that new and more popular methods seem likely at times to push out the poor, shrunken, weeping, mediæval Lent. There are no pages in saintly biography which are passed over with such shuddering contempt as those which record the bodily austerities with which temptations were met. No lives would be regarded as so utterly and culpably useless as those of the Hermits and Pillar Saints. And yet a life spent in repairs, or menaced by harassing temptations, might suggest that even fasting might be entitled to a fair trial by a man who wished to be practical in his religion, as in everything else. The fact that holy men found bodily discipline to be effective might suggest the thought that perhaps after all the coarse temptations to satisfy evil longings might be most effectively met by actions which showed that even pain would be preferable to such a pleasure, and that the gratification of the senses was not even a thing to be desired; while S. Simon on his pillar was at least a valuable protest to the age in which he lived, that men in the world must make it a place where virtue could live and holiness be attainable, and that the only attitude which a Christian can adopt towards sin is to stand completely aloof from it. It must be a serious question with a man, whether he should wait to be attacked, or whether he should not with his own hands cut down all the sheltering points of advantage which would harbour the enemy. In a warfare against obstacles like this, a wise man will not hesitate also to use the divine helps which have been put at his disposal. Confession of the sins of the past is distasteful to the natural man; we shrink from its humiliation, and doubt its efficacy or importance. The whole of this question will be treated in a subsequent volume, with proper regard to the history, doctrine, and practice of formal Penitence. But the dust of controversy and the bitterness of suspicion have contrived to shift attention upon the danger and shame of the Confession, and to turn it away from the comfort and blessing of the Absolution. It is when the soul is harassed by recurring falls, or vitiated by the taint of past sin, or weakened by tampering with the sovereign will, that it finds itself in need of outside help, such help as God has put into the hands of men to dispense, because that by reason of sympathy they can reach out to the needs of their fellow-sufferers, and apply the remedy where it is most wanted.

Here then is a second manifestation of 'the Flesh' as an obstacle to progress, where it displays itself in recurring falls which mar an otherwise good life, or where it lingers in insult and menace round the outlying regions of life, and wishes to remain as a tolerated evil in the shape of sinful thoughts in the heart, where it was once admitted as an honoured guest.

3. There remains to be considered the last and serious obstacle which the Flesh can become when a low standard has been set up within, and the shrines of Nature-worship share with the temple of the living God the high places of Jerusalem. The Flesh may reign supreme in the heart, with all its deadly consequences; it may assert itself from time to time with all the violence of a storm which beats down the fields of ripe corn; or it may exist side by side with a religious life, which it has degraded and corrupted, until the very moral sense is weakened, and sin, having lost its terrors, is no longer regarded as an object of hatred, nor attacked with all the forces of an earnest endeavour after holiness. This, perhaps, is the most dangerous development with which the Christian has to contend, when the Flesh has made common cause with the Spirit, which it is ever driving out further and further in the force of its unnatural compact. A Religion which has been emptied of all its strictness is perhaps a more dangerous obstacle to encounter than the more open developments of evil in antagonism to Religion; because evil sheltered under a religious garb can penetrate to regions where simple evil would be viewed with suspicion.

Disregard for the sanctity of the marriage tie is perhaps the most serious and fundamental display of this principle, inasmuch as marriage reaches back to the very foundations of society. This will be fully treated in another volume of this series, and it is unnecessary to enter on it here. It is only necessary to say, that anything which will tend to destroy the plan of God, Who is thus building up the family, must needs be an abomination and a curse. At the present moment, when selfish luxury is abnormally and painfully developed; when it becomes more and more difficult to live in what is regarded as even social respectability on moderate means, when, instead of the glad cry of the Psalmist, 'Happy is the man that hath his quiver full of them,' each child is regarded as a fresh deprivation of a luxury, or a fresh step towards poverty; when men study social questions apart from Religion, and seek to regulate life by pleasure instead of duty; then very serious results follow, and are following. Marriage was instituted for one purpose, and from this it never may be deflected. Our own Marriage Service has a warning on the very first page of its opening address—a warning which a false refinement forbids us now even to read— which we should do well carefully to weigh and consider. Marriage as an integral part of God's plan is a very different thing from marriage as part of the selfish gratification of a luxurious life. A tremendous blow will be inflicted on England if it ever becomes widely believed, as is being now industriously propagated among our working classes, that large families are a mistake, and that marriage can be diverted from its proper purpose. All public opinion is unanimous in despising the man who lives to eat, instead of eating to live. But this is a light offence as compared with that where marriage is viewed apart from its responsibilities, and the solemn blessing of God is invoked on a union as to which His Holy Word is by no means silent, and the verdict of history clear, to those who can read it.

This is an extreme manifestation of the lowering of the moral tone which takes place when 'the Flesh' has fastened itself on the law of marriage, and produced a contented acquiescence in its degradation. But short of this there are sundry manifestations of the same spirit which are terrible obstacles to the advance of true Religion. There is the breaking down of strictness, under the sacred name of liberty, and the letting in of evil under the plea of freedom, which make it impossible for any high level of religious life to be attained. There is a great revival of Religion; sternness and strictness characterise the first earnest enthusiasts; the early Evangelicals, for instance, and the early Tractarians are alike in this; and then an age of slackness sets in, names take the place of things, party watchwords the place of religious verities, strictness becomes unpopular or is evaded, and then, multiply as they may the means of grace, keep up if they will all the old exercises of Religion, there still remains only the same dead level, there is the crack across the integrity of life, beyond and above which goodness cannot rise, as grace flows away from the broken cistern. Want of strictness, when Christ is allowed a niche in the Pantheon which holds all and every deity, is an insidious danger, full of evil. No one can afford to allow that attitude of life to be assumed by him which is symbolised by the standing 'in the thievish corners of the streets.'

To do nothing is to be open to all mischief,—to drift, trusting to chance, is to go down with the strong stream over the cataract. It is a dangerous time when 'the Flesh' has got its say as to the observance of Sunday, and contrives that God shall be robbed of His tithe of time and devotion on the strictest principles of Catholic orthodoxy. It is a dangerous time when 'the Flesh' has managed to secure a system of fasting which seems to comply with the requirements of the Church, while it has only made a change of dishes, and compounded with delicacy as a substitute for sufficiency. It is a dangerous time when 'the Flesh' has managed to insinuate the idea that a little knowledge of the world is as necessary to the full perfection of life as adulteration is necessary, more or less, for the spirit too volatile to stand the climate without it. Men and women are thus persuaded to go as near as they can to sin, and think they have done wonders if their wings are not singed. It is a dangerous thing when 'the Flesh' has diminished the claims of authority, whether it be the parental authority, or the authority which age and position imparts. The history of the Greek word ὕβρις is a morally instructive one; it begins with meaning 'insolence,' it goes on to signify deadly sin, and finally it sums up, in one short designation, that attitude which is the consummation of all irreverent life—when a man can best be described in these fatal terms, that he fears not God neither regards man.

This attitude of the Flesh, when it has allied itself with reason and wrapped itself up in decent disguises, may speedily corrupt the moral atmosphere, and make Religion more and more difficult. 'Blessed are the pure in heart: for they shall see God,'[1] is a Beatitude which carries with it a serious damnatory clause. To be religiously short-sighted is a grievous calamity. And yet a state of public opinion may set in, in which, imperceptibly and insidiously, the higher vision of God may become impossible. Innocence is parted with here and there in obedience to a motive of prudence, dictated apparently by the highest principles. Children are taught all the dark secrets of life, and are old before they are young. They are inoculated with the plague, lest, perchance, they should afterwards be stricken with it; and some die, and more are blind, and the world is poorer; for the Flesh, like Herod, having failed to kill purity, has slain innocency, while a further loss is inflicted on the world in a depraving of delicacy and beauty. Satan, if any one, understands the value of ritual; he can do a great deal with pictures which affront modesty, in the interests of art; with dresses which shock propriety, in the interest of what is rational; with decorations and surroundings which are striking, realistic, and suggestive, which nobody is afraid of. And at last the world wakes up to find that his ritual is ugliness. He trades on ugliness, he drags his victims down until they love ugliness, and even what is physically foul and disgusting; whereas God is a God of beauty, always and everywhere; wherever He moves He is surrounded with beauty. Surely to the destruction of innocence and the spread of corruption must be opposed the beauty of a holy life. 'Whatsoever things are true, whatsoever things are honest, whatsoever things are just, whatsoever things are pure, whatsoever things are lovely, whatsoever things are

[1] S. Matt. v 8.

of good report; if there be any virtue, and if there be any praise, think on these things.'[1]

And innocent childhood, robbed of its superhuman beauty, is followed by a youth of mere material development. The following of nature, the worshipping of muscle, the shrinking from hard enterprise and self-denial, may end, and does end, too often, in spiritual atrophy and a blinding of the higher perceptions. And instead of a well-regulated life, in which the passions subserve the will, guided by reason under the influence of the Spirit, the will is irresolute and tottering on its throne, swayed by every blast of passion, and moved by every passing whim; while the straggling rays of the Spirit are caught up, distorted, and quenched in the drenching mist known as 'the Flesh,' which hangs in dense folds over the life, which has parted with God without knowing it, and is incapable of attaining to that Religion which it still professes to honour and admire. The grossness of sensual sin is the best warning against it. The collapse which it brings with it is swift and certain. The lingering taint which it sometimes leaves behind, even when it has been subdued, is disabling and disheartening, and requires to be vigorously dealt with and overcome. But the settled incapacity which comes from its dominion in the heart, where it reigns unrecognised and kills by a subtle influence, is perhaps to the ordinary Christian the most deadly form of all. It is an obstacle to Religion which every earnest man must deal with, while he hears the stern voice of the apostle, which reminds him that 'to be carnally minded is death.'[2]

[1] Phil. iv 8. [2] Rom. viii 6.

CHAPTER IX

DOUBTS

'Exhort him to be true and earnest with himself, and to take care that he be not bribed to disbelieve things which his conscience tells him are true, by doing acts which his conscience tells him are wrong.'

ONE of the most painful trials to which a man can be subjected is loss of faith. Every one can sympathise with the victim of an accident, who has thereby lost his power of eyesight. We feel a sincere compassion for a man who has suddenly lost the capacity for enjoying all this beautiful scene in which God has placed us. And yet it may be that the loss of spiritual insight in one who has been accustomed to trace out the hidden things of God may be a pain no less acute, no less worthy of our compassion. Men resent, and resent rightly, the harsh denunciations of scepticism which are sometimes in vogue, or that it should be supposed that unbelief is always rooted in some moral fault, intellectual pride, or spiritual indolence. Faith must always be a difficult and delicate thing, subject to accidents and incapacities of all sorts. If there be some form of doubt which can lay no claim to the title, there is, on the other hand, a great deal which can be called 'honest.' There are honest inquirers after truth, who either cannot see, or, seeing, fail to appreciate, or, appreciating, fail to trust the claims of Revelation. And it is no answer to their assertions, and no contribution to their better understanding of the truth, to impute to them motives short of the highest, or to refuse to recognise in them a love of truth as real and as noble as our own. But it is not of these that we are now called upon to think. A wide subject like Religion might be used as the label of a whole theological library. We are concerned now rather with the aims and the difficulties of those who describe themselves as religious men, not with the idea of Religion in the abstract, nor with the difficulties of those who cannot accept it, who disbelieve its axioms and challenge its postulates, and are thus unable to accept its conclusions.

I

And among the difficulties which beset religious men doubts are some of the most serious. They come in the form of a religious reaction, most often; either when a man, who hitherto has taken things on trust, begins to investigate for himself whether these things are so, or when, being required to take a step forward as the logical result of what he has hitherto believed, he suddenly wakes up to find that the substructure is not safe; he is required to build on the foundation gold, silver, and precious stones: he finds that his foundation is little better than wood, hay, and stubble. He may arrive at this conclusion as the result of a genuine conviction, for which he is to be pitied and helped, or it may be that he is himself responsible for the conditions which have brought him to this distressing state, and that the help he needs is moral or spiritual rather than intellectual.

There is no greater triumph for the enemies whom we have been lately considering, within and without the soul, than to cause by a defeat a revolution in the government at home. The defeat at Sedan meant the destruction of the Imperial Government in Paris. A moral defeat in an outlying region of spiritual warfare is sometimes followed in like manner by a complete overthrow of those religious sanctions and forms of government, which either were powerless to help, or had singularly failed to recover or restrain. A religious reaction, from whatever cause it comes, must be expected and provided against by any one who wishes fairly to meet the dangers which are sure to encounter him and menace him in the practice of Religion. We may have to encounter and work through a series of trials, which range from chilling disappointment to paralysing despair. It is a terrible thing when experience seems to fail. If Religion is what it pretends to be, it must be capable of being verified in ordinary experience. 'I have tried it,' says the perplexed soul, 'and have found it wanting. Moses told me that my life in Egypt was really a bondage, that I was meant for something better than serving Pharaoh; the flesh-pots and the settlement in the land were deceptive; man is no slave, there is a promised land to which I must press forward, a land flowing with milk and honey. I believed him, I followed, I passed the Red Sea, I cordially accepted the Theocracy. And where is the Land of Promise, and the land flowing with milk and honey? If I have shaken off the bondage, I have also lost the flesh-pots. True, I heard the voice on Sinai, I heard the thundering and saw the blaze of light. But do let us be practical. This is the wilderness after all, and my soul loatheth this light bread. " Up, make us gods which shall go before us; for as for this Moses, the man that brought us out of the land of Egypt, we wot not what is become of him."[1] This is a voice by no means uncommon, bitter with disappointment and running off into hostility; the voices of men whose religion is an extinct volcano, the very men who were most enthusiastic in that night of the Lord much to be remembered, when they came out of Egypt into a higher life; men who have drunk of that Rock which followed them, and have witnessed the discomfiture of Amalek. Men whose voices joined in the eager cry, 'What is it? What is it?' as the bread of God lay round the host, are now plodding along, footsore and weary, out of heart, eager to take up with any fresh god or float any new enterprise, disappointed shareholders in a falling investment, ready to join in the bitter chorus which ever rises from the ranks of those who have tried and failed, who are as those who have tried some much-valued remedy and found it powerless to avert disease. There are a large and much-to-be-pitied class of men, men who welcome Religion as their great hope and stay against sin which they hate and detest; men who really feel keenly the bondage of Pharaoh, the tyranny of evil habit; men who too often have been at the mercy of quacks, whose very misery has made them credulous. It is a terrible thing for them when they begin to fear that they have encountered another failure, and are doomed to another deception. Religion has not kept its promise. They are eagerly on the look-out for another god.

Clearly Religion has to meet these, her disappointed followers; she must have some account to give of a

[1] Exod. xxxii 1.

state of mind so painful and so plausible. If she is able to keep her promises, she must lose no time in showing how this can be done. If the wilderness has taken the place of the Promised Land, she must show what it all means. Where does the fault lie? Is it in delusive promises only meant to keep us quiet and lure us on? Or does it lie in some moral or spiritual defect in those who expect from Religion that which she never promised to give, while they fail to do their part in securing the blessings which lay ready to hand, but fell short of their destination for want of ability in those for whom they were intended to grasp them? Are we being taken in by Religion? or are we failing in our duties? Are we merely visionaries swayed by a strong sentiment, and the victims of imagination? or are we short-sighted, the victims of accident, misuse, and spiritual disease or debility?

If we took at this a little more in detail, it may perhaps be more easily understood. For no one would hesitate to say that doubts are a very real hindrance, and a religious reaction a well-known form of spiritual trial. Which is to blame, religious delusions or spiritual short-sightedness?

'I used to be told, and at one time I felt, that in the Bible, at all events, I had an unique book, the Word of God. Here was a collection of writings which must be put on a higher pedestal. "The Bible is not like any other book: no other book comes to us with a claim authorised by the Church of our Baptism as containing the Word of God; or containing so constant assertion of its claim to be heard as the Word of God; or as cited, one part of it by another part, by a sort of mutual testimony, as of divine authority, or as constantly upheld by the long consent of the Christian ages as the Law and the Testimony."[1] I was told that God's Word was a lantern unto my feet and a light unto my paths; that it would throw light on the piece of ground just before my feet as I walked along in its light, feeling my way by the help of its gleams. There was light in it, as I was told, and patience, and comfort; when I was in difficulty I felt that I was helped by it, when I was in doubt I might be guided by it, when I was in sorrow it would cheer me. I could say from the bottom of my heart, "How dear are Thy counsels unto me, O God: O how great is the sum of them."[2] I used to be told that underneath its plain surface there were mysteries, that there was 'the going of the Spirit' amidst its simple writings. I used to believe that every word was true, that, written aforetime, it was written for my learning, and that whether I understood it or not, I might say with the apostles on the Mount of Transfiguration, "Lord, it is good for us to be here."[3] But now I am beginning to doubt this. In the first place, I am told that it is a work of a very composite character; that some of the books were written long after the time when, and not by the authors by whom, they were supposed to be written: "the Psalms of David are the hymnal of the second Temple." The laws of sacrifice, the details of the wilderness-wanderings, the tabernacle, are all harmless fictions, examples of inspired romance. There is a large element of myth in the Old Testament; our blessed Lord Himself "used as evidence matter that is not evidence, either by intentional perversion or hazardous interpretation." It is difficult to say what is inspired in Holy Scripture,

---

[1] Bishop of Oxford *First Charge* p. 11.   [2] Psalm cxxxix 17.
[3] S. Matt. xvii 4.

or what is not. I am told it makes no difference, that all critics are agreed, that only learned people can decide on these matters; that I must, in obedience to the historical sense, readjust the old order of Law and Prophets, and speak of the Prophets and the Law. And when I have separated the several constituent threads which make up the narrative, gauged the direction of the prophetic mind, allowed due weight to the love of the supernatural and the exaggeration of affection, then I may attach whatever importance remains to a precipitate of inspiration, certainly as an influence which cannot fail to elevate, if it be only by bringing me in contact with a splendid product of the past, couched, a great deal of it, in magnificent language, and translated into the most rhythmical English.

'Inspiration, I have begun to feel, further, cannot be confined to these venerated products of ancient literature. Why should I not equally elevate my mind by reading Shakespeare, or meditating on the poems of Browning or Tennyson? I must readjust my relation to the too credulous creations of my uninstructed past. A sacred book like this is, after all, very much like other sacred books, but, for all that, I cannot repress a feeling of acute disappointment. The modern Bible may be a monument of literary skill, and may fill us with wonder at the ingenuity of critics who are able to discover, *e.g.* that " the story of Gideon is a jumble from the writings of seven different people." Still, it is not the same Bible as it was before, and I am shaken by it. Which then of these two attitudes represents my better self? Was I at first merely reading fancy into facts, and peopling a blank space with imaginary figures; while, like a child, I was mistaking the roar of the air in the convolutions of a shell for the murmur of the voice of God from off the sea of God's eternity? Or is it that I am failing in my spiritual eyesight, going back from positions which I used to occupy, merely catching at inferences from the attitude of modern thought to justify a position which I had already taken up on other grounds, and swayed by other motives? A believer who thinks he ought to rectify his position, even if he is wrong in his supposition, is one thing; the man who takes advantage of the shifting circumstances to have no position at all, is another.

'Or let us take, again, the most Holy Sacrament of the Altar. There was a time when we took Christ simply at His word. He had promised, "He that eateth My Flesh, and drinketh My Blood, hath eternal life; and I will raise him up at the last day."[1] He had said, "My Flesh is meat indeed, and My Blood is drink indeed."[2] We felt indeed strengthened and quickened by the Holy Sacrament. Our souls were indeed refreshed by the Body and Blood of Christ, as our bodies were by the bread and wine. It was a point of contact with the unseen; it was help from above. Here was the manna lying round the encamping host of Israel, to feed it in the wilderness. Here was the cake of barley bread which tumbled into the host of Midian. Here was "the corn of the mighty, and the wine that blossoms into virgins."[3] With S. Bernard, walking up and down in his cloister, before celebrating the Holy Mysteries, we could sing, with the same show of sincerity:

> "Jesu, the very thought of Thee
> With sweetness fills the breast;
> But sweeter far Thy Face to see,
> And in Thy presence rest."

---

[1] S. John vi 54.   [2] S. John vi 55.
[3] See *Sermons on the Blessed Sacrament* Dr. Neale Sermon v p. 35.

But whither has this confidence and joy departed? "After all, this is an ordinance about which there is a great deal of disputing. Some would tell us that the Sacrament of the Lord's Supper is a pious commemoration of a great event in past history. Why should they not be right? Some tell us that the presence of Christ is in the heart of the receiver. Transubstantiation, Consubstantiation, imply puzzling disputes. A great deal is being said about Evening Communion, and about the dangers of superstition. Perhaps we are coming too often to this mysterious Sacrament. It is possible that a great deal of our past fervour was fictitious, although it was not meant to be such." We can scarcely believe that we once believed, or doubt that we really doubted. When another explanation of the facts is possible, why should it not be true? When reason can take the same phenomena and arrive at a different conclusion, why should she not be listened to? Once more, was I mistaken in the past? was I too ready to acquiesce in what I was told? Or has something happened? Has there been an experience of which I am only partially conscious? A visionary past, or a spoiled present—which is it?

'Or, once more, let it be the whole conception of Religion. We know the eagerness with which it was pressed upon us; we were prejudiced, in fact, towards it; we lived amidst baptized people, who caused us to be baptized at a time when neither our consent could be obtained nor our reason acquiesce. We were bent into habits of prayer, and always led to assume the existence of God, and the necessity of acts of devotion. We were confirmed as other people were, and our minds thus were warped still further in the direction of a narrow faith. We became communicants, we tested the powers of the priesthood, we threw ourselves into the system of the Church. And was it all fancy that we believed in the truth of what we were told? Was it fancy that on Sundays we thought we had clearer views of heaven and heavenly things? that on that day we could see shining afar the turrets and walls of the blessed city undimmed by smoke, unclouded by the dust of toil? Was it fancy that the burden of sin fell off at the word of Absolution? Was it fancy that Confirmation left us stronger and better than we were before? Was it fancy that the answer to prayer came with marvellous certainty, and that there was an atmosphere of supernatural peace, which surrounded our life, and made it possible to hear the sounds of heaven and the voice which spoke to us?

'But now I look back on all these things and wonder if it was all real. There is the Buddhist,—how wonderfully devout he is in his religion, how elevated his thoughts, how sanctified and self-denying his life! Look at the Mussulman kneeling on his carpet, wherever he may be, absorbed in prayer. What an example he sets to ordinary Christians! And yet these are what we call false religions: why should not my religion be false too?'

Are we face to face with the blank despair which must sooner or later overtake inevitably the victim of a delusion? Or is it the repetition in the individual soul of that which is so much in vogue in certain parishes of our large towns? Religion is neglected, the clergy do not reside in their parishes, the services are few and carelessly offered, the congregations diminish until the church is empty. What is more evident?

The church is not wanted, there is no congregation. 'Pull it down, instead of perpetuating a failure.'

What has Religion to answer to this melancholy doubt which so grievously asperses her? 'It is painful to be told that anything is very fine, and not be able to feel it fine. Something like being blind when people talk of the sky.' Religion cannot but sympathise, but she is bound to say that the witness is not true. It was no visionary Bible to which she directed our aspirations, and round which she bound our affections. It may have been that a minute attention to the texture of the canvas, and the mixing of the colours, and the strokes of the brush, somewhat diverted our attention from the beauty of the composition. The picture was meant to elevate us and help us: we have been wondering all the time how it was done. Dr. Pusey has said on criticism of the Psalms, 'When any of us can truly say with the Psalmist, "I am [all] prayer," and we are so wrapt in prayer, that our whole being should be prayer —not till then should we criticise the Psalmist, and then we shall have no mind to do it.'[1] No; the fault is not in the Bible, but in our attitude towards the Bible: we have wearied of it, and then have listened to anything which seemed to justify our weariness. The Holy Communion has lost nothing of its power; those were real meetings with God, which nerved us with strength, and refreshed us when weary. Even when most dazed we felt that it was good for us to be there, and witness the tranfiguration of might. 'What think we?' says Hooker. 'Are these terrestrial sounds, or else are they voices uttered out of the clouds above? The power of the ministry of God translateth out of

[1] *Spiritual Letters of E. B. Pusey* p. 175.

darkness into glory, it raiseth men from the earth, and bringeth God Himself down from heaven ; by blessing visible elements it maketh them invisible grace, it giveth daily the Holy Ghost, it hath to dispose of that Flesh which was given for the life of the world, and that Blood which was poured out to redeem souls.'[1] Even when our souls were weighed down with grief, we felt it was good for us to be present where the Blood of the Passion was poured out, and we were able to feel that the Body was given for us, the Blood was poured out for us. It was no delusion, no unreal sentiment. We were not following cunningly devised fables when we were made partakers of this life-giving Sacrament. And so with Religion. No one ever attempted to conceal from us that the way was steep and long, swept with storms, blind with fog, intersected with cross ways, and infested with false guides. No one ever attempted to hide from us that it was possible to become weary in welldoing, and that there were some who would not endure unto the end. Religion is not unaccustomed to the sight of her votaries turning round upon her and saying ' We have been deceived,' and upbraiding her, and saying that the path is but a sheep-track, and neither leads onward nor leads home. But the fault is not in Religion, it is in those who have neglected its guidance and despised its warnings. In times of despair and gloom, when Religion seems falling from us, and our Leader seems lost to us, and we grope about, without light, and without God in the world, there is one thing that may recall us to ourselves, and help us to start again, and that is the knowledge that there is such a disease as spiritual blindness,

[1] Hooker *Eccles. Pol.* Book v lxxvii 2.

and that spiritual things are spiritually discerned. It may very often happen that dryness and despair and a sense of failure are after all merciful pains, which warn us that all is not right within, and that some vital organ of heavenly influence is choked within us, or severed by accident, or maimed by disease.

When S. John is speaking of Isaiah and the dread commission which he received, to preach a blinding gospel and a hardening message and words which would injure where they were meant to ease, he says, 'These things said Esaias, when he saw His glory.'[1] As if the very brightness of the vision which had so startled and overpowered him had forced upon him the conviction that the God of beauty is also a God of wrath, and that the light which illumines is also fire that burns, and that the very nearness of heavenly things entails a corresponding carefulness in those who deal with them. An inexperienced man, before now, who has looked at the sun through a telescope without the precaution of shading and reflecting, has paid the penalty by immediate loss of eyesight. It is only too possible, especially in an age like this, which scorns precaution and shrinks from nothing, to blind our spiritual eyesight by an unguarded vision. A controversial age pushes its way, piling upon each side of it a moraine of doubts. Everything is looked full in the face; there is nothing sacred. The Bible is treated like any other book. The Sacraments are dragged into the law courts, or discussed in the public papers. Prayer is handed over the counter to be tested as a form of appreciable production. The doctrine of Reserve was not invented in the interest of charlatans who need

[1] S. John xii 41.

the darkened room for the exhibition of their manifestations. It was again and again insisted on by our blessed Lord that holy things must be fenced round; the devils were not allowed to testify of Him; after any singular display of power, the most frequent injunction to the recipient of His bounty was, 'See thou tell no man.' The miracles were to veil truth, not to popularise it. In the ancient Church 'the Holy Mysteries' summed up the attitude of the faithful towards the most solemn rites of their religion. There were the frequent expulsions, which guarded against the presence of those unprepared. In the mediæval Church we have the same hiding under symbolism, the barrier of screen, and gloom, and mystery. Now all is open; a schoolboy who learns no doctrine can discuss the probability of a divine inspiration of Scripture. The Holy Mysteries are celebrated of set purpose at the hour when the largest crowd is likely to be present; whether prepared or unprepared, baptized or unbaptized, is in many cases not even considered. Further, in our modern ways, Religion and worldliness are brought so close together that the theatre overnight almost touches the altar in the morning; the mouth which but lately was full of gossip of the world is pouring forth the praises of the Psalter; novels and theology jostle each other in close juxtaposition. To him who knows how to consecrate his eating and his drinking, and his every work, this may be a right condition of life. But it must be credited at the same time with producing some of the distressing doubt which comes from gazing at the bright glory of God with unshaded eye, unaccustomed and untrained, and still filled with the floating vision of the world. When we blame Religion for deceiving us, we ought not unfrequently to be blaming our own heedlessness of vision.

But besides this, the dawn of doubt may synchronise with a damaged sight in yet another way. 'Overfamiliarity breeds contempt,' may have, and does have, a very sinister meaning in Religion. It is a serious thing, as every thinking man knows, to make a resolution and not to keep it, because it damages the spring of the will; so it is a serious thing to follow out our religious duties carelessly, to let practice fall very far short of theory, to use only half-power, as it were, to trust in quantity rather than in quality, to frequency rather than to earnestness. To do this brings us under the sinister power of repeated impressions. Mr. Ruskin has told us that 'custom has a twofold operation; the one to deaden the frequency and force of repeated impressions, the other to endear the familiar object to the affections. Commonly, where the mind is vigorous, and the power of sensation very perfect, it has rather the last operation than the first; with meaner minds, the first takes place in the higher degree, so that they are commonly characterised by a desire of excitement, and the want of the loving, fixed, theoretic power. But both take place in some degree with all men ; so that as life advances impressions of all kinds become less rapturous, owing to their repetition.'[1] Nothing is more difficult in Religion than to overcome the deadening effect of repetition, and it becomes only too possible, that if we go on praying the same prayers, reading the same Scriptures, frequenting the same Sacraments, without any attempt to deepen our hold of them, or to elevate our appre-

[1] *Modern Painters* vol. ii chap. iv p. 33.

ciation of them, we shall pave the way for that disgust which welcomes doubt, as a useful solution of a difficulty, and the parent of a welcome change. We must not, it is true, expect the childlike awe of our first impression to remain, the thrilling joy of a first spiritual experience to continue in exactly the same degree. But frequent use should deepen, not deaden, the impression, and will do so if we have habitually used our full powers, and not worn ourselves out by the use of privileges which have lost their beauty, because we have never appreciated their fulness.

Doubt has a more serious origin still, which has already been partly hinted at. If men are too ready to credit others with it, and to blame where they ought to pity, still it is well known there is such a thing as moral short-sightedness, which is a fertile origin of doubt. It is astonishing in this connection how much pure ignorance has to answer for. So many people have formed such a contemptuous estimate of the Religion which they profess to follow, that they despise accuracy of statement and definiteness of creed, and think that as Religion is a subject of which every one knows something, so every one may call in question even fundamental truths. Men forget what the apostle calls 'the proportion of faith.'[1] And from a culpable ignorance of that which it is in their power to know, or, not knowing, to refrain from misrepresenting, they damage the roundness and exquisite balance of Religion, and then form a dislike of the deformity which they have produced, begin to doubt the credibility of that which they have been taught, and blame the faith, and not their own perverted estimate of it.

[1] Rom. xii 6.

Certainly a large portion of the misbelief of the world, such as induces people to doubt some of the salient principles of the Catholic faith, has arisen from this straining of proportion up to the breaking point, and from some ignorance of the delicate bearing of one truth on another, leading them on to mistake and doubt the very structure of the Faith itself. Prejudice or dislike has a great deal to answer for, again, as a fruitful cause of doubt. And in this connection error is no doubt a fruitful parent of mischief. We have a conspicuous example of this in the fact, that owing to superstition and tolerated abuse of Catholic truth and customs, there is hardly a doctrine of the Church which does not stink in the nostrils of the ordinary uninstructed Protestant. Why should there be any objection in itself to such a doctrine as Baptismal Regeneration, except for the mechanical ideas which have been supposed to attach to it? No one would have objected to the doctrine of 'the Real Presence,' had he not been terrified by a gross version of Transubstantiation. Confession, again, is in itself only reasonable. Prayers for the dead appeal to the most simple feelings of natural human piety. Superstitious accretions have so fastened on to these things that the Church cannot make her voice heard through the dense folds of prejudice. Short of this, there are certain doctrines which indolent human nature hopes may, after all, not be true, which carry with them, if they are true, certain serious consequences in practical life; here, once more, is a very frequent origin of doubt. The doctrines of the Church have no chance against an alliance of prejudice and ease. The expurgated Religion of the world has always a great deal to say against one who is guilty of the unpardonable offence of being too zealous, or who attempts to add anything to the obligations of Religion.

While there are darker moral obstacles still even than these. 'Blessed are the pure in heart: for they shall see God,' we have already seen, carries with it a far-reaching significance. It has been said, with great truth, ' No one, I believe, can really know his own heart, without knowing also that he is by nature capable of almost any sin, and that there is within him a constant pressure, sometimes gentle, sometimes vehement, tending to make light of the responsibility for sin, and to weaken belief in the justice and love of God. This pressure, if once we yield to it, tends directly to unbelief in revelation ; for the morbid conscience longs above all things to slumber, and in the full brightness of revelation it cannot rest. If we are once convinced that God has spoken, all hope of peaceful repose in sin is lost; and therefore he whose heart inclines to sin instinctively veils himself from the knowledge of revelation, just as the sick man tosses uneasily until the stream of sunlight is curtained from his pillow.'[1]

It certainly should be a first investigation with all of us, Is my soul spiritually healthy? Is there any reason far back in the moral life which may account for this blurred vision and darkened outlook? The poor man looked to Jesus Christ to heal his palsied limbs; Jesus said to him, 'Son, be of good cheer; thy sins be forgiven thee.'[2] So it may be that when we come to Him to dispel our doubts, He first addresses Himself to heal our sins.

---

[1] Wordsworth *Bampton Lectures* p. 13.
[2] S. Matt. ix 2.

II

But there are many who do not rest at this point, who listen to what Religion has to say in her defence, but are unable to admit that the fault lies in themselves. 'No,' they say, 'we have read all that can be said; we are not ignorant on the matter at all; there is hardly a modern German book which has escaped us; all the best magazine articles dealing with this subject we have eagerly scanned. Controversy is by no means unattractive. We know what the Church says, and we know what is said against her. Neither are we prejudiced. We look with dislike on the vulgar generalisations which can only deal with such broad ideas as "Publicans and Sinners," "Popery," "Jesuits," and the like. We know the poetry of Religion, we know the beautiful lives of some of its followers; we can appreciate, we can distinguish. No; we are not prejudiced. Neither is it anything within. We know that none of us are as good as we ought to be, and that every one has his weak points; but we thoroughly disbelieve in the artificial and unnatural. No; it is more and more unceasingly driven home to us that there is no communication to be depended on between us and the invisible. When people think they see the hand of God in the world around them, they are only mistaking a fated evolution for design. No nation ever saw so much in Nature as did the Greeks. Imitate them if you like, personify your fancies, and clothe the products of your imagination with forms, but never forget that they are fancies and imaginations. Call the thunder, if you will, the chariot of God, but never forget that it is thunder. Call the lightning the making bare of His arm, but never forget that it is lightning. Sing your *Benedicite* if you will; it is a good thing to add to the poetry of our conceptions; but do not imagine that when the birds sing they really praise the Lord; they do it in obedience to the dictates of Nature, or perhaps because they are in pain. All this that you say about the two books of God, the book of Nature and the book of Revelation, is very fine; but we are beginning to know pretty well the main secrets of the universe. And as to the book of Revelation: if the knife of the critic has slit the parchment and made it dumb, this cannot be helped; at least you know now what made your drum give its grand sound. Still, if we have made the mistake of dogmatising once, we will not fall into a similar mistake again. You may be right; it is just possible that God may have dictated or inspired sacred writings, only we cannot see it ourselves; God may be moving in this great world beneath its veil of cunning workmanship thinly spread before His presence, only we cannot see it. We do not wish to deny, we only wish to say we do not know. We doubt very much whether it can be asserted that in spiritual matters there is any body of absolute truth carrying with it all the responsibilities which accompany what we mean by that term, or any such collection of the laws of spiritual nature as true and as real as those which form the foundations of natural science.'

'"What is truth?" said jesting Pilate, and did not stay for an answer.'[1] Whether Pilate was jesting or not may well be open to doubt; or whether a sudden

---

[1] Bacon's *Essays* 1 of Truth.

vision of deeper responsibilities opened out before him; or whether, in the perturbation of the moment, he only half-mechanically caught up and uttered the last word that fell upon his ears; or whether he had some lurking wish to hear what could be said on an interesting philosophical question—however this may be, certainly he did not stay for an answer; and the great question remains unanswered by Him Who, being the Truth, could alone define for us in its entirety the nature and scope of Truth. The existence of entrenched Doubt within the enclosure of our lives cannot be an indifferent thing; we cannot mask it, and go to fight other foes; we cannot go on to do our ordinary work, as if it were not there. Is this the explanation of things to which we ought to listen? Is this the scientific attitude which we ought to adopt towards the Religion of our youth? We need not be atheists, or irreligious, or even sceptical, while we simply act as those who suspend their judgment, and who are ready to do things which do not commit them, and things which are not extravagant; and welcome all honest wayfarers, who in an absolutely pathless waste are as likely to be right as they are. 'What is truth?' There is the voice, of course, of the jeering crowd, which need not now detain us. It is a sad spectacle to see such large masses of men the victims apparently of a complete reaction. They contemptuously shout, What to us is the idea of God, or the revelation of God, such as you profess your Scriptures to be? What to us is your Church or any Religion whatever? We do not wish for heaven, and we are in no fear of hell. 'Let us eat and drink, for to-morrow we die.' 'Let us die, for to-morrow we eat and drink.'

These, from whatever cause, are the heathen of our large towns. Some have allowed their evil passions to hurl them with fury against those fragments of truth which they know as possible hindrances to the reign of unbridled desire. Some are the unlovely product of a system of education which believes in the doctrine of unprejudiced choice. Some are pure heathen, men who have not been confronted with truth which they have rejected, but rather men who cannot be said to have rejected what they have never even heard;—like our modern philosopher, who refused to be called an atheist because, as he said, he had never been taught to believe in a God. Here is a great body of men who have decided definitely as against truth, and may serve to show us the practical working of this theory, in the unbalanced region of passion and ignorance. We may hear also the same cry from the moralists, who are impatient of our expenditure of intellectual force, not only on a nonentity, but on that which may easily set up a damaging hindrance to the manly αὐτάρκεια of a well-regulated life. 'A moral life,' say they, 'is the true conception of Religion.' We have already considered this earlier in the book, and while we know that a man cannot be religious if he is immoral, we know a man may be outwardly, and to a certain extent inwardly, moral without being religious. And the question really is, whether, supposing God to have spoken and Christ really and truly to have lived and died for us, God does not require something more from us than He did from a respectable man in the ages before Christ lived and preached His Gospel. We may pass by the moralists also, and ask rather, Is there such a thing as a true Religion, or whether that which entered first as a doubt is to remain as a fixed attitude of the soul? At least, we are told, if Religion is to be admitted at all, it must be a Religion as broad as human nature. All forms of Religion are indifferent, because they are all so many expressions of the same thing. An earnest man may sometimes express himself towards the Supreme Being in the terms of Paganism, sometimes of Mohammedanism, sometimes of Christianity; it does not really matter. If a man follows out what he believes to be true, it will bring him sufficiently within sight of God. But suppose for one moment that God has spoken, suppose for one moment that Religion, and Theology the science of God, is in any degree like some one of the exact sciences, does experience, however gained, go for nothing? We find in these that each has its Bible, compendiums of exact truth, and he who enters on their study now enters on it enriched with a heritage of precise fact, wrung very often from Nature by laborious experiment, given as a gift of God in the wonderful secrets of what is known as a discovery. And Religion, after centuries of spiritual investigation and communing with the Unseen, must, to say the least of it, be able to show some facts which can be put by as definitely ascertained in the library of Theology. Surely it is not to be supposed that every generation has to find anew its religious data, or start on an absolutely untrodden field, or, at least, where the foot-marks never rise beyond the dignity of a sheep-track, and end in nothing. The Christian Religion, the Religion about which doubt is thus being felt, asserts most strongly that it is based on a Revelation of awful facts from God, a Revelation which leaves us better or worse than when we heard it. God has spoken, and what He has said is true, fixed, and unalterable. And so important is this, that it is a doctrine again and again insisted on in this Revelation, that if it be accepted as from God, then rightly to believe it is necessary to salvation. 'Believe on the Lord Jesus Christ, and thou shalt be saved.'[1] 'He that believeth on the Son hath everlasting life: and he that believeth not the Son shall not see life; but the wrath of God abideth on him.'[2] If God hath spoken, it is not for man to say 'I did not know.' Therefore the question has to be decided high up, 'What is truth?' Has Christ spoken, or has He not? If so, what He says, and all He says, is truth: truth which brings with it its damnatory clauses, which we may not slight; truth which must be preserved whole and undefiled, without partiality or arbitrary selection; truth which, in view of God's majesty and our manifold needs, 'except a man believes faithfully he cannot be saved.' 'I am the Way, the Truth, and the Life.' Without the Way we cannot go; without the Truth we cannot know; without the Life we cannot live. 'I am the Way Which thou oughtest to follow, the Truth Which thou oughtest to believe, the Life by Which thou oughtest to live.'

Doubts entrenched in the heart, which have persuaded us to reduce Religion to its smallest dimensions, which have pulled down Sacraments, Holy Scriptures, the Supernatural, and made our religious life like a desecrated church, only a beautiful shell, from which the inner consecration is gone—these are very serious hindrances, and have to be dealt with in a struggle which means death to one or other of the combatants.

[1] Acts xvi 31. [2] S. John iii 36.

Evidences are the usual remedy for doubts, but in the end we must fall back on our own experience. There are some people who have no manner of doubt; who can see Jesus bound, carried off, powerless, insulted, condemned to death, and yet never waver; who can stand by Him in the moment of His keenest degradation, and wait patiently for the glory to be revealed. It is always there. It is sure to come. Pilate felt it when the divine Captive was brought before him. See how his whole life is tossed and agitated at this great crisis in his career, when he is brought face to face with the supernatural. It may be that when a man is tossed with doubt, when Religion seems failing him, as Baal failed his worshippers, where there is no voice nor any that regardeth, that he should go and stand on the edge of the supernatural. Let him fall back for a moment on those places where the ground shelves abruptly, and he is looking out into the waving mist of space. Such a point is death. Here, at least, everything falls away, all human hope, all human support. Why should I die? Why should I be plunged into the seething, tossing world, and be a personality, and reach out on all sides of me in wonderful correspondence, merely to be snapped off and die into nothingness? Immortality is almost an instinct of the soul. Is this a capacity of correspondence without an environment? When this world falls away, as I know it does from the dead man, is it an abyss, a plunge, and a thud, and then nothing? Or is there a life out there veiled by the fog, and wreathed in the gloom, towards which my hope of immortality reaches out as an appetite towards its satisfaction? Death is a point where the passionate earnestness of vitality, and the instinct of a life which cannot utterly die, drives me into feeling what a life which I can neither prove nor gauge by experience may possibly mean.

But this is a point which, after all, as yet can only be imagined, although we must all come to it. But are there not other points as well in which we touch the supernatural? In a previous chapter the presence of a power of evil, outside us, has been insisted on. It can hardly be doubted by any one who has had any experience of spiritual warfare, that he has to encounter some tremendous pressure, which fastens on him out of the gloom. 'We wrestle not against flesh and blood, but against principalities, against powers.'[1] Not only is the darkness of death a touching of the supernatural, but the fierce winds which rage around the crags, and press down our footsteps, and push us back, and force us almost to the ground, are a token of a supernatural power working outside us. It is possible to go even further. Often and often men arraign the goodness of God, and say, How can the fact that He is all-loving be reconciled with the fact that He assigns His children to everlasting punishment because they have displeased Him? It is sometimes said that many have given up their faith on this ground alone; and yet what is that universal belief, that *pheme*, as it were, from the unknown world, that subtly-growing impression of *Nemesis* following on crime? What are we to say of the awful punishment which even in this world dogs the footsteps of sin, of the grim fact that some sins against the laws of nature are never forgiven by nature, even in those who repent and obtain remission of their sins? What are we to say of the punishment,

---

[1] Eph. vi 12.

lingering on to the third and fourth generation, where innocent children are punished for the sins of their ancestors? Are we not here in the presence of some mysterious law working outside us, some mysterious law of attraction, which draws down from an unknown quarter punishment on sometimes successful sin. The lightning's flash through the gloom and the roar of the thunder of God's wrath are a message from the supernatural world which lies around us.

But there are closer experiences yet than these. Few are so unhappy in their religious past that they have never found any help in prayer. Many can speak of wonderful answers to prayer in their own persons, and of touches of supernatural light. Where men have taken God literally at His word, they have found Him absolutely true. Here is a supreme point where heaven touches earth, and where God vouchsafes to reveal Himself to the soul.

Doubts are crippling, disabling things. They sometimes represent a mysterious agony allowed by God in His good providence to assail us. But oftener they represent the unhealthy action of a maimed life, which, beginning in a spiritual deadness, settles down at last into an attitude of blank despair. They are best met by baring our souls to the Sun, before Whose healing beams the blight and mildew die away, and health and vigour return with a new and stronger life of faith.

CHAPTER X

DIVINE HELP—THE ATONEMENT

> 'Strong Son of God, immortal Love,
>   Whom we, that have not seen Thy Face,
>   By faith, and faith alone, embrace,
> Believing where we cannot prove.'

THERE is a vision of the prophet Isaiah[1] in which he represents himself as gazing out into the country of the enemy, along the road by which Jerusalem had often seen the avenging armies returning from the punishment of their foe: 'Who is this that cometh from Edom, with dyed garments from Bozrah? this that is glorious in his apparel, travelling in the greatness of his strength?'—from Edom, the congenital and perpetual enemy of Israel, with his red shame of pottage put before privilege, his red slaughter of his brethren, and now the red vengeance which had fallen upon him. What news of him? How does he stand now? Just as the Christian sometimes gazes at his old congenital foes —the World, the Flesh, and the Devil—and wonders what new attack they are preparing along the old tracks watered with his blood, and torn with marks of conflict, so here the prophet gazes out to see what

[1] Isaiah lxiii 1.

the avenging armies had done in punishing violence—to see the return of the conqueror from the land of the enemy. And what does he see? A solitary figure, unsupported by armies, unarmed and undismayed, splendid and sweeping in his blood-red raiment, swaying to and fro in the fulness of his strength,[1] filling up, as it were, the whole landscape as he draws near to Jerusalem. And so to us there comes a vision, ever welcome, ever opportune, telling us of the quarter in which we must look for relief, and the source and power of victory. 'Who is this?' Salvation comes by One, by One alone, not through precept and rule, but by a Person. Our army of ethical instructors may go out against Edom; we look for great things from an instructed nation. Honesty, recommended as the best policy, will disarm the predatory instincts which prey upon society. Prudence and an acquaintance with the laws of health will serve to keep back the assaults of evil desire. Again and again, sick at heart, we have seen our armies go out with colours flying, and glittering in steel, in all the strength of education, progress, self-development, self-reliance—strong in the sense of citizenship and of manliness, alive to the beauty of art and culture, of civilisation and refinement,—and Edom has swallowed them up. One conflict with the Devil, one day's march under the influence of the World, one skirmish with the Flesh, is enough. Sad and weary, we look out at the window as the newspapers issue their long report of failure. Where are the millions we spent on education? Where are the progressive doctrines, so salutary and sound? Where is the determination of the character

---

[1] See *The Book of Isaiah* by G. Adam Smith D.D. *in loco.*

trained to choose the golden mean between the extremes of error? Why tarry the wheels of culture, the love of the beautiful, the admiration for the true, the desire for the good? Have they not sped? Have they not divided the spoils? Again and again we have looked, only to see a champion fleeing for his life; another failure, and another shame; the true betrayed, the beautiful disgraced, the good disowned, under the strange power of that red Edom, our brother and our foe. 'Who is this?' Victory has come through a Person: a Person Who has not rested content to throw down precepts and there leave them, but has devised means by which precepts may be developed into action. He is alone; He only could pay the price of sin in the mystery of the Atonement; He only could deliver His brother and make agreement unto God for him. He is alone in the supernatural means which He has devised for the sanctification through Religion of the nature saved by the Atonement. His raiment is stained red with marks of conflict; through Him blood becomes wine, and wine becomes blood. The Blood of the Atonement becomes the wine of the Eucharist; the wine of the Eucharist becomes the Blood of the Saviour; the blood of struggle and conquest becomes the wine of vigorous effort and excellence: the very marks of the struggle showing the vitality of error. Our foes are not foes that can be met by copybook headings of morality, nor by prudence, and precept, and caution. They are alive and vigorous: it is a conflict of blood. See! the Victor sweeping on in His raiment! The marks of blood, of a treading-out of good, of conflict, are sprinkled on the glorious apparel of the

Church. The Font speaks of death, and the Altar is red with the perpetual sprinkling of the Blood of the one great sacrifice. The raiment of the Church is stained with the blood of her conflict. Her praises are *Te Deums* on the battle-field; her prayers are wrung out of anguish. Who is this sweeping on in His raiment? The very beauty and outward adornment of the Church is a garment which is spread over the stern conflict of the Conqueror in overcoming sin, and is glorious with the stains of battle, and red with the wine-juice of victory, as He sways on in the wealth of His strength; now driving out Satan from his most familiar haunts, now shaming the World out of its half-hearted efforts, and laying low the empire of the Flesh.

And the answer with which He greets us is this: 'I that speak in righteousness, mighty to save.' So He comes towards us tired and disappointed as we are, with the hard conflict, almost beaten, wellnigh in despair, wearied with Edom, who seems to know our weak points in the devilish opportuneness of his temptation, the cold cynicism of a sneering world, and the almost irresistible power of the flesh in subverting and warping the will. Here is His victory, which will come through Him Who is righteous to reward us, too righteous not to punish us, but mighty to save. The great and precious truth becomes clearer to us as the strife gets harder, that grace is stronger than nature, holiness stronger than sin, and that there is only one absolute power in the world, and that is wielded by Him Who is 'mighty to save.'

I

The forces which are arrayed against us, when we try to carry out the precepts of Religion, we have already seen to be most powerful. It may be doubted, whether even yet we quite realise the true nature of the obstacles to be overcome. It was said of Mummius, the general to whose lot it fell to sack Corinth with all its treasures, that he was so ignorant of the real value of the beautiful things that came into his possession, that he only suspected their importance from the high price which was offered to him for their purchase. Perhaps we shall only be able to form any sort of estimate of the power of evil, when we see the long series of helps which God has provided against it, culminating in the Atonement, and the system of grace which has followed from it. When we see the struggle with which our freedom was won, and the price which was paid for that freedom, we shall better see how surrounded Religion must be with difficulty. It is of the very last importance that we should have a firm grasp of what is meant by 'the Fall.' We have some sort of idea what a fall means in a man's moral and spiritual life, how utterly it upsets all his relations to the world; we see an image of it in the case of a crime committed against the law of the land. The deed is done—be it theft, murder, forgery, or some other crime—and at once all the relations of the man towards the world are altered. Before, he was a citizen of a free state, now he is a criminal. The post which enabled him to transact his business and communicate with his friends, now sets in motion the agents of justice who are on his track; the telegraph hinders his escape; the railway facilitates his capture more than his freedom; the police, the law, public opinion, are all turned round to be his enemies. He is like an engine which has left the rails: all that before facilitated its progress now forms a series of obstacles, and accelerates its overthrow. So with a moral fall: the things which should have been for the sinner's wealth turn out to him to be an occasion of falling. And unless he is stopped, he rushes on to destruction, the very things which were meant to help him only ministering to his downfall. We can trace something of the causes which precipitate a fallen man; it is not so easy to estimate the condition of a fallen world, a world in which all the machinery has become bent and misapplied; beginning with man in his distorted exercise of the will, and ending in the general creation, which was made subject to failure, not willingly, but by reason of a mysterious participation in human degradation. It will make a great difference in our estimate, whether we look upon this world as gradually passing on by improvement to perfection, starting from a rudimentary state, and slowly reaching out to the crown of progress: or whether we regard it as having fallen out of gear, fallen from a perfection—undeveloped, potential perfection, it may be—into a state of confusion and disaster: in one word, whether the Fall is a fall downwards, or, as some contend, a fall upwards.

Clearly, a true estimate of the real nature of our malady is almost a necessary prerequisite to its alleviation. It must again be repeated, that the difficulty of moral goodness in itself needs some explanation. The failure, noticed above, of mere precept and example, deserves more than a passing word of surprise, or even sorrow. In ordinary matters, a man, when he has resolved to do a thing, in business or in enterprise, is able to carry it through by sheer force of determination and by attention to those rules which have been laid down for his guidance; but in the region of moral and spiritual effort we see again and again the strange spectacle of apparent impotency. *Video meliora proboque deteriora sequor* has its Christian counterpart in the fervent cry, 'When I would do good, evil is present with me. . . . O wretched man that I am! who shall deliver me from the body of this death?'[1] Clearly goodness is not an affair of taking the best advice and following it. Morality is not to be regulated by a good digestion, plenty of exercise, and life in the open air. The sense of self-interest even cannot be trusted to keep a man straight. Man will injure himself not only with his eyes open, but in the face of even strong restraints. God Almighty in His love has scientifically treated evil, and has allowed us to see the salient points of His treatment, the origin of the evil, as far as it concerns us to know it, the steps devised to meet it, and the provisions made against further relapse. The only thing that prevents the world of the Fall from being the world of the Restoration is this, that from the very beginning the freedom of the will of man has been respected. Man was free to bring about his own fall: man is free now to resist his own salvation. So that we only see, as it were, a partial restoration here and there—patches, so to speak, of a restored world, men and women here and there who have yielded their wills to God. And if it be wistfully asked, Is God

[1] Rom. vii 21 24.

once more going to reign in a world rescued from its imperfection, is the earth really to be filled with the glory of the Lord as the waters cover the sea? the answer perhaps is, that Solomon's temple is being raised of stones made ready before they are brought to Jerusalem; that here in the forests, there in the quarry, now in this generation, now in that, the Gospel is being offered to all the world, and the New Jerusalem is slowly rising up elsewhere, and when all nations have had their chance, then will the end be—an end, as far as this world is concerned, where only a remnant will be found, and the Son of Man will be unable at His coming to find faith on the earth.

Why is moral and spiritual life so difficult? How has Christ helped us, how is He helping us, against the difficulty? What is there wanting on our part to enable us to realise this scheme of restoration, which starts from the fragments of a fallen world and builds up the magnificent city of the New Jerusalem?

In the first place, we are conscious that there is a great mystery about sin, which we very imperfectly understand, which yet affects us very nearly in our moral and spiritual struggles. Sin, the apostle has told us, is lawlessness.[1] It is 'creature-love turned away from God.'[2] But is it merely a violation of the positive orders of an omnipotent Being? If God had not said 'Thou shalt not kill,' would it have been morally permissible to slay our fellow-men? If God had never said 'Thou shalt not commit adultery,' would the laxity which we trace all around us in the observance of the marriage law be at the most an undesirable social offence? Surely we feel that the law of the Sabbath,

[1] 1 S. John iii 4.   [2] See Ellicott *Salutary Doctrine* p. 6.

as embodied in the Fourth Commandment, stands on a footing different from that of the rest of the Decalogue. We feel, as to the great fundamental laws of morality, that God orders them because they are right; that they are not merely right because God orders them. If God had never issued His laws as to murder, adultery, dishonesty between man and man, as to the guidance of the tongue, respect for authority, and respect for Himself, where He is known to exist, we should have instinctively felt that the violation of any of these things was wrong. And so there would seem to be an absolute right and wrong in the nature of things, which God Almighty Himself respects; so that it is not a mere form of anthropomorphism, it is not merely clothing God in human dress, and applying to Him human motives, when we speak of 'must' and 'ought' and 'can' and 'cannot' in connection with His action. The Atonement itself, as we shall see presently, pre-supposes something of this kind. Why, it may be asked, could not the Omnipotent God, by one act of His sovereign will, obliterate all guilt, and take away the accumulated sins of the world, which we are told were mounting up in all their baseness and guilt before His divine purity? Why was it necessary that God Himself should become incarnate in order to expiate by the sacrifice of a sinless One the sins of a sinful world? The Atonement, and the reason assigned for it, must always make us feel that when we talk of sin, whether in its power or in its guilt, we very imperfectly realise what it means. And this will account for the reckless way in which men expose themselves to its influence, and also for the light way in which they allow themselves to arraign God's treatment of and wrath upon sin. There are few things, for instance, which so stagger men's faith, if they believe in the Old Testament at all, as God's command in Deuteronomy xx 16 to extirpate the Canaanites for their abominations, and the way in which it was carried out, as, *e.g.*, in Joshua x 39. There are several justifications advanced, as we know, but most of them are inadequate. May we not see a deeper reason than those commonly advanced, in its connection with the absolute law of right and wrong? In the first place, the destruction, extirpation, the punishment of children for the sins of their parents, has continued ever since those early times; it is going on all around us now. No one arraigns God's justice for the destruction of Jerusalem by Titus, which God claims in prophecy to be of His ordering; nor for the catastrophes which accompanied the breaking up of the Roman empire; nor for the plague or fire of London; nor for the great 'assize of nations,' a modern war; nor for the terrible sufferings which sinful parents inflict upon their children even still to the third and fourth generation. That which strikes the imagination in the case of the Canaanites is that God should employ conscious agents, viz. men, to be His executors of wrath. It is against the principle involved in it in its effect upon the Israelites that men inveigh. And they forget that there were distinct objects in the extirpation thus ordered, all of them having to do with the mystery of sin,—the first being that sin must be punished; the ever recurring mystery, which, as we have said, reached its highest exhibition in the Atonement. Then it was not only ordered on penal, but also on conservative grounds, that a holy nation should be kept alive out of whom Messiah should spring;

while the punishment was committed to human agents for a purpose, that they should ever be reminded, by the punishment of which they were the agents, of God's awful wrath on sin, and of the terrible vengeance which would overtake them if they sinned in the same way (just as in the punishment of stoning, the witness had to be the first in execution). And so the sense of this punishment would be a continual warning to them all their days, while they would be kept by these thoughts from the demoralisation of a massacre, and also would be spiritually upheld in carrying out the decrees of God. The Israelitish wars, it must be remembered, were not always exterminating,[1] while in those which were connected with the mysteries of the punishment due to sin, the Israelites would not have the difficulty, which we should feel, in believing themselves to be God's agents, in carrying out His wrath, which He now commits to the wind, the flame, and the earthquake, or to men who do not know themselves to be His agents. In those days God's presence in the world was more immediate, at least to the Jew. God was gradually driven further and further out of the world, from the time when He communed with Adam and the patriarchs, until the Incarnation, since which time He has been raising men to heaven rather than bringing heaven to earth. Sin must be punished is the underlying principle which dictated the extirpation of the Canaanites. It was so with the Law of the Goël, again. The avenger of blood was retribution personified. It was something of this kind which underlay the wild act of Jael, that 'dark patch of passion,' so strangely praised by Deborah the prophetess. Sin

[1] See Deut. xx 10 18.

must be punished. We have already seen the working of this law in the retribution which followed on the pardoned sin of David. A repentant drunkard expiating the sins of a misspent youth in a suffering old age illustrates the same truth. The heathen world meets us with their firmly-rooted consciousness of Nemesis following on even successful sin; the Erinnys may be trusted to correct the inequalities of human justice. In our own lives we are conscious that every sin leaves its mark, every lapse tells its tale in our life, even a mistake involves us in a tangled maze of consequence. The broken law must be respected. There is an eternal 'ought,' which has to be reckoned with. In the highest development of an artistic spirit we may trace a manifestation of the same thing: an artist, a musician, or a scholar, who is guilty of an error in his respective art, if he is a true artist is as much pained by the offence against abstract art as he is by any consequence of ridicule or loss which follows his mistake. 'Ought not Christ to have suffered these things?' said the mysterious Stranger on the Emmaus road. Sin is linked round a mysterious catastrophe involving the breach of fundamental law. This is not put right by a man simply saying, with various degrees of sincerity, 'I am sorry.'

II

As we advance in our contemplation of the nature of sin, we are bound to consider the mysterious law of Sacrifice. Sacrifice meets us at the very gates of Eden, and spreads out widely into most of the religious systems of the world, culminating, as the most efficacious of all, in human sacrifice. Blood is poured out before the Lord. 'It is the blood that maketh atonement by reason of the life.'[1] A life was given; life springing from the divine fountain of life was offered. God's gift, God's best gift, as it then would have been estimated, was offered to God; and the purpose for which it was offered was for the remission of sins, and for the averting of the wrath of Almighty God. Here was an attempt to throw off at once the sense of defilement, and also to do something to repair the outraged majesty of law which had been violated by sin. This system reached its climax in the Levitical law, which it is now the fashion so strangely to disparage. 'It is characteristic of Hosea,' says a modern writer, 'to class sacrifice with idols. Both are senseless and inarticulate, incapable of expressing or of answering the deep feelings of the heart.' And with commentators like these we always find also the apology, although it does not always take that form, for the wrath of God. It is the same spirit which, carried a little further, attempts, as it were, to patch up sin; which encourages people to believe that sin is a sort of theological spectre, dressed up in the interests of priestcraft, or at the best is only the product of an overstrained estimate of human perfection: man, being what he is, must expect to have a slight twist somewhere, and these imperfections, looked at in the right way, very often give character to an otherwise monotonous individuality. It is suggested that if people attended more to perfect their conditions and their surroundings, and to 'getting themselves out,' the world would be

---

[1] Ellicott *Salutary Doctrine* p. 82; Lev. xvii 11.

a better place than it is ever likely to become by hopeless attempts made to force nature into an unnatural setting, or to make a creature fly in the air as a spiritual being, when by every law of its nature it was meant to cling to and have its perfection out of the earth. A writer of some experience has lately said, when discussing the apparent alienation of masses from the Church, 'My opinion is that the deep-lying cause of failure is the absence in this generation of the consciousness of sin.' Men are so proud of man's achievements, the meanest man as he walks the streets says to himself, as he looks at the triumphs of science, 'All power is mine.' He has no fears to make him conscious of inferiority. He riots in the possessions of his generation, and asks not how he came, and whither he is going. There is no wide consciousness of sin, and consequently there are few eager questioners saying, 'What must I do to be saved?'; few who put the Church to the test. But sooner or later, if a man is in earnest and finds God, there comes this sense of sin, so strange and mysterious, with its dread remorse; the sense of personal sin, which will cleave to a man, which will give him no rest until, quite apart from merely starting afresh, and turning over a new leaf, he steals up to God, and puts himself at the foot of the Cross, and says, 'Against Thee only have I sinned, and done this evil in Thy sight.'[1] 'Lord, I love, I would love more warmly; Lord, I believe, I would believe more firmly; Lord, I grieve, I would grieve more deeply.' This longing of the heart God met in the Israelite with the vast system of sacrifice, of which we have the record in

[1] Psalm li 4.

Leviticus. We see the sinner dedicating the animal selected for sacrifice at the door of the tabernacle.[1] We see him laying his hands on the victim's head, thus mystically transferring his sins to the head of his substitute.[2] We see next the slaying of his victim, still by the offerer, signifying that death comes by sin, and that the sinner deserves death in the Lord's presence as a satisfaction to His holiness. Then there follows the sprinkling of the blood by the priest, before God,[3] prefiguring the Atonement, followed by the consumption of the body of the victim in various ways. But there are two facts to be noticed about this, elaborate and helpful as it was: first, that all this intricate system appertained only to the remission of what we call now venial sins, such as sins of ignorance and ceremonial defilement; that there was no sacrifice known under the Law which availed to the remission of the guilt incurred by the breach of any one of the Ten Commandments. And further, that for any sin there was only then brought about a πάρεσις, not an ἄφεσις. Sin was overlooked, or not imputed—it was not taken away —and we find the Jew still at the threshold of the Gospel holding out mute hands towards his deliverer, and saying, 'Come, O Lord, and tarry not. Do away the offences of Thy people Israel.'

At last the true meaning of this system of Sacrifice became clear. The prophets had laboured to emphasise its inward meaning. The blood of bulls and goats could never take away sin: and yet all the world was guilty before God—not of a contempt which could be purged by submission, not of a

---

[1] Lev. i 3.   [2] Lev. iii 2-13.   [3] Lev. i 5; xxii 11.

breach of positive law, which He Who imposed could also remit, but of a violation of the eternal law of right and wrong, of sin in the abstract, expressed in rebellion against Him Who created, orders, and governs all things. But how could the whole human race expiate the sin of which they were guilty, in which all shared? The whole human race made reparation to God, in the Person of Christ, Who, by His Incarnation, represented the whole race of man, Who by His obedience even unto death washed away sin, and sealed redemption to mankind; and although the whole race of human beings could not assemble, as it were, under one roof to express penitence and make reparation, still through this, their Representative, all human beings do make a real and all-sufficient satisfaction. In Him the whole human race suffers, and although we may dismiss, and ought to dismiss, the idea of the innocent suffering, while the really guilty escape scot-free, still there is a sense in which we must not shrink from speaking of substitution, and of One bearing our sins, while we escape; because in every representation, the individual who submits himself submits to a larger share of the responsibility than of right belongs to him as an individual. And so we may speak of Christ as bearing the brunt of pain and sorrow which comes to Him as the Representative of all the world; as the One Who alone could be the Representative of all the world—of the world as it ought to be in the eyes of God; because, in Himself sinless, He represented the ideal world, while in taking up the sins of mankind He represented the actual world. And in this way also He reconciled the Father unto us, in doing away with 'the tension introduced by sin between the love and righteousness of God.'[1] So by the fact of the Atonement, the relations of God to man, and man to God, were adjusted, and a blow was given to the dominion and power of sin.

III

How then does the Atonement help us in the practice of Religion? Is it anything more than a theological subtlety, which, when it has been discussed among controversialists, is of interest, doubtless, to them, but leaves the practical Christian very much where he was before? No, by no means. The world before the Atonement is quite a different thing from the world after the Atonement. The moral atmosphere is different. Spiritual sounds can now be heard which could not be distinguished before. It is possible to breathe freer and for longer intervals the pure air of heaven. The debt has been paid, the balance re-adjusted, there is no longer any need for the despairing cry which pushed aside as impossible the ideal of the highest life. The Atonement is a steadying doctrine; it enables men to fight the battle of life without the paralysing sense of being overmatched. Christ has spoiled principalities and powers, triumphing over them in His Cross. The virgin-peak of holiness has been scaled by One Who, if He was perfect God, was yet perfect Man. Life is easier, holiness is possible, the prince of this world is judged. But much more than this: the Atonement secures to us real and substantial blessings in our own life. It is by the Atonement

[1] See Wordsworth *The One Religion* p. 219; Ellicott *Salutary Doctrine*: The Atonement 'The Gospel of Experience' pp. 174 175.

that, in the words of Holy Scripture, we are justified. 'Justification is the free gift of Christ, whereby He restores to us our lost inheritance of grace, and in restoring it cleanses every stain, whether of actual or original sin, though concupiscence still remains for our trial. But it is more than a simple restoration of our perfect birthright, for we are raised by Justification to a higher state than that from which Adam fell, and made, through union with the Redeemer, partakers of the Divine nature, whence the Church sings, *O felix culpa, quæ talem et tantum meruit habere Redemptorem.* We receive the Spirit of adoption, whereby we become joint heirs with Christ, and sons of God.'[1]

To be justified is to be made just or righteous, that is, made to conform in life to the standard of what is absolutely good and true, which result is attained by faith, which receives at God's hand the perfect righteousness of Christ. Faith is the hand which the soul extends towards heaven, or with which it grasps the Redeemer's Cross. Christ Jesus, the only perfect One, is the source of Justification to all His brethren. 'It is not that this righteousness is credited to them by a legal fiction without being conveyed. . . . It is conveyed by His Spirit and His Sacraments.'[2] And so 'Justification is used for the initial act on the part of God, in a process of which sanctification in its fullest sense is the gradually accomplished result; and in crowning our merits God crowns His own gifts.'[3] So that from the Atonement there comes this very real gift into our soul, the gift of

[1] Oxenham *Catholic Doctrine of the Atonement* pp. 103 104.
[2] Liddon *Sermons on Some Words of S. Paul* pp. 186 195.
[3] Oxenham p. 228. See also Dr. Gibson *XXXIX Articles* vol. ii pp. 395 396.

righteousness, the acquittal from sin, and the capacity for holiness. But further, at the end, when holiness is perfected, we are accepted 'in Christ.' All through our life, whatever good we do is of Him, and accepted in Him. 'In all the servants of Christ, God sees the image of His Son.'

And yet He Who made us without ourselves, and who regenerated us without ourselves, will not save us without ourselves, without our conscious and deliberate acceptance of His salvation. And the very difficulty we have in accepting these great truths, and linking them into our practical life, shows how easy it is to slip away from them. How easy it is to accept Christ as a model, and to forget that He is a Saviour; to honour Him as a martyr, and to ignore the Atonement. Spiritual indolence, on the one hand, wishes to leave all to Christ, to speculate on human nothingness, and to forget that this is the verdict of God on our supreme and most finished effort; that there is another verdict which awaits work not even attempted, and the burying of the one talent of human merit because it was one. On the other hand, the thought of Justification as a necessity, or the idea of any merits except our own, or the possibility of any falling short in human development, are repugnant to the progressive spirit of a confident pride which, knowing nothing of sin, does not seek for sanctification; which in the proud contemplation of its own excellences can conceive of nothing to be atoned for, and neither knows nor cares aught for salvation or the being in Christ. We can see how the apostle S. Paul was conscious of this danger, and how earnestly he repudiated it, in his impassioned words, 'God forbid

that I should glory, save in the Cross of our Lord
Jesus Christ, by Whom the world is crucified unto me,
and I unto the world.'[1] He had no doubt whatever
as to the appropriateness of the Cross as a symbol of
Christianity. It would be strange, were it not for the
considerations such as we have examined above, that
the Cross should have emerged into such eminence,
and have overtopped all other symbols of Christianity.
Men refer, it is true, to the Cross as found among
pre-Christian and heathen nations: the Egyptians, the
Mongolians, and the Buddhists. There is nothing in
itself remarkable in this, for it is a common and an
obvious sign in many ways. So Justin Martyr in the
second century triumphantly appealed to its universality. 'Consider all the things in the world,' he says,
'whether without this form there is any administration, or any community, possible to be maintained.'
He points to the sails of the ships, the spade of the
labourer, the very figure of man, the standards and
trophies of the army.[2] People who delight in paradox
may amuse themselves in tracing the mere survival of
heathen custom in the Christian use of the Cross.
But to the Christian it is no bare or arbitrary sign; it
is a symbol of, a reference to, an actual fact which
took place once in the history of the world, and of
certain consequences which flow from it, of the greatest
moment to his life; and whether heathen have used
the symbol before or since, has nothing to do with the
question. It is our Lord's own summary of the burden
which His religion would lay upon His followers,
and of the grace which would ensue from that burden.
S. Paul uses it also in the same way as a summary of

[1] Gal. vi 14. [2] Just. Mar. *Apol.* I 55.

Christian life and teaching. And at the present day the thoughtful man, when he speaks of the Cross, has passed far away from the mere material symbol; he means more than a tragic incident in the past, he refers to a living system, which makes demands upon him and regulates his attitude towards God and holy things. It is the most common of all Christian symbols: it tops the spires and towers of our churches, it surmounts the orb and sceptre of kings, it is traced on the brow of every Christian child; but also it represents a system and an attitude—a system of God's dealing with men, and their attitude towards the Saviour of their life. And this is why S. Paul is so eager and so emphatic, so indignant, that he would thrust it forward and brandish it in the face of his opponents. He is confronted with our old enemy, that enemy which is never so dangerous as when it masquerades in the garb of Religion—the World. Christianity then, as now, was unpopular. Then, as now, there were those who would make selections out of it as a system, and weave them into whatever happened to be the popular form of Religion, while they disliked it as a whole. It is always easy for those who dislike trouble to make a selection out of Christianity, and make it a graceful appendage to something less stern, leaving out its absoluteness, its exclusiveness and severity. But the early Christians saw that Christianity could never be a tolerated religion at the price of its integrity. Again and again it might have been admitted as a *religio licita* in the Empire, had they agreed to renounce its claims to be an absolute religion, and to supplant all others. S. Paul knows how to classify this sort of feeling, these unworthy offers when advanced by Judaism. It is the World, the World following out its Religion. It is the World, which disbelieves in anything stronger than a view, or more pronounced than an opinion, and which shudders at a difference, and looks upon a definite statement as a display of bad taste. 'Let all be mixed up together, the best in Judaism and the best in Christianity, and do not let us push to an extreme the unpalatable doctrines which offend our common sense of religion.' 'Zeal for the law!' says S. Paul. 'Zeal in conciliating public opinion! I know of no such thing. I have only one thing to be proud of, and that is the Cross of Christ. By means of it I dread the World, as if it were a crucified, an abhorred thing; and the World dreads me as if I were a creature of shame, and cursed with the ban of one who hangs upon the tree.' And this is a frame of mind which is common in all ages of the Church, not the least in our own. There is much in Christianity which is beautiful and fascinating. No one can deny that it has shaped and coloured civilisation itself; but there is also much which is stern and distasteful, and which makes large demands on faith and conduct. What is easier than to excerpt the glorious precepts of Christianity, its simple morality, its human kindliness, and to put on one side all that gives offence? The Christ of the Gospels in the simple idyll of Bethlehem or Nazareth, Christ in His Incarnation, the end of the evolution of man—every one will accept this, and it will produce no conflict, offend no prejudice, and alienate no earnestness. And yet S. Paul, and the Christian Church with him, could only say 'God forbid.' The Cross of Christ, the offence of the Cross, that which sharply separates off the Church and the World, is the only thing worth contending for, the only thing worth possessing—because the Cross, more than anything else, represents a system. It means also, as we shall see in the next chapter, power; it represents a grateful recollection of a supreme trial and degradation which the Church is anxious and longing to turn from humiliation into glory; but emphatically it represents a system,—a system which cannot be broken without serious damage to its integrity and proportion. Its stern side represents its extreme value and greatest efficacy. As with the old sacrifices discussed above, so in the great Sacrifice of the Cross, Christ surrenders Himself in the councils of Eternity as the Victim, the Lamb without spot, slain from the foundation of the world.[1] He offers Himself to bear the sins of all mankind. On His head, as on the head of the victim, were laid our offences. 'He bare the sin of many.' He died once for all upon the Cross, the 'one sufficient sacrifice, oblation, and satisfaction, for the sins of the whole world.' In heaven He ever lives to make intercession for us, while the Church pleads His Sacrifice here below. He gives still of His Blood shed and of His Body broken for the life of the world in a Sacramental mystery. To take out the Cross is to take away the whole system of salvation as the Church has received it; while to say that the Gospel is in the Sermon on the Mount rather than in the Mystery of Calvary, is to misunderstand and to misapply the whole scheme of our Redemption. It is something done for us, not something told to us; good news, not good advice; salvation, not reformation. And therefore an emphatic 'God forbid' is the only attitude which

---

[1] 1 S. Pet. i 20.

we can assume towards a Christianity without the Cross. It is useless to point to what it has done, if we then proceed to rob it of the power by which it has transformed the world. It is, no doubt, a stern reminder. It means a perpetual protest against an easy life decorated with religious terms and flavoured with a sentiment of piety. It means a stern expiation, a constant warfare, an exhibition of a crucified life in which the hand of faith which is held out to receive the blessings of Atonement, Justification, and Sanctification, is itself pierced. Christ has done all—that is quite true—for those who are also contributing their all. Our share of the world's debt is paid, in so far as we are able to appropriate Christ's merits. Our own sanctification is possible, only as by the Holy Spirit the life and power of Christ is developed in us. It is recorded in the life of S. Martin, that, as he prayed, a figure of supreme majesty and sublime beauty stood before him, and claimed his adoration and his homage. But the saint, looking fixedly at him, asked, 'Where is the crown of thorns, where is the print of the nails, where are the marks of sorrow, and the sign of the Passion?' And then the evil illusion vanished. We do not worship beauty, we do not worship mere grandeur, we cannot stop at the Incarnation. We must go on from Bethlehem to Calvary. We are followers and worshippers of the Crucified. We are sons and daughters of the Cross. For by the Cross the world was redeemed.

CHAPTER XI

DIVINE HELP—THE CHURCH

> 'To be saved is, of its own inherent nature, if only we understood it, to be saved into a church; to be saved into an assembly of the firstborn—a city of God.'

We have now examined the revolution which Christ effected in the methods of conducting our spiritual warfare, and working out our higher life, by His Atonement. We have, however, as yet considered but half of Christ's Redemption plan, if we may with reverence discuss so profound a mystery.

If we were to suppose a case, in which a man of deep benevolence and of unlimited capacity for exerting that benevolence, were to meet a poor sufferer, weighed down with debt, oppressed with a long and disastrous past, with no present resources, and no hope for the future, we should imagine him, when satisfied with the genuine nature of the case, if he wished to do more than merely satisfy a passing need, setting himself to accomplish two things. First of all, he would ascertain the nature of the liabilities by which the past exercised such a sad influence upon him, and, if possible, he would pay off these, and set the sufferer free. Then, in the second place, he would think no system of present relief complete which did not provide against a repetition of these calamities for the future. Like the Good Samaritan in the parable, he would first bind up the wounds of the sufferer, pouring in oil and wine; he would then take him to the inn and provide for his safety and maintenance during his recovery. So we are accustomed to think that our Lord Jesus Christ, when He took upon Him to deliver man, did in the same way two things; in the words of the children's hymn,

> 'He died that we might be forgiven,
> He died to make us good.'

He is the author of the Atonement, whereby He takes away the sin of the world; He is also the author of Sanctification, whereby He keeps those who commit themselves to Him from falling into deadly sin and missing the way to eternal life. The first of these great schemes has been glanced at in the preceding chapter—what it means and what it implies; the second we must endeavour to set forth in the following pages, even if it be possible only to put out a suggestion of this great and important scheme of Sanctification, which Christ has left to us. It may be said, on grounds both natural and historical, 'It is because man is social that "the perfect man" is to be realised, not by the single Christian, but by the whole Church.'[1] It may be said broadly and simply, that Christ's scheme of sanctification may be summed up in one word—the Church. It must be our effort to justify and safeguard this statement, to secure it from unworthy conceptions, and from the still more unworthy fears of those who, because once burnt, refuse to approach the fire either

[1] Gore *The Mission of the Church* p. 10.

for heat or light,—a proverb, be it observed, of the irrational or semi-rational portion of creation, not of man, who can think and connect his process of reasoning. To borrow an illustration of Archdeacon Wilberforce,—there will be some people still who resent the construction of high-roads to the royal dwelling across the common where hitherto each had believed himself to be at liberty to make his own way. But a little further acquaintance with the roads, their easiness, their safety, and their directness, will convince him that liberty to go wrong is not always an unmixed blessing, and that individual freedom is dearly bought if it means an inability to profit by the fruits of a wisdom higher than our own. It will take a long time to convince men that the Church is anything else than a body of people who have banded themselves together to develop and propagate certain opinions which are profitable to human interests and minister to human pride, inasmuch as human agency is thereby represented as in some way co-operative with divine grace, with a tendency to supersede it; a society whose aim it is to set up lords over God's heritage, barring the free right of appeal to Him: to put men and human ordinances between Him and them, and to aggrandise themselves by appeals to human ignorance and human weakness, until power, riches, and influence carry them to a height where it is difficult to discern in the Pontiff, surrounded with magnificence and loaded with wealth, carried in state before admiring crowds, any semblance to the meek and lowly Jesus, sitting on an ass, and a colt the foal of an ass.

It is perhaps needless to say that this conception is both false and unworthy, and that no system must be judged by its exaggeration or corruption, but in itself. The Church is no combination of those who think alike on the same subject, united by a common purpose in the furtherance of a common design. 'We are sometimes asked to think,' says the present Archbishop of Canterbury, 'that the Church only exists in the union of believers, and has not a reality of its own. Now it is perfectly clear that in the New Testament the idea of the Church is not that. Men talk sometimes as if a Church could be constituted simply by Christians coming together and uniting themselves into one body for the purpose. Men speak as if Christians came first and the Church after; as if the origin of the Church was in the wills of individual Christians who composed it. But, on the contrary, throughout the teaching of the apostles we see that it is the Church that comes first and the members of it afterwards. Men were not brought to Christ to believe in Him and His Cross, and to recognise the duty of worshipping the Heavenly Father in His Name, and then decided that it would be a great help to their religion that they should join one another in that worship, and should be united in the bonds of fellowship for that purpose. In the New Testament, on the contrary, the kingdom of heaven is already in existence, and men are invited into it. The Church takes its origin, not in the will of man, but in the will of the Lord Jesus Christ. He sent forth His apostles; the apostles received their commission from Him: they were not organs of the congregation; they were ministers of the Lord Himself. He sent them forth to gather all the thousands that they could reach within His fold; but they came first, and the members came afterwards; and the Church, in all its dignity and glory, was quite independent of the members that were brought within it. Everywhere men are called in; they do not come in and make the Church by coming. They are called into that which already exists; they are recognised as members when they are within; but their membership depends upon their admission, and not upon their constituting themselves into a body in the sight of the Lord.'[1]

So we shall find that the Church is an integral element of Christ's plan, if we may so speak with reverence. 'It is the society established by Him and in Him on earth, in view of salvation. In its larger sense, it is the society of God's creatures who have a share on earth in the effects of redemption, or who in heaven have remained faithful to God.'[2]

Before we proceed to discuss the Church as God's kingdom, or city, or spiritual society, it will be necessary to examine briefly that most sacred and mysterious conception of the Church, which we owe to S. Paul, and which finds an echo in our Prayer-Book in more than one place, which speaks of it as 'the Body of Christ.'

There is always a danger, if we take up these terms without stopping to consider them, that they should be absolutely meaningless to us; there is always the risk, if we attempt to explain them, of misunderstanding or depreciating them. There are some terms, especially in Holy Scripture, which we can rather feel

---

[1] *Twelve Sermons preached at the Consecration of Truro Cathedral* pp. 17-20.

[2] A. P. Forbes Bishop of Brechin *Explanation of the Thirty-nine Articles* Article XIX.

than explain. It is possible that this may be one of them. It might be said that the Church 'is spoken of as a body, because thought of as a whole through the abstracting power of reason. Yet why should it be called the Body of the Lord?' Christians may be the body of His realm in this sense, but not His own Body. S. Paul would seem to say that the members of the Church are the spiritual members of Christ. Christ in and through His Church imparts to His servants His own life; and in the unity of the Church, all these many Christ-informed members became one body in Him, He being the head, they the members.[1] And so while each individual would be helped to rise to the full powers of his being by being vitalised by Christ, so the whole body, compacted as it were of the members of Christ, would reach out to the world, not only with all the greatness of a community, but with all the supernatural energy of the life of Christ.[2]

But it is rather as a divine Society that we must consider it now, designed to help mankind. For while 'the principle of Rationalism is, that man's improvement may be effected through those gifts which God bestowed upon him by creation, inasmuch as sufficient means of intercourse with the Supreme Spirit were provided by the law of his nature—the Church deals with man as a fallen race, whose original means of intercourse with God have been obstructed, and which needs a new and supernatural channel for the entrance of heavenly gifts. And this channel has been provided through the Man Jesus Christ.'

[1] See Wilberforce *Incarnation* chap. xi.
[2] See *Explanation of the Thirty-nine Articles* by A. P. Forbes Bishop of Brechin, as above.

So that perhaps to make the conception of the Church a practical one to the ordinary understanding, it would not be wrong to describe it as a sort of spiritual benefit society. No one can live without God. The ordinary man of the world owes it to God's help that he is not the veriest criminal, such as those who prey upon society. But the highest type of spiritual excellence, the most complete form of help for human infirmity, is to be found in the special organisation devised by Christ for that purpose. As a rough and simple illustration, let us take an example out of ordinary country life. Here is a man who has met with a severe accident, his power of earning his daily bread is gone, his wife and children are suddenly deprived of the help of the bread-winner; and yet he exhibits no despondency, his wife and children continue to be clothed and fed, the doctor attends to his needs, medical comforts are provided. On inquiry you learn that he is a member of a provident club, which supplies him with the help of a doctor, with wages during his enforced idleness, and will continue to minister to his needs until he is able once more to do his work and earn his own daily bread. Here, on the other hand, is a man who has met with a similar accident, his conditions are the same, but his case is very different; his wife and his children are starving, he himself is dependent on such precarious aid as he can get, and is left to parochial care and public charity. He, you learn on inquiry, belongs to no benefit society, and either through indolence, or in a spirit of isolation, has elected to pass through life simply trusting to his own exertion, and to the chance of avoiding disabling calamity. Such, in a figure, is the difference between a member of the Church and him who stands outside it. He may say that he means the same thing, and is facing the same way; but the one is in the receipt of certain covenanted spiritual blessings, which help him in life's journey, and minister to him in life's troubles; the other neither feels their necessity nor desires their aid; and he, even if he avoids calamity, fails to attain to that spiritual height which we associate with Christian excellence. It is in this sense that we maintain that the Church is a great benefit society ordained of God for our sanctification and help.

We may now proceed to trace the preparation for the Church, and the organisation of it when formed, before we proceed further to particularise its methods of help. There had been a kingdom of God upon earth before this, temporary indeed, provisional, ready to vanish away, which yet represented a distinct stage in the ordering and disposing of the approaches of God to man and of man to God, leading up to the Incarnation, and to the extension of the Incarnation through the Church and Sacraments, in the full kingdom of the Spirit, where God dwells with man and in man. There have been at different times tendencies unduly to elevate the Law as a perfect, final, and satisfying scheme, as we see in the Judaism combated by S. Paul; and, on the other hand, there has been a tendency to minimise it and depreciate it altogether, as we see in the present day, when an attempt is made to represent Judaism as having merely taken over its distinctive features of worship from the neighbouring nations, which represent Religion in its childhood and swaddling-clothes of superstition; while the ceremonial accretions, as they are stated to be, are only the ritual daubs wherewith the decaying and effete religion, which was really played out, tried to hide its hollow cheeks and lifeless countenance. If 'the Law' be nothing more than a dialect, so to speak, of ancient religious language, it is interesting to the student of comparative religion, and that is all ; but if it represents a stage in divine economy,—if, that is, it is what it professes to be,—then we may see in it a very definite stage in the development of the plan of God for the human race with reference to Himself. 'The Law,' Judaism, whatever we may like to call it, represents a pale, a religious precinct, within which certain representatives of the human race were collected, where they might draw near to God, listen to Him, receive His approaches, and form the point of contact, as it were, the place in human nature, where God would alight when He came in the Incarnation, in the body prepared for Him. So we find in Judaism in no sense a catholic religion, but a religion of privilege, a receptacle in the first place for the Divine message. 'Thus saith the Lord,' the Lord speaking by the prophets : 'Hear now the word of the Lord,'—these were proclamations which made Judaism to the human race, in a real and true sense, that which the oracle of Delphi was to the false religions of the world. Here God speaks, here the Holy Ghost speaks by the prophets, here God leaves not Himself without witness. The world is prepared, those who have eyes to see may see the mystery which is revealed here dimly, there more clearly, by type, by figure, by prophets, that out of a despised little country, in humble guise, to suffer, to die, to be buried, God would come. It was no small preparation for a fuller state of privilege that there should be a place in the world where supernatural truth should be revealed to faith, and where men should hear, instead of the faltering accents of opinion, or the faint questionings of human hopes, the dogmatic utterance, 'Thus saith the Lord.' This was a real preparation for the *Ecclesia docens*. And no less may we see God's purpose in the Ceremonial Law. This really represented the setting up of a place of meeting, where man could approach God with reverence, *i.e.* where God could meet man without its being a source of judgement and even harm to him. It has been said that solemn ritual was forced on the Jewish Church, just as solemn ritual is forced on the Christian Church. What gave the first impulse to the building of the temple, with its stately ceremonial and gorgeous magnificence? It was the direct result of the solemn lesson working in David's mind, taught by God in the judgement on Uzzah, that holy things cannot be unprotected and left exposed to profane touch,—just as the early Church found that the profaned Eucharist, with its judgement of death, suggested the barrier of awe and solemnity, such as ritual and careful reverence produce.[1] Thus the Ceremonial Law was a step again in setting up a place where God could talk with man, without fear of profanation or the awful penalties which await the irreverent looking upon God; while of course it was more than this: it was the placing in the world treasure-chests of sealed mysteries, which the key of the Gospel would afterwards unlock. It was to saturate the religious life of the world with religious truth, which had no meaning in itself until it found its fulfilment in Christ; while a third and more important development still was effected by 'the Law,' viz. the attempt made thereby to treat the awful phenomenon of sin. Here was the

[1] See Willis *Worship under the Old Covenant* p. 220.

barrier between man and God; here was the awful debt mounting up which necessitated the tremendous remedy of the Atonement. And to the Jews, the peculiar people of God, was promulgated the Moral Law in the Ten Commandments, 'containing in a compendious form an exhaustive statement of human duty towards the Author of our being, and towards our fellow-creatures.' But this was not all. The Law, which man failed to keep, and was unable to keep, showed him his guilt, and his inability to be righteous before God; while in the tremendous system of Sacrifice there was the strongest possible exhibition of the evil of sin, in the constant symbolism of death as the penalty for trangressions, and of the consuming wrath of God, like a devouring fire wiping away and licking up all that was tainted or charged with defilement; while behind it all there lurked that appalling fact, which we have already glanced at, that no sacrifice under the complicated Levitical system availed to atone for wilful sin. There was, after all, no remission of sins, as sins, under 'the Law,' and so 'sin by the Law became exceeding sinful,' and man was left at the threshold of the Church, at the foot of the Cross, unhealed and uncomforted, where his helpless impotence, and his craving for forgiveness, reached out in eloquent appeal to the Saviour of the world.

Such a system could be, and was, only preparatory. A Spirit-bearing Body, of which 'the Law' was only a sketch, was to become a reality in the Gospel. Forgiveness of sins was to become a realised possibility, the barrier between man and God was to be broken down, and the power and presence of Christ as the Atoner and Sacrificer were to be brought home to the soul through the medium of the Holy Spirit, in the Church, with its communion of life and its fulness of grace, for which all that had gone before had been the gradual preparation. 'It is not good that the man should be alone.' 'Adam' has expanded from his individual existence into the exhibition of a vast community-life, in which he reaches out to, and is enriched by, other lives and interests,—by saints living, saints departed, by Christ Himself. We shall be able the better to appreciate the difference between the individual unit, and the same as a member of the Church, by a glance at that great political organisation which marches like a solid phalanx across the pages of ancient history, the Roman Empire. If a man could claim that he was a Roman citizen, then he could feel welling into his own life the advantages which were gathered up, as the contribution of the lives of its citizens, its government, its resources, its laws, its army, its civilisation, all which went to form that great conception, Rome ;—the privileges of a club, such as that we were considering above, on a large scale ; so that any Roman citizen who came to a provincial town, where a group of Roman citizens met together in a body, was forthwith a member of the group; and the group was simply a fragment of 'Rome,' cut off in space from the main body, but possessing its vitality and self-identity as fully as when it was joined to it.[1] So the Holy Spirit, when He leaped down into the world on the day of Pentecost, put men into connection with a great spiritual environment, or, more truly, vitalised the old machinery of the Jewish Church for that purpose. A morality higher and deeper, and at the same time attainable, was proclaimed.

[1] Ramsay S. *Paul the Traveller* p. 125.

Rites which were not only significant, but effectual —which could really take away sin, and not merely exhibit its power,—were displayed, opening up the approach to God. So that if a man could say in truth, 'I am a Churchman, I am a member of the Church,' he could claim the full benefits and protection of a supernatural endowment more fully than a Roman citizen could claim the privilege of that which was meant by ' Rome.'

As we gaze at this Church in its earliest manifestation, in the records which are left to us; as we witness the first formation of this 'Spirit-bearing body,' this pale, this precinct, in which the Holy Spirit became the atmosphere, by means of which the sound of God's voice, and the warmth and glow of the life of Christ, could reach the soul; we see, first of all, what appears to be a chaos of χαρίσματα or special gifts of the Holy Spirit, poured in, as it were, with a vast flood of grace over the infant community. The apostles stand out as the possessors of all power and authority, lodged in themselves, not with a divided jurisdiction, but each with a complete right of superintendence over the whole Christian community. They had their ministering disciples and subordinate helpers. So S. Paul and S. Barnabas made use of several, mostly young men, as assistants, who reported to them on the condition of the Church communities; they did certain duties, such, for instance, as baptizing, which the apostles, as Christ had done before them, usually committed to others, while they reserved to themselves the right of laying on of hands; while underneath them there was the community in possession of extraordinary spiritual gifts, distributed by apostolic hands among all; and so at first we shall find no ordered ranks of a ministry as later; there is a distinction of gifts rather than a distinction of offices.[1] In this condition of things there was not as yet any fixed form, definite arrangement, or gradation of ecclesiastical offices; the need for them was not yet experienced. But gradually the age of spiritual gifts passes away, and we discover the appearance of Church officers, such as Bishops and Deacons, and an organised system of ordination to fixed offices. It is as if the Holy Spirit had entered at first with a great flood spreading over all, which, as it subsided, or rather as it became more diffused, exhibited the different channels into which it sank, to be by them derived to the Church in the ordered flow of fixed ordinances. And so we see, first, the order of Deacons becoming fixed, as it were, and then that of Presbyters or Bishops, and finally, the Episcopate in the form in which we know it at the present day—at first not marked off as an office, although it existed as a fact, as, for instance, in the person of S. James. It is true to say generally, with reference to this, that for some time, and until the apostles began to be removed by death, 'the Episcopate slept in the Apostolate.' In the Church of the living God, as in the world around us, order is essential. And whenever we set ourselves to study (as will be done more at length in a subsequent volume) the carefully adjusted machinery by which that order is attained, we are studying the framework of the organisation by which life flows into the Church, and is derived through the Church to the individual soul, making us one with Christ, and inheritors of all spiritual blessings. The Church has always therefore laid great stress on the

[1] Eph. iv 11; 1 Cor. xi 28.

integrity of her orders—that is to say, on the fact that she possesses an apostolically constituted ministry. Bishop Moberly has well pointed out the great and important position of the apostles in this respect in the economy of the Holy Spirit. He says: 'It seems to me important to dwell for a short time on this point —I mean the condition of the Twelve during the short time that elapsed before they began to teach or baptize or bring others into the communion of the Body of Christ. In them conjointly dwelt for the present the fulness of the Holy Spirit, in so far forth as He was given from Christ to be transmitted for the sanctification of mankind. Personal graces, administrative graces, all the diversities of gifts to be given in many divisions to men in the Church through human agency, were to issue from that great gift which, hitherto undivided except to twelve holders, rested for such transmission upon them alone. As in the case of the miraculous feeding of the multitude of four or five thousand, the Lord gave to His disciples, and the disciples to the multitude, so the gifts which were to sanctify the innumerable company of the members of the Body of Christ in all future ages should flow down from one single source through twelve channels. Governors and governed, teachers and taught, graces inward and graces outward, all Christians should desire the orderly communication of the covenanted indwelling of the Holy Spirit through the agency of those twelve men, on whom the tongues sat, like as of fire, on that great day.'[1]

The question, then, of Holy Orders is no academical question to be debated among the dogmas, or main-

[1] G. Moberly Bishop of Salisbury *Bampton Lectures* edit. 1 pp. 40 41.

tained in the interest of ecclesiastical bigots who wish to lord it over God's heritage, but it touches the very machinery of spiritual gifts, by which certain definite and clearly defined blessings are transmitted to the Church. Many people fail to see the importance of a question which is discussed from time to time,—the validity of Anglican Orders. Holy Orders and the possession by a Church of valid Orders in the direct succession from Christ, is a question of vital importance, whether, as has been said, we hold 'the Episcopate to be enjoined by the revealed will of God, or, like Archdeacons and Capitular bodies, to be a feature of our Church arrangements, which, however admirable, may conceivably be dispensed with without sacrificing anything organic in the conditions of communion with Christ.'[1] It is all part of the unconscious indifference, so painfully evident in theological discussions, which regards spiritual matters as by their very nature incapable of precision or careful limitation. A man of business, who knows the importance of a definite phrase in a deed which concerns transmission of property, a man who will insist, as trustee, or as governor of a benefit society, on literal compliance with most stringent rules, and a subordination to carefully elected officers, as a prerequisite for receiving the precise benefit of that particular society, will yet tell us that it cannot be anything but an indifferent matter what is the exact form in which we dispose ourselves to receive God's benefits. No doubt God's general benefits may be received generally; but Christianity is not a system of general benefit, but a system of special benefit, devised for man at a period of special need; and

[1] Liddon *Clerical Life and Work* p. 297.

accordingly we find, as we should expect, that, acting by a reflex influence, where the supernatural Church is rejected there is a rapid tendency to reject a supernatural Christ. 'How can these things be?' very soon becomes shifted from an objection to Baptismal Regeneration into a formula which challenges Christianity all along the line. It is always easy to pose as a champion of pure Christianity by raising a cry of sacerdotalism. But, apart from the fact that the Jewish religion as revealed by God Himself was sacerdotal, and therefore sacerdotalism in its most extreme form cannot be intrinsically wrong,—apart from the fact that sacerdotalism, so called, is merely carrying out in the region of the spiritual life a principle by which benefits are conveyed to us every day of our lives in the political, legal, medical, artistic spheres, where the few are made by the natural ordination of God's will the trustees and dispensers of God's gifts to the many,—apart from this, it must be remembered, that if on any showing God has given a definite system of ordinances, an appeal to be separately treated is really asking God for a distinct personal favour, and so far from being a sign of humility is a mark of pride. The Church is too deeply rooted in the principles of God's providential dealings with men, too firmly based on history, too closely bound round the Christian life, to leave room for us to treat it as an open question, or indeed regard it as anything else than an integral part of God's redemptive plan, part of His scheme to deliver man.

It remains that we should examine this a little in detail, and show how far the Church is from being an arbitrary arrangement, which possibly might be superseded, improved, or otherwise altered by a more modern conception of human progress and the development of the race.

The initial difficulty which had to be encountered in any system of morality devised for the better conduct of the race, was this: that man, with the best desires and intentions, was unable to carry out that course of action which his better judgment told him was the highest and the best. It is, as we have seen, a strange difficulty which has always to be encountered, that man will knowingly do with his eyes open, things which will result in harm and loss to him. The great thinkers of the world discovered that there is in man a predisposition to what was evil; that man left to himself is the most depraved of all creatures in every form of depravity. This we know and distinguish under the title of original or birth sin, and it is recognised even by those who shrink from theological terms and have no concern about sin, as hereditary taint, if not necessarily in the nature of all men as a natural obstacle, yet to be discerned in most men as a legacy from their proximate ancestors in the shape of a warp, predisposition, or bias to certain sins or blemishes. Even those who most believe in birth-sin, in sin which is by nature, must also recognise this fact as a superadded difficulty in the terrible weight of heredity, the very thought of which sometimes serves to keep a man down, and check all aspirations after better things. What is the use of contending against that which a man cannot help? What is the use of attempting to overcome that which is in the blood? A murderer may thus easily bring himself to believe that his punishment is a mistake, and his execration by society an inhuman perversion of that which ought to take the form of pity for his misfortunes; and the more ordinary sins which beset our humanity may very easily be allowed to remain within the circle of the heart, untouched and almost unnoticed. They are the heirloom of misfortune, and the sad characteristics which must ever distinguish a member of a tainted family. With this doctrine of birth-sin belonging to the children of Adam, and of further hereditary taint descending from parents, Christ, we may say with reverence, had first to deal in delivering man. He must make men capable of goodness; and therefore in His divine Benefit Society there stands at the entrance, as the initial requisite, binding as a necessity on all who wish to be saved, the Divine command, 'Ye must be born again,' and the Sacrament of New Birth, Holy Baptism, by which this is effected. As we are by nature born in sin, so we are by Baptism made the children of Grace. The effect of Baptism has been treated of at length in the third chapter, and we see at once how it is thus lifted out of being an arbitrary enactment, once imposed by Christ as a graceful symbol, and now in the interests of sacerdotalism riveted on the necks of an enlightened people. The insistence again and again in Holy Scripture on its necessity, the clear indication that not even a great conversion like that of S. Paul was sufficient without it, the instant submission to this ordinance by the jailer of Philippi, who had asked, 'What must I do to be saved?' and had received his answer—these, and other passages of Holy Scripture, show how the early Church understood their great commission, to make disciples of all the nations by baptizing them into the Name of the Father and of the Son and of the Holy Ghost, putting them, as it were, by Baptism into a sacred enclosure whence they could reach, and be helped by, God Who is a Father, God Who is a Redeemer, and God Who is a Sanctifier, and so attain to that highest of all possible ideals of character known as Christian life, far elevated, as we have seen, above morality, and yet instantly dying down if any breach takes place in the commonest and simplest integrity of the moral life. To those who will enter the Church of Christ, Holy Baptism, if received by the hand of faith, will give that nature which will enable the Christian to produce in his poor, weak, crumbling humanity that image of Christ which would have been impossible without it.

As the child grows up still within the sheltering life of the Church; when his nature now begins to develop and becomes weak and plastic; when Satan grapples with it, and the winds of the world wrestle with it, and the flesh in all its softness enervates it,—when, in addition to this, God, Who did tempt Abraham, knows that He will have severely to try him who is to be an heir of salvation, with trials under which he may bend and crack: then, at this period of his career, at least in the Western Church, is provided the ordinance of strengthening known as Confirmation, in which this young life is made firm by being attached to the strong prop of the Church, and invigorated by the gift of strength, in the imparting of the Holy Ghost through the laying on of the hands of the Bishop. The most superficial glance at all the ordinances of the Church will show us how one and all they are charged with strength; how inevitably this must be so in carrying out the policy, so to speak, which saves men and women, not by taking them out of the world, but by strengthening them in it against its evil. It is a distinct loss which we in the English Church have incurred in regarding this rite, as it is too often regarded, simply as an edifying ceremony of renewal of vows, such as might take place at any parochial mission, for the advantage of those whose hearts have been moved ; a misconception which has come about largely from the fact that in the revision of the Prayer-Book in 1662, this renewing of vows was made part, and a very edifying part, of the service of preparation. Confirmation is much more than this : it occupies a distinct place in the economy of divine Grace as stored up in the Church. And it is a curious irony of fate that those who are most loud in decrying even a harmless doctrine of good works, should again and again be found to be minimising the operation of divine Grace in favour of human co-operation through the heart, the intelligence, or earnest resolution.

Further, as original sin was dealt with by Holy Baptism, so clearly it becomes necessary to treat, in some way, actual sin. The child, as he grows up, is not only conscious of the weakness which remains, even after the New Birth in Holy Baptism ; he also falls into the commission of actual sin. And against this, a special provision is made in Christ's Church, a special help is given against a special difficulty, in what is known as Absolution. Men, particularly in times of controversy, are so engaged in arguing as to the precise meaning of certain terms put into our English Prayer-Book in the sixteenth century, or they are so engaged in contemplating the imaginary horrors of Confession, and all the anguish it would mean to themselves, that they forget altogether what is meant by Absolution,—whether there is such a thing at all, whether it is a remedy against actual sin, whether it was so designed by our Blessed Lord Himself. However difficult it might be to attain it, however painful the process of Confession, any man who was in earnest would at least give it a trial, if he found he could not overcome the sense of guilt, or the power of sin, without it; and having tried it, he would be in a position to see what a marvellous remedy Christ has here left to us. The nature of this Absolution is forgiveness and something more than forgiveness. It is a remedy which heals and strengthens at the same time. It is forgiveness pronounced by God, Who is the real Absolver, using the instrumentality of His minister. In the same way, every time one of Christ's ministers baptizes he forgives sins, still not in his own name, but in Christ's. It is the same delegation of authority with which we are familiar in one of the most ordinary processes of everyday experience, where the pardoned criminal is released from jail, virtually and really by the Crown, which alone has that authority, but actually by the jailers, to whom the authority has filtered down, through various methods known to the law. So that if we were asked, 'Who can forgive sins but God only?' we should unhesitatingly say, 'No one.' But as, when this question was first asked, the multitude glorified God, Who had given such power unto men, so still we may recognise the tenderness and gentleness of God, Who has thus met the cravings of the human soul for an answer to the heartfelt expression of its penitence, and has lodged this power in the hands of men, who, sinners themselves, can sympathise with their fellow-sinners, and help others out of the abundance of the consolations wherewith they themselves are comforted of God;—while the message brings with it that which, in addition to forgiveness, helps to the breaking off the chain of sin and evil habit, together with grace to make a firmer stand against the wiles of Satan for the future, when God has once more set the poor sinner's feet upon the rock and ordered his goings. If it be asked whence this power is derived, the answer is simple, that it comes as part of the Holy Spirit's living endowment in Ordination, in words which either mean what they say, or else should be removed out of the Prayer-Book as a needless stumbling-block and a mockery: 'Receive the Holy Ghost for the office and work of a Priest in the Church of God, now committed unto thee by the imposition of our hands. Whose sins thou dost forgive, they are forgiven; and whose sins thou dost retain, they are retained.'[1] A provision for the forgiveness of actual sins is part of Christ's endowment in His great spiritual Benefit Society called the Church. If it be contrary to the spirit of the Anglican branch of it to compel a sinner thus to make use of this Confession, it is equally contrary to its spirit to compel him not so to use it. Every one knew in the sixteenth century what Absolution meant, and the term was retained to describe the same benefit which goes by that name throughout the whole Catholic Church. It can only be denied by a non-natural use of terms. It can only be refused to those who need it by a faithless breach of trust on the part of those to whom God has committed the care of the remedy.

[1] The Form and Manner of Ordering of Priests, *Book of Common Prayer.*

But life in the Church is not all repair and struggle with sin; there are definite means provided also for spiritual growth, the highest of which, as will be seen in a subsequent volume of this series, is the Holy Communion. In fitting in this great ordinance to the present brief survey of God's benefits as provided for the use of men in the Church, it will be necessary to speak only of one aspect of it. Only a few years ago, as is the case even now in some parts of the Church, the Holy Communion was regarded as an unusual and even dangerous thing, standing altogether outside a man's ordinary life, to be received at rare intervals, perhaps only at the very end of life, when the turmoil of trouble and temptation had swept by, when there was nothing to distract, and nothing to agitate the halcyon calm which was the only possible condition under which to enterprise so great a thing. And consequently this holy feast was not for the young, nor for the busy, nor for the tempted; it was the feast at the end of the day, not the food for the work of life. The difference between these two conceptions is vital; certainly, reverence and guard as we must and ought this most holy feast, it is perverting it from the purpose for which it was placed in Christ's great Benefit Society if we cease to regard it otherwise than as food for the work of life. 'He that eateth Me, even he shall live by Me,'[1] said our blessed Lord. By this we grow, by this we develop within us that divine nature which makes us living branches in the sacred Vine.

It would be possible to show further the many blessings still which belong to those who are members

[1] S. John vi 57.

of the great Society: the attention bestowed all through life, the spiritual physicians which wait on us, the word of caution and advice which cheers us, the care in sickness and in health which is bestowed upon us, the regulation of the family, and the guarding of its sanctity, the preparation for death, that supreme moment which awaits us all. Most certainly, he who breaks away from the unity of the Church is guilty of a great deal more than a wrong use of his right of private judgment. He is breaking down the hedge in schism, and preparing the way for others to follow him, and he is also depriving himself of the full blessings devised for his sanctification.

CHAPTER XII

THE EXPRESSION OF RELIGION—WORSHIP

'Gratias agimus tibi propter magnam gloriam tuam.'

IF Religion is a personal relation towards a personal God, Who has revealed to us so much as may be known of Himself, and how He wills to be approached; if under the helping guidance of God, not only a moral life is possible to us, but also a life of great spiritual excellence; if a great pattern of holiness has been put before us, the realisation of which is barred by obstacles within and without; if, at the same time, God being stronger than any opponent which can rise against us, the way of heaven is open to us, and the very highest life of holiness has become a possibility in the kingdom of grace—it remains to be seen how the life of Religion will display itself, what will be its outward expression, and fullest development. We have seen how a man may be religious; what will he be, how will he behave himself, when he is religious?

The manifestation of Religion is twofold: it will express itself in relation to God, and it will express itself in the personal life. It will reach out towards God in worship, and it will exhibit the manifestation of a life of goodness, within the sphere of personal influence in which God has placed us. Of these two, it will now be our aim to consider the first in the present chapter. To consider worship as the expression of Religion towards God in its most perfect aspect.

It will be obvious to any one who pauses to think, that not only is worship a subject which is very much misunderstood among us, but also that it is by no means easy to feel, or, feeling, to express, what is the underlying principle of worship. Why should God seek to be praised for all He does? Why should He demand from us as His right the constant expression of an adoring wonder that He is what He is, and does what He does? We say of the greatest of men, that the greater he is the more he shrinks from praise. We see how the Incarnate God submitted to the two extremes of indignity—human birth and human death. He did not abhor the Virgin's womb, He overcame the sharpness of death, and in the life which He lived between these two points, He submitted to be the outcast of the people, He retired from honour, and shrank from praise. Further we see how humility, humiliation, self-abasement are inculcated upon us, with an iterated persistency as the marks and methods of Christian perfection. Why is there this fundamental difference of attitude between God and man? Are we to say here once more, 'I will not call that moral in God which is immoral in man'? or are we speaking of two different things? or has man intercepted and misapplied that which was meant for God, and, like the bird in the well-known fable, decorated himself with ornaments beautiful in themselves, but incongruous to his nature, and obviously not belonging to him?

These are questions not easy to answer, or at least

to answer intelligibly. And we may need some little patience to unravel the matter.

God, we can see at once, is no greedy potentate, sitting on a throne of ease, demanding the extravagant praises of His subjects, and the hollow insincerity of empty phrases from prostrate slaves.

What does 'Worship' mean, our English word? It means, to think, to declare worthy. Worship is worth-ship. It is to surround with a halo of glory and honour all that we know, see, or feel of the working of God; to say that God, wherever He is, and however He manifests Himself, is to be declared worthy. Why? It would be sufficient to answer, 'because God has so demanded it of us'; or 'because man, if he once feels the presence of God, cannot do otherwise.' Moses, even when told to do acts of reverence, already trembles at the sight of God. Isaiah feels out for a barrier to place between himself and God, such as that symbolised and proclaimed by the 'Holy, Holy, Holy' of the Seraphim. But still God may allow us to ask why? If we look around us, we shall see a vast system carrying out the will of God, albeit there are marks of failure, albeit there are broken wheels, and twisted rods, and friction, and collapse; still to us, as it was to the ancients, it is a vast cosmos. All is carrying out an ordered plan, all is subservient to a guiding will. And to those who have ears to hear, there is a great hymn of praise ceaselessly ascending to God from all His works. Surely we cannot accept the statement that 'the world seemed richer *then* (*i.e.* in Pagan times) and brighter to all men than it has seemed since; but of all men it seemed richest and brightest to the Greek.' The Benedicite is not an unmeaning iteration of an irritating formula. It is the hum of the great world-machine ceaselessly doing its work, where 'the heavens declare the glory of God, and the firmament sheweth His handywork,' where all things sing at their work, and their song is conformity to the will of God, which is the sign and test of their right working. Is not this so with some nicely-adjusted machine? The delicacy with which it does its work, the ease, the absence of friction, the gentle hum, are a sign to the practised ear that it is rightly discharging its proper functions, and carrying out the object of its existence; whereas the jar, the groan, the jerking motion, the unevenness of action, are as certain a sign of something amiss and incomplete in the mechanism. Its perfect action is, as it were, its praise, and its praise is conformity to the law of its purpose.

The adoration, the worship of Creation, of the Universe, is, therefore, the glad expression of conformity to the purpose for which it was adapted by the great Creator, an unconscious worship, the hum, as it were, of perfectly working machinery. But man has free-will, he has a power of resisting God's purpose, and of bending creatures out of their ordered design, and therefore as he works, he must send up to the great Author of all life and work the conscious expression of conformity to His will. He too must sing as he works, he must pass on to God any praise or adulation which is directed to himself and means that the immediate machinery which surrounded him is being deflected from its main purpose, just to turn his own wheel with a velocity which threatens to upset proportion, establish friction, and damage the great cause of God. All things carry out the will of God, and sing as they do so. Man, as he works, must ever be lifting himself up to God. God is worthy; this is His scheme, His order, His plan. Only thus, by constant reference to God, constant submission to Him, will he be able to throw his rebellious self into the great scheme of God. Worship will thus be a constant referring back to God on the part of those who are made conscious participators in His plan, and are in constant temptation to thwart it. God is the central force round which all things revolve, by attraction to which all things are kept in their orbit; but with man this attraction is a conscious reference to Him, which takes the form of worship.

If worship be then, in language disentangled from metaphor, 'the conformity of the human will to God's will in glad adoration,' if it be the Amen-Alleluia contributed by the whole personality to God's action,[1] it will clear the conception a little further to see what worship is not. There is no doubt that in the reaction against the old ideas of Public Worship a great change of feeling took place. Formerly worship very often consisted of an objective ceremonial action, of the nature of a court pageant, in which the worshipper took a general share by his presence, without attempting to enter personally into the meaning of every word said, and every action done. As a reaction against this, great stress was laid on the minute individual participation of the worshipper in everything. And worship was made to consist more of the simultaneous homage of praying individuals than of a concerted act to which each contributed a part. No doubt perfect worship would be a combination of both these ideas. We feel,

[1] See Holland *The City of God* p. 78 etc.

on the one hand, that it must be a great deal more than a mere assisting at a public recognition of God, as if He were merely an earthly monarch, whose reign extends no further than the outward precincts of a well-ordered life; while on the other hand, worship must clearly be something more than the public expression of homage on the part of so many individuals. And it is in this latter direction especially that we shall find many misconceptions of worship, extending even to its complete negation. Granted at once that worship must be in 'spirit and in truth'—that is, of a God Who is felt and known, by that part of our being which holds, or is capable of holding, intercourse with Him. Granted that worship cannot be the mechanical performance of certain functions, attendance at a roll-call, or an æsthetic elevation of the imaginative faculties towards a Higher Being; still there are conceptions of worship held by religious people, which are equally derogatory to its higher glories. The name of worship has been carried into regions where its very nature is forgotten. Look, for instance, at what in modern parlance is sometimes called 'a place of worship.' There is a large room surrounded by tiers and tiers of seats encircling a pulpit, with galleries capable of containing more listeners still. Our first impression on beholding it is, 'What a magnificent auditorium!' And we picture to ourselves a man moving thousands with his eloquence, or, at the best, speaking in their name to God. It is a strange perversion of the idea of 'worship,' which makes it consist in the hearing of a sermon delivered by a man, or in prayers for sundry needs, or at the most in the singing of a few hymns, many of which are purely subjective in character, or very often prayers in metrical rhythm. It is all part of human selfishness which considers the worship of God, the declaration of His worth, to consist either in the receiving of good advice, or of seeking only fresh favours and advantages for the manifold needs of life. We have seen in our own time the disastrous effect of theories such as this on the church-going habits of the nation. If worship only means going to a place where, as the worshipper phrases it, he can get most good; then as he begins to dislike the effort, or feels the unreality of his action, he speedily discovers that the sermon of the best preacher can be purchased for a trifle and read at home, that he can pray by himself as well as in company if he wishes to do so, that the hymns may be enjoyed in the comfort of his own room as well as in the discomfort of a public building, and, as he puts it, he can read his Bible and have his good thoughts at home; and he feels that perhaps he runs less risk of being a Pharisee than do others, because he makes no professions. He started with the idea of going to church to get and not to give. And now, although he does not know it, he is tired of being sent empty away, because he came to worship with no appetite for heavenly things. Worship had no real place in his life, and its hollow substitute has speedily become distasteful from its very hollowness.

Worship, if we read aright, as distinct from prayer, moral instruction, and moral elevation, has always been considered such an important thing that God has made special provision and special demands for it. Man must feel God in all that he does, refer to Him, and subordinate the will to His in the assent of worship, which mounts up as the homage of a work done not only without friction, but in joy.

Hence we read that man has been encouraged and ordered to have places of worship, places, that is, where he looks out upon God. In the earliest ages Cain is said to have gone 'out from the presence of the Lord.'[1] Abraham, we read later on, 'stood yet before the Lord.'[2] Rebekah, we read, 'went to enquire of the Lord.'[3] A tent was set apart by Moses before the building of the Tabernacle, where every one repaired who sought the Lord.[4] We have then the building of the Tabernacle, which is familiar to all, and the great stress laid upon the building of the Temple, and the honour thereby conferred on him who built it; while we are accustomed in our own day to feel the peculiar sanctity of a consecrated church, in its arrangement, its symbolism, and its beauty, designed thus to elevate the heart and lift it up to God, and keep the soul in constant dependence on Him, while it recognises His glory, and justifies His action, and submits to His will. It is only the desperate shifts of a blind fanaticism which have tried to dissociate holy places from the worship of God. Forms of worship again have always been objects of great care and reverence. The most ordinary attention to Holy Scripture will show how much God insisted on minute requirements with reference to the law of sacrifice, and that ceremonial with which He was approached. While nothing can be more remarkable than the wonderful care displayed in the structure of the great Liturgies of the Church, of which Dr. Merivale says, 'The farther we inquire (as to their language), it seems to remount higher in primitive antiquity.'[5] These form a study in themselves of

[1] Gen. iv 16. [2] Gen. xviii 22.
[3] Gen. xxv 22. [4] Exod. xxxiii 7.
[5] *History of the Romans under the Empire* chap. liv vol. vi p. 445.

the greatest interest, and bear witness to the very large part which worship played in the service of the Church, and how intensely important everything was felt to be which was in any way connected with it. While there also stands out clearly this principle, that the worship of God will always be associated with effort: it began in sacrifice that looked forward, it is continued in sacrifice that looks backward. It is no light, easy thing—it is the Liturgy, the great public act; and while all creation is putting up its hymn of praise, as it works unconsciously with God towards the perfecting of His plan; as the angels in heaven always do Him service, while they express their glorious recognition of His infinite worth, by veiling wings, and poised effort, and adoring voice, in the midst of smoke, and trembling, and the pulsing strains of Alleluias beating in rhythmic waves before the Throne; so man no less has felt that God's worthiness can only be expressed with effort, that worship must be more than a passing recognition on the part of those who think seriously, or the singing of a hymn, or the praying of a prayer. It is on the look-out for the places where God has promised to make Himself known, it approaches Him through recognised channels, and in ordered ways. The worship of God is a solemn action, needing a solemn effort, claiming all the powers of spirit, soul, and body. Without it Religion will very easily become a system of self-pleasing, and while looking away from God, will rest either with complacency on self, and become pharisaical, or else with suspicion on our neighbour, and become contemptuous. Life without Religion must sooner or later be a failure, at least in view of its own highest possibilities, and

Religion without worship will be driven in on itself and become barren and unfruitful. 'My soul truly waiteth still upon God': it is the voice of the soul which offers all its activities to the higher purpose of God. 'We give thanks to Thee for Thy great glory': it is the voice of the adoring Church, which, having exhausted every other theme which Creed or Scripture supplies, casts itself down on the simple beauty of God. Life in all its complexity, God's mercies in all their changeful variety, work in all its victories and failures, need this as their final consecration. 'We worship Thee because Thou art so glorious.' Complete satisfaction is to be found in God's complete perfection.

II

In thinking of worship more in detail, and of that which is required of the worshipper, there is an incident in Holy Scripture which certainly merits more attention than it sometimes receives. That the adoration of the infant Jesus by the Magi should be poetical, does not conflict with the fact that it was real; that it was dim and mysterious does not prevent us from seeking to penetrate its inner teaching, which caused the Evangelist under the inspiration of the Holy Ghost to record it in his pages for our learning. We seem in this incident to see some of the most characteristic acts of worship: not the least, that these mysterious strangers leave their home and track the desert, not on a political or a mercantile mission; as far as we are told, with no ulterior motive whatever, but simply to declare His glory and honour, Who they had reason to believe to be born King of the Jews. This surely is of the very essence of worship.

> 'Not for the sake of gaining aught,
> Not seeking a reward,
> But as Thyself hast loved me,
> O ever-loving Lord.'

But it may be possible and helpful to range under the symbolism of their gifts some of the characteristics and requisites of worship, the excellences which are required in those who bring them, and the exceeding difficulty, worth, and importance of all that can lay claim to so dignified a name.

The treasures of the Eastern worshippers contained, in the first place, gold. Worship will be costly, but it will also be beautiful. 'Nothing is more foolish, if not more selfish, than to plead that we may be indifferent to outward worship because God is spirit. At the very time when the Psalmist celebrates the King's daughter as "all glorious within," he immediately adds that "her clothing is of wrought gold." In the Revelation of S. John, the most precious stones, the most costly metals, and the richest dyes are employed to set forth the splendour of the bride, the Lamb's wife; and, surely, if Mary expressed by a lavish gift her homage to her Lord when He was preparing for His burial, much more may we be lavish in our gifts when we follow in the train of One, Who has ascended up on high, in all His royal dignity. The thought of danger to which we are thus exposed may make us careful how far we go, but is no argument against a course of conduct rooted in the conception of the Church's being. Such danger is simply that which must be met on every side so long as the flesh lusteth against the spirit; and the only way to avoid it is to see that the worship of the Church be a witness to her Risen Lord in the completeness of His exalted state. Let her express as far as possible in her worship what He is, and her path is sure.'[1] From time to time, men who have bodies, imagination, art-perceptions, tendencies of all sorts which can hinder, if they do not help, think that they can best honour our Lord by giving Him a maimed worship, by approaching Him as if they were simple spirits, as if the rich endowment of life in its manifold treasures neither came from Him, nor were susceptible of being tithed for His worship. But quite apart from this, beauty and the sense of beauty are in themselves mysteries. 'Beyond that which is useful, and that which is true, and that which is good, and that which is orderly and well-proportioned, and that which is beneficial and salutary, there clings obstinately to the soul of man this idea of what is beautiful in its infinite forms and degrees.'[2] 'God has given to the great masters of art the power, the tremendous responsibility, of creating beauty; beauty which none can challenge or dispute; beauty which is independent of human mortality, and exercises its spell on successive generations.'[3] Surely in the mystery of beauty we have the robe of glory which conceals the presence of God. The great truth witnessed to in the words quoted above would be strange unless we believed that the sense of beauty comes from God. Man apparently cannot long do

---

[1] Milligan *The Resurrection of our Lord* p. 215.

[2] See R. W. Church *Cathedral and University Sermons* 'The Sense of Beauty' p. 118.

[3] *Ib.* pp. 121, 122.

without it. He feels the coldness and bareness of this world. He wishes to paint its naked walls, and curtain its sharp angles with forms of beauty. And as we know, and perhaps we are now painfully conscious of it, an advancing civilisation and a selfish luxury may seize upon this instinct and pervert it to our harm. God, ever since the days in which He ordered Moses to make the ornaments of His sanctuary for glory and for beauty, seems to have laboured to lift up our hearts, by beautiful objects, to Him Who is beauty itself; whereas sin is always ugly, even when it most seeks to bedizen and decorate its foulness. God is always beautiful. The most simple operations of Nature: the sea rolling in before the storm; the sun sinking below the horizon; the birds and the insects as they flash through the air in pursuit; the trees and plants as they are developed or matured for food; the very smoke of our industries when it has passed up into the air; the terrors of the Alpine summit; the calm of the country lane—all are wrapped round with beauty, and all lead up to God. And therefore, without a fear of His reproach, or a sense that an alabaster-box which was valuable has been broken, or of spilt ointment which might have been profitable for the support of many poor persons, we pour out upon our sanctuaries and their services those gifts of God which His wisdom has given, to those who possess them, for glory and for beauty. Believing that in so doing we are declaring His worth Who gave us those rich things; believing that in so doing we are seeking those things that are above, that we are giving the art of our time its proper orientation by consecrating it to God; that in so doing we are helping the worshippers, giving something which may elevate them out of that which is too often the squalid setting of their lives; and further, that we are making our churches into shrines more ready to be joined, without a sense of incongruity, to the golden city of the pearly gates. But still, God first; His honour, His glory first.

Amidst much that can be said, and ought to be said, as to the united worship of united voices in what is known as congregational singing, still there is the place for an offering to God on behalf of the congregation of the most perfect production of musical art which can be procured. The whole question of musical worship is strange and mysterious, when we come to consider it. It seems to rest on the postulate that, in approaching God, we must steady, modulate, and arrange not only our thoughts and words, but the very tone of our voice. Thus we give to Him as a solemn offering the most beautiful variations and combinations of sound which it is possible to produce as an offering to His Majesty. It would surely be as foolish to limit church music to services in which an ordinary man can join with his voice, as it would be to limit church decoration to pictures and ornaments which an ordinary man could appreciate, or church architecture to erections which an ordinary man would deem sufficient. True, this has its dangerous side; as Rahab, and Babylon, and Tyre come with their beautiful offerings to Zion, there is a danger. The skilled choir, the splendid organ, the thrilling orchestra, leave the theatre and the concert-room and come to the church, who fondly and thankfully says, 'This and that man was born there: he is a child of Zion.'[1] Every one

---
[1] Cf. Psalm lxxxvii.

knows something of the danger of thinking that he can mount up to heaven on the wings of beautiful melody, and of imagining that while we are only satisfying our æsthetic sense, we are worshipping God.

The birds which have fluttered into a large cathedral through the open door or window on a summer's day, try vainly to get out and feel once more the breath of the warm air and the delightful freedom of heaven. They beat against the painted glass, and dash themselves against the carved ceiling, but it is not the air, it is not the ever-receding vault of heaven, it is a prison in which they will die. The light streaming through a painted window is, after all, not the open air of heaven, nor the confinement of the church its broad expanse. If we misuse church worship, we shall dash our souls to pieces against its very beauty, and be starved by the gold which cannot feed us.

And so the Magi, beside their gold, brought incense. Our worship has to melt away into the worship of heaven, to be translated into its language, and be mixed with its intercession. We have already glanced at the great stress laid upon the form of divine service. And we shall find accordingly that the worship of God is no mere arbitrary arrangement left to the device of men, which might conceivably have been different; but is arranged by the order of Christ Himself, so to link together in one the worship of earth and heaven. The pleading of the great Sacrifice of Christ we believe to be the centre of divine worship in heaven. The Eucharistic Sacrifice in which we are united with this, is the Church's great service on earth. This is her Liturgy, her great public work. Round this revolve the other divine offices, each of them shining with a star embedded in them from the Holy Eucharist, in the Collect, each of them taking its radiance and glory from the great central act of our Religion. Men are always taking liberties with God. If He gives them much, they try to take more. If He wills to be approached in one way, they insist on approaching Him in another. We need, after all, a medium for our worship, in which it may reach heaven. It must be put in the censer of the Great Priest, and offered by Him with much incense. God has ever willed to be approached with sacrifice, and with sacrifice He is approached still. 'Through Jesus Christ' end all our prayers. The Sacrifice of the Cross, still perpetually pleaded, is the medium of our acceptance with God. In this we have our means of access to heaven. In the Eucharistic sacrifice, the sacrifice of the Altar, the sacred enclosure is as it were extended, and either heaven descends to earth, or earth mounts up to heaven, so that we can plead here, in our Eucharistic intercession, the all-prevailing blood of sprinkling in a service which is one with the service in heaven. This subject will be fully discussed in the volume of this Library which treats of it particularly; it will be sufficient here to quote the testimony which is given by two recognised Anglican divines. The first is Hooker, who says: 'The fathers of the Church of Christ . . . call usually the ministry of the Gospel *priesthood*, in regard of that which the Gospel hath *proportionable* to ancient sacrifices, namely, the Communion of the blessed Body and Blood of Christ, although it have properly now no sacrifice.'[1] Some have drawn the mistaken inference from

---

[1] Hooker *Eccles. Pol.* v 78 [2].

this that Hooker wished to deny, or at least to minimise, this great doctrine. But Mr. Keble, when commenting on the passage, well points out that it is quite true to say that the Gospel hath properly now no sacrifice, *i.e.* no such sacrifice as had been mentioned before under the head of ' ancient sacrifice.' But he goes on to say that ' he who thinks most highly, and therefore least inadequately, of that holy and divine sacrament cannot well say or conceive anything of it higher than this, that it is in the strict sense of the word, "that which the Gospel hath proportionable to ancient sacrifices." ' It stands, that is, in the scheme of reality, in the same position as sacrifice did in the scheme of types. In fact, it would be much in the interest of truth that the many admirers of *The Christian Year* should go on to read what Mr. Keble has to say in his learned and important treatise on Eucharistical Adoration.[1] The other Anglican divine who gives us his testimony to be quoted here is Jeremy Taylor, who says : ' We celebrate and exhibit the Lord's death in sacrament and symbol, and this is that great express which, when the Church offers to God the Father, it obtains all those blessings which that sacrifice produced. Themistocles snatched up the son of King Admetus and held him between himself and death, to mitigate the rage of the king, and prevailed accordingly. Our very holding up the Son of God, and representing Him to His Father, is the doing of an act of mediation and advantage to ourselves, in the virtue and efficacy of the Mediator. As Christ is a priest in heaven for ever, and yet does not sacrifice Himself afresh, nor yet without a sacrifice could He be a priest, but by a daily ministration and intercession

---

[1] See Keble *Eucharistical Adoration* pp. 69-71.

represents His sacrifice to God ... it follows, then, that the celebration of this sacrifice be in proportion an instrument of applying the proper sacrifice to all the purposes which it first designed.'[1] These quotations may tend to show how continuous is the tradition that the incense of Christ's intercession must accompany the offering of the gold of beauty; and that worship is not an arbitrary approach to God, left to individual caprice, but the Church's solemn action, learned from Christ, and linked on to the worship of heaven. And considerations like these will show us how very important it is that the Lord's own service should occupy its proper position as the very pivot on which all worship turns. The fact remains that in the English Church a choir-office, venerable, intellectual, and exceedingly beautiful, has been allowed in too many places, and for too long a time, to occupy the position of the Holy Eucharist in the worship of Sunday. One of the difficult problems of the day, which yet awaits a satisfactory solution, is how to reconcile the fact of the Holy Eucharist as the great Christian service open to all, as their heritage and birthright, with the other set of ideas, of which we see traces in primitive antiquity, of the mysteries to be guarded and shielded with reverence and reserve behind the barriers of screen and fence, with many expulsions of the unworthy, and much discipline. The early Church would be startled at the sight of Christians contentedly putting up with a choir-office on the Lord's Day. Would it not be equally startled at a celebration of the Holy Mysteries in the presence of the modern representatives

---

[1] Jeremy Taylor *Works* vol. iii Discourse 'Reception of the Sacrament' p. 29.

of the Catechumens, the Energumens, and the Penitents? But apart from this question, which still awaits a satisfactory solution in a portion of the Church where discipline is terribly lax, there is a previous question often fiercely discussed, on which a word may be said here, under the head of worship, pending its more complete discussion in a subsequent volume. Is the Christian allowed, and if he is allowed, is it desirable for him to plead the Sacrifice at times when he is not prepared to communicate? Opportunities for Holy Communion are immensely multiplied; may he use them merely as opportunities for intercession and worship? It is customary to say that 'non-communicating attendance,' as it is called, has a formidable foe in Mr. Keble, who wrote as follows:—' I cannot but doubt the wisdom of urging all men indiscriminately to be present at the Holy Mysteries; a matter, as far as I can see, left open by the Prayer-Book, and in ordering of which it may seem most natural to abide by the spirit of the ancient constitution, which did not willingly permit the presence of any but communicants, or those of whom they had reason to believe that they were in a way to become such.' And he goes on to deprecate the idea of some special quasi-sacramental grace attaching to it, in which perhaps he would seem rather to be deprecating, on the one hand, the idea of mere attendance at the celebration as being in any sense a means of sacramental grace or of receiving any blessing beyond that attached to earnest prayer; and on the other, the habitual non-communicating attendance of *non*-communicants, *i.e.* of those whom he calls 'all men indiscriminately,' many of whom perhaps have never received, or meant to receive, the Holy Communion in their lives; men who correspond to 'the gazers and lookers-on' who were ordered out in the exhortation in the Communion office of 1552. We have already seen what a serious question this is in view of the primitive reserve and jealous guardianship of the Mysteries. But surely this is a question quite distinct from the attendance without communicating on the part of the faithful communicant who is unable, or for some ceremonial reason not qualified, or unwilling from a feeling of reverence, to communicate on some given occasion. With reference to this second class, it has been proposed from time to time to insert a rubric in the English Liturgy forbidding the presence at the Holy Eucharist of those who do not intend to receive. But such a proposal has never won its way to acceptance, and the fact that the proposal is made shows that, as the Prayer-Book now stands, such a practice is not forbidden. It may, no doubt, be conceded that in the primitive Church the practice was for all to communicate at least every Sunday and Holy day; and that the only exceptions were in the case of those who were excluded, not being suffered either to communicate or to be present, for some special reason. But on the other hand we have to face the fact that the custom of non-communicating attendance is universal throughout the whole Church, east and west, except among a section of the English Church; and not only in the Church, but also among Presbyterians, as we are told by Dr. Milligan, 'our children in Scotland remain in church during the celebration of the Supper, because they are not strangers. Those also are not strangers who, though they may not communicate on the special occasion, do communicate on other occasions or at other hours.'[1] As to the benefits of non-communicating attendance, while recognising to the full Mr. Keble's disclaimer of a quasi-sacramental character attaching to it, yet as a method of praying, surely it has a great advantage. Whatever we may say about the ancient Church, there remains the fact that it did allow the last class of penitents (the *consistentes*), whose penance was all but ended, to be present as a privilege ; and that the ordinary church-goer of to-day may at times be in a similar position, when reverence, in the absence of discipline, prevents him from claiming his privilege, and yet allows him to feel the desire of being associated with the great pleading.

However this may be, here certainly there would be an opportunity for prayer, which in the highest sense would attain to the epithet used by Mr. Keble of 'earnest and faithful'; prayer offered at the time when the Church is performing her most characteristic function of interceding in union with her Lord, in offering the one great sacrifice in which heaven and earth join, while the great and mysterious Presence that we have with us at such a time is a call to a high and prevailing intercession ; the whole position perhaps being summed up by S. Augustine in his letter to Januarius : 'Let each one do what he piously believes according to his faith ought to be done. For neither of them dishonoured the Body and Blood of the Lord, but emulously vie with each other which shall most honour that most life-giving Sacrament. For neither Zacchæus nor that centurion contended with each other, when one of them gladly received the Lord into his house, while the other said, "I am not

[1] Milligan *The Ascension* p. 304.

worthy that Thou shouldest come under my roof"; both honouring the Saviour in different and, as it were, opposite manners, both obtain mercy. For the one, though honouring the Sacrament, does not venture to receive daily; the other, though honouring the Sacrament, does not venture to let a single day pass without receiving it. Contempt is the only thing that Food dislikes."[1]

It has been said that from the analogy of the Jewish sacrifice, the sacrifice cannot be complete without communion, and that no one can have part in the sacrifice without communicating. It is true that the priest at least must always receive, and that the Church desires communicants for the fulness of the rite;[2] but it is not true from the analogy of the ancient sacrifice, that communion is necessary to a participation in the sacrifice. In the peace-offering the offerer must partake, but he never did so in the burnt-offering and sin-offering.[3] And this, too, is remarkable, that the daily sacrifice was a burnt-offering of which the people never partook, although it was the daily service; the peace-offering, of which they did partake, being only occasional. 'They could not eat without offering, but they continually offered without eating.' So that while it may be admitted that the best course is to communicate as often as possible, as far as reverence and most careful preparation permit, still, at the same time, if a man fears to do this from reverence, or because he may not receive the Holy Communion twice

---

[1] S. Augustine *Epistle* liv *to Januarius* chap. 3.

[2] 'Si qui sunt communicandi in missâ (id quod optat ecclesia')
Roman Rite.

[3] Willis *Worship of Old Covenant* pp. 139, 150.

in one day, he may be present without receiving as a matter of Christian liberty, and attain thereby a secondary benefit, never the same as if he had communicated, and yet a blessing real and unmistakable, because he had been present at the sacrament of Christ's Presence, at the service of intercession in union with the pleading of the great Sacrifice, whose precious offering mounts up before God, as the incense which sanctifies the gold.

And the last ingredient, so to speak, of worship must not be forgotten—the myrrh. We have seen how in the sixteenth century this was the nature of the reaction that set in, that Religion came to be regarded as no mechanical compliance with outward acts of devotion, but as requiring at every stage the intellectual and moral acceptance of the worshipper's whole being; that presence at a long and imposing religious ceremony, for instance, would not in any way suffice, unless the consciousness of the worshipper went along with it; that Religion can be no separate thing standing outside a man's life, in which he serves God for a certain period, while for the rest he serves himself and his own lusts: that sin cannot be just mechanically shuffled off, when it has reached a certain height of iniquity, as a man might clear out a dust-heap at certain intervals, but that forgiveness of sins is conditioned always by an earnest effort on the part of the sinner to be rid of them altogether, and to subdue the tendency towards them. The reaction set in, and rightly, against a mechanical Religion, and led, as is so often the case with reaction, in some cases to a discarding of 'mechanism' altogether; and superstition on the one side was met by unbelief on the other. Still, in considering worship as the expression of Religion, we must never forget this side of it. It is asserted by those who disparage the divine economy of the Church, that all the faithful are priests. In a sense, of course, this is right and true. But to assert this truth carries with it the necessity of asserting a further truth, that this priesthood as well is entered by an ordination. The mere æsthetic ceremonialist, the musical critic, the protesting critic, who simply goes from church to church to see if there is anything to which he objects, the careless, the indifferent, the unholy—such as these cannot rightly offer the great service of worship which ascends to God. It has no myrrh in it, nothing which keeps off the corruption of a careless life, and the manifold pollutions of the world. It must always be a serious thing when great attention to the minutiæ of divine worship is not accompanied by increased devotion and personal holiness. Æstheticism in itself means nothing, and is good for nothing. It serves to disguise the sternness of Religion and the horror of sin, and leads to the divorce of Religion from morality, so that 'Religion does not merely cease demonstrating against vice, but enters into an alliance with it, betrays her office, and becomes her own enemy, while immorality loses its last chance of cure.'[1]

So must worship be guarded, as in itself a divine and holy thing; an exercise in which only the religious man can profitably join, for he alone will know how to open his treasures.

---

[1] See article 'The Divine Mechanism of the Eucharist' by Daniel Radford *Church Times* August 26 1898.

CHAPTER XIII

THE EXPRESSION OF RELIGION—GOODNESS

'Serve God and be cheerful'

'The joy of the Lord is thy strength.'

We have now considered Religion as it expresses itself in its most characteristic way toward God, in Worship: it only remains that we should glance at that further and fuller expression of it in the life of devout goodness. Here, if anywhere, we shall find Religion at work. It is easy to simulate the outward proprieties of worship, and throw a cloak of devotion over a very sordid inner life: it is not so easy to maintain a life of consistent hypocrisy so effectually as never to be startled by the roughness of life out of the polite homage which one pays to virtue, or allow oneself to forget it among the seductions of life's pleasures. 'By their fruits ye shall know them,' said our blessed Lord; and Religion, and Religion only, can produce those fruits which are the distinguishing marks of Christianity, and the products of its highest excellence. Christianity is not a system to be dabbled in, but a life to be lived in strict attention to the requirements of its great Founder. No system of attention to its most important details; no mixing of its precepts with those of other Religions; no eclectic enlargement of an undenominational Pantheon, which places what is good in Christianity side by side with the best in other systems, will suffice. Nay more, Christianity under such conditions may do absolute harm to him who so uses it. It is a system whole and complete in itself, whose creed has damnatory clauses, which deals with hell as well as with heaven, with punishments as well as with rewards. And, further, it is the life of true Religion, that must ever be the highest form of apologetic for Christianity. A life which cannot be rivalled or surpassed elsewhere, will draw men irresistibly to the system whose principles produce such fruit. If men are to be led to be Christians, it will not be by being shown that Christianity is historically true, that intellectually it is a system of which no intelligent man need to be ashamed, but rather by the exhibition of a power of life which cannot be found elsewhere, or on any other condition.[1] It is one of the saddest of spectacles, as we have already shown, to watch men gazing at their splendid systems of morality, which really lie just outside their powers of attainment. Men had been told over and over again what was beautiful, and their inmost conscience approved the superior beauty of moral excellence; but no one had succeeded in strengthening the power of the will. But in the Christian Religion we can appeal to the world around us and say: Here in the life made possible by the Holy Spirit, men can find just this power which they need; here is the supernatural power over natural passions and forces; here is a Religion, and not a morality, or rather a system in which the two go together; here

[1] Milligan *Ascension* p. 276.

is the exhibition of the highest possible ideal for man, and the capacity at the same time for attaining it.

Jesus Christ asks, no doubt, in His Religion for the surrender of the whole being; but to one who so surrenders himself, He promises a life which cannot fail to commend itself as the best life for man, a life in which his composite nature finds its truest and fittest development.

I

The life in which Religion expresses itself is described by S. Paul, in his Epistle to the Romans[1] as 'in the Spirit.' There is a life in the flesh, and there is a soul-life, but the life of the Christian is life in the spirit. S. Paul describes the soul-life, the life of the natural or animal man, in the second chapter of the First Epistle to the Corinthians, in which we see him distinguished from the spiritual man, mainly in this, that he is one whose governing principle and highest point of reference for all things is the $\psi v \chi \acute{\eta}$, the animal soul; in whom the spirit is borne down and overweighted by the animal desires and judgments, by that side of the incorporeal nature which is turned earthwards. Not that necessarily such a man is of purpose irreligious or directly vicious, but that simply the animating principle is turned earthwards, instead of in the direction of the spirit.

With the life which is lived in the flesh every one is too familiar. In this we see men whose appetites and desires, so far from being under the control of the spirit,

[1] Rom. viii 9.

have beaten down reason, and have overthrown the directing principle, which undertook to control them, without help from on high. It is a terrible expression in which S. Peter[1] speaks of those whose eyes are 'full of an adulteress'; as if they had become so completely absorbed 'in sensual thoughts and desires, that the eye, the most expressive feature, seemed to realise the presence of some object of the desire, and to be intently gazing at it.' Any one may see for himself, on almost any day, examples of lives like this lived in the flesh, or of lives lived under the dominion of the soul-nature; they help us the better to understand what it must be to live in the spirit, a life in which all the powers of correspondence are, as it were, directed heavenward in the power of the renewed spirit, which is the true link connecting the whole being with the world unseen, as the flesh connects it with the world of matter.

And accordingly when Nicodemus came timidly and tentatively to our Lord as 'a teacher come from God,' he was shown at once that it was not a doctrine so much as a life, which was in question; he 'must be born again':[2] that as his natural birth put him in correspondence with the world of phenomena, by which gradually his life would be developed and formed, so he must be placed by an action as real and important as birth, into correspondence with spiritual phenomena, by which once more his spiritual life might be formed. It is, therefore, by being 'in the spirit' that a man attains to that form of life, which is unlike any other, which by its transcendent excellence is a living apology for Christianity, which

---

[1] 2 S. Pet. ii 14.   [2] S. John iii.

THE EXPRESSION OF RELIGION 281

can say, Centuries of speculation have been spent in finding the true end of man; here you find it; here it is exhibited before you; here is a type of life unlike any, even the highest in pagan antiquity; here is a type of life which was unattained, and apparently unattainable, by the people of God, of whom the Old Testament speaks; and this life is the product of Christianity. 'By their fruits ye shall know them.' We claim for Christianity that it is the Religion for man, because it has produced and does produce the highest type of life possible to man, in the life and conversation of those who claim that they have studied and weighed well our blessed Lord's promise, and in and by the power of the Holy Spirit have obtained a supernatural strength which has braced up the will, and delivered them from the dominion of passion, and the tyranny of selfish desire, and enabled them to be themselves.

II

In examining the character which the apostle S. Paul delineates as developed in those who are truly religious, we shall find him speaking of what he calls the 'fruit of the Spirit,'[1]—that habit and frame of life which springs up by the power of the indwelling Spirit, like fruit; that is to say, 'one rich, central, harmonious development from one rich, central principle germinating and fructifying into a result of purity and peace.'[2]

While the flesh produces works, the Spirit develops fruit, springing up from the operation of those seven-

---

[1] Galat. v 22. [2] Dr. Moule *Veni Creator* p. 191.

fold gifts with which every Christian is familiar. And we note that the several virtues of which the apostle speaks in this connection are all parts of one thing, 'Not separable characters, but a character,' not different lines of development from which the spiritual man may choose, one here or one there, omitting the rest, but all interrelated in a divine completeness in the fulness of the spiritual life. This is the life which is the expression, in the man himself, of true Religion; and in following the guidance of the apostle we shall best see its component parts.

Prominent in the 'fruit of the Spirit' there will be found the element of Love, the great and characteristic virtue which was insisted on by our blessed Lord as the very substance of the Christian life. We have already considered it as one of the theological virtues; it will only be necessary therefore to glance at it in its ordered place in the matured character. There are two strong currents in human nature, perhaps two forms of the same thing, but setting up a subversive principle whose power can easily be detected; the one is wilfulness and the other selfishness. Wilfulness is the intense desire to have our own way; and selfishness, like some vigorous growth in the vegetable world, which drives to the utmost limit of its capacity the gospel of the survival of the fittest, makes a man push his coarse fibrous roots into the soil from which feebler plants draw a precarious sustenance, until he has sucked all the goodness into himself, heedless lest another should dwindle and decay, reckless of his expansive shadow or swelling girth. The Spirit of God corrects both these subversive tendencies by the growth of love; a feeling amounting to a passion pervades the heart, drawing it towards God and His Holy Law, such as we detect in the unfathomable depths of Psalm cxix. The love of God, ruling in the soul, produces a passion counter to the barren wilfulness which sterilises all purpose and design around it, and in the place of the love of his own way puts in the heart of man the love of the law of God. The way of God, the commandments of God, are no longer a stern order to be evaded, or carried out in a bare literalism, but become the plan of which the heart approves, towards the execution of which it tends. Impatience, or its counterfeit—resignation, disappointment, rebellion, all yield to a joyful acquiescence in the will of God, not only as the best for the individual, but as the plan and design of life, which it is a joy to follow and a pride to promote. Love turns the wilful marauder, who pillages life's treasures for self, into the feudal soldier, who places himself absolutely at the disposal of his Lord. While with regard to our fellow-men, and the world around us, when we once realise the large part which selfishness and want of love play in its miseries, we shall see how this growth of 'the fruit of the Spirit' strikes a blow at the individualism which looks upon the world as a treasure-house in which the fewer the claimants the richer the distribution of the spoils; while it leads us to feel that all we need for our life is a marching ration, not a luxurious banquet of enervating pleasures, that such expansion of our sympathies which we at present allow must be infinitely extended until it reaches the whole world. Family claims must reach out into friendship for a few; friendship for a few must expand into univeral goodwill; and universal goodwill must needs include even the love of enemies.

Apart from the intrinsic beauty of this character, it will be seen at once how much more useful such a life is, how it contributes to progress and general well-being. And lest it should be thought that this is an easy virtue, which can speedily develop itself without supernatural aid, when once its excellency is pointed out, it is well to remember that it is not altogether natural to man to love. Love is a virtue which requires submission, and submission is not always given without an effort. There are times when God seems to order that which is clearly opposed to our inclination, and more than this, what at the moment does not command the assent of our reason. That Abraham should slay his son, or be ordered to do so, still staggers the faith even of those who are not prejudiced by the strong love of a father for his child. That God should make men the instruments of His fierce wrath even Saul hesitated to believe, and men at the present day can still scarcely credit. In ordinary life we cannot always at first even command the submission which is the preliminary of love, or so obey the command of God that we would not wish it to be otherwise. And if we need submission towards God, we shall also need sacrifice when dealing with our fellow-men. The soil beneath the roots of our neighbour's growth means, it is true, that which the natural man might covet for himself; the leafy canopy which we throw out is after all only a sign of life, but still we must look, not only at our own things, but every man on the things of others. With the growth of the life of the Spirit we should be able to tell the unbeliever that, at least, we had solved the great social difficulty of the day. Love would repress selfishness, which finds its expression in grasping or in discontent, and each would seek the good of each, as between those who are members one of another.

Added to this Love, there is a further development of that life of the Spirit which is the expression of Religion, known as 'Joy.' If Love on analysis proves itself to be a fundamental virtue which opposes itself to vices which have made against human progress, Joy, although less obviously, is part of the equipment of life, which has been eagerly sought for, but has too often eluded the search. It will readily occur to all to notice how dominant is the note of Joy in the gospel. 'These things have I spoken unto you, that My joy might remain in you, and that your joy might be full.'[1] 'Your sorrow shall be turned into joy.'[2] These are but samples of this great teaching in the New Testament. And yet one can understand how easily it may be believed that Joy is an ornamental virtue, placed rather too high in the list; that S. Paul is like a poor architect, who begins to ornament his tower in the lower stage, where there should rather be only an exhibition of strength. And yet already the hollowness of culture, and the emptiness of mere civilisation, in this end of the century, feels that joylessness is a good deal more than a scratch on the varnished surface of pleasure. It is true that the bright polish of joy is absent, but this is caused by a break in the machinery within, and is a symptom of something worse than itself. An age which has lost enthusiasm, which feels deeply on no subject, is betraying a grave symptom of paralysis. An age which parades its pessimism is surely preparing for the time when there will be taken from him that hath not even

[1] S. John xv 11.   [2] S. John xvi 20.

that which he seemeth to have. An age which has lost hope has lost the power of real progress. And as in the past, so in the present, it is not without a distinct effect on that part of the world which still looks out for a Saviour, that the Christian exhibits in the life which is lived in the Spirit, the fruit of Joy. Joy is a sign of harmonious working within, of a life which has found, as far as may be in this world, satisfaction ; and as to the Christian, so to the world, ' the joy of the Lord is your strength.'

The life of Religion as lived in the Spirit exhibits a third fruit, known as Peace, a virtue so rare that it is hardly appraised at its proper value. Here again Christianity showed its heavenly origin by appealing to the real yet unexpressed wants of the human heart. If Joy was a proclamation of the gospel to a world which had worn itself out in the race for pleasure, Peace no less was a message to the longings of a storm-tossed humanity. 'Come unto Me, all ye that labour and are heavy laden, and I will give you rest.' 'Learn of Me; for I am meek and lowly in heart: and ye shall find rest unto your souls.'[1] 'Be careful for nothing; but in every thing by prayer and supplication with thanksgiving let your requests be made known unto God. And the peace of God, which passeth all understanding, shall keep your hearts and minds through Christ Jesus.'[2]

A tranquillity of order, which is not the self-repression of the Stoic nor the hedonism of the Epicurean, but springs up in the soul as naturally as fruit on a fruit-bearing tree, this again is an expression of Religion eloquent of its origin, from its very rarity and

[1] Mat. xi 28, 29.   [2] Phil. iv 6, 7.

unearthliness. He who is living in the Spirit has found out a great truth, that in the world he must have tribulation, but that he is living in touch with One Who has overcome the world. He can bid adieu to worry, with its dividing, distracting cares, he can cast aside discontent, because he is confident in the higher wisdom of God. And so, undisturbed, he goes to meet the difficulties of life; he faces temptation undismayed, although conscious of his weakness; he meets trouble, sorrow, and disappointment unmoved, although he feels their bitterness.

'These things I have spoken unto you, that in Me ye might have peace.'[1] Here is a secret which many would gladly learn of the Christian soul, how it is that in the most adverse surroundings Christians are still able to shine as lights in the world, because God has encircled them with His own atmosphere, and shut them in with His own presence; 'Thou shalt hide them privily by Thine own presence from the provoking of all men: Thou shalt keep them secretly in Thy tabernacle from the strife of tongues.'[2]

Another fruit of the Spirit which is developed in the life of Religion is Long-suffering. Here again experience will justify the wisdom of God. How different a list this is from the ordinary equipment which the man of the world deems necessary for life, and yet how much more truly is it the equipment which is suited to his needs! The one fault that is damaging his usefulness is impatience, which takes the form of inability to endure the preparation which God finds it necessary to bestow upon him; or impatience which finds vent in anger with the world, with environment, or

[1] S. John xvi 33.   [2] Psalm xxxi 22.

with self. There are many splendid instruments of God which are being dashed to pieces against their surroundings for want of the power of bearing the discipline of life. But here, formed by the Spirit, is a character which can assimilate the discipline instead of being broken by its severity. How strangely perplexing it was to the persecuting heathen in the early days of Christianity! Was it an incurable obstinacy, or was it patience, firmness, and heroism which kept alive that dispersed remnant of the people, amidst suffering, ignominy, and hatred, until, believed to be extirpated, they ended by converting the Empire? We can see what a force there is still in Christian heroism, which elicits unwilling admiration from those who witness it. We are surprised sometimes to witness the power which underlies simple endurance, the victories won by suffering, and the crown which patience knows how to assume when she has had her perfect work. Long-suffering may very possibly be a much more necessary virtue than we are apt to think. How many are failing of the highest because they cannot stand the discipline of character which God knows that they need: 'Woe unto you that have lost *the power of bearing*; and what will ye do when the Lord shall visit you?'[1] We read sometimes in the newspapers of suicide which has been caused, it is alleged, by trouble; or vicious courses which have been taken up through want of success in life. How little men seem able to bear the stern rigour of the discipline which God puts upon them, while they mistake chastisement for vengeance, and discipline for causeless anger.

We little realise how many Sauls there are who are

[1] Ecclus. ii 14.

THE EXPRESSION OF RELIGION 289

beginning their career of wilfulness by an irritable impatience which refuses to let them wait for Samuel and the slow measured tread of God's approach; how many Jonahs there are still, who are bringing on themselves the providential storm, by their hasty flight to Tarshish away from uncongenial duty. We are but little conscious of the many victims of discontent, who prefer Egypt with plenty to eat, to the wilderness with God and the light food of the manna. Impatience even with self is preparing many a soil for the devil's sowing, to whom God has whispered in vain, 'Fret not thyself, else shalt thou be moved to do evil.'[1] There are foes of mankind who make havoc of his peace and prosperity, which every one can see; so common, that they have been labelled as 'human nature,' and buoyed like obtruding rocks which cannot be removed. It can then be nothing short of a revelation of a higher world, if the Christian is able, not in pious sentiment which he does not feel, but in actions of which he does not speak nor appear to be conscious, to exhibit a life which has turned pain into a Sacrament conferring grace under a rough and repelling exterior; a life which has turned the Cross into a throne where Christ crucified reigns from the tree, and in which His followers glory in that which makes them ashamed of the world and hateful to its luxuriousness; a life in fine which has turned suffering into an education, and weakness into the material of strength. If mankind only knew it, one of the greatest powers which a man can have is the power to suffer without being broken, to endure without snapping under the heavy hand of God, Who still as of old chastens those whom He

[1] Ps. xxxvii 8.

T

loves, and chastises every son whom He wills to receive.

Once more this Spirit-life blossoms and bears fruit, as the Religion within pours its vigour and sap through the branches, and produces Gentleness. Often it must have seemed that the Christian ideal is too tender a thing for this rough world: that the Sermon on the Mount is unpractical, and that rougher and sterner virtues are required for the hard contact with the facts of existence, which life in this world makes inevitable. The offering of the other cheek, the non-resistance to evil, the giving to every one that asks, the refusal to use oaths at all, and similar counsels of the kind, we are told must be largely discounted, and on a large scale altogether ignored, else life would be impossible. This may be so, if things are to remain always as they are. But we often make the mistake of taking things which Christ said to His inner band of disciples, and expanding them into principles of action for the whole world, which as yet has barely mastered the elementary precepts of morality. In the same way usury was forbidden to the Jews among themselves, as members of a family, when it was not forbidden to them in dealing with other nations. Look upon Christians framed as Christ would have them framed, and members of a family. Then none of His commandments seem unusual or strained. Brothers and sisters would be taught everywhere not to settle their differences by blows, but by mutual concessions. Brothers and sisters in the family would give absolutely to them who asked of them, and would lend to them who wished to borrow. Brothers and sisters would think it quite unnecessary to ratify their assertions with oaths. So when, and as long as, society represents a body of Christian brothers and sisters, the commands of Christ may be literally, nay must be literally, followed; and the work of the Church must always be directed to setting up this family in the world, in which the precepts of Christ may run in all their perfection, while the code of dealing with the world outside must always remain somewhat modified, although founded on the perfect precepts of the family. Such a virtue is Gentleness. In its perfection it is seen within the circle of Christian life, while in a modified form, balanced by judicial resentment and discipline, it is a power which is strong for good in all the world. Experience joins with Revelation in saying, 'Thy gentleness hath made me great.'[1] 'Them that are meek shall He guide in judgment: and such as are gentle, them shall He learn His way.'[2] There is still a great power in gentleness, even in the rough world. Beautiful as it is within the peaceful enclosure of the Christian family, it is also a force of the greatest potency in the world. Gentle goodness or benignity is a virtue which we should all do well to cherish. There is no lack of agencies for good which owe their origin to human activity: but it is from Christ, from the Spirit-enlightened life, that men have learned some of the noblest forms of benignity. It is one of the glories of Christianity that it has taught tender respect for the suffering in mind and body, in that product of Christian love, at all events in its complete development, known as the hospital. To Christianity, once more, we owe the tender care and respect for the very young and the very old, for the unfortunate, for the lower animals—in fact, for all

---

[1] Ps. xviii 35.   [2] Ps. xxv 8.

creatures as coming from the creative hand of God. So Christianity teaches us to honour humanity wherever we see it, and to respect life wherever we encounter it. So that this goodness, which is called benignity, or, as here, gentleness, is one of those signs of the indwelling Spirit of God, which make Christianity 'a lengthened shadow' of Him Who shed all around Him the grace and tenderness of His presence. Gentleness, kindness, whatever term we use in which to express this virtue, leads us back to the way of God, and is an eloquent token of His inner working; while those in whom this tender grace has thus expressed itself will insensibly be led to study not only what kind actions they are able to do, but also the manner in which they are able to do them. They belong to the very aristocracy of holiness. 'Thy gentleness hath made me great.'

And gentleness such as this passes, once more, by an almost imperceptible shade of meaning, into another fruit, called Goodness or Beneficence, the active carrying out, as it were, of benevolence. We are all of us stored in some particular way with help for our brother. God makes men, and different classes of men, the repositories of help for others. There are priests of wealth, and priests of science, and priests of instruction, and priests of consolation, as well as priests of His own peculiar grace. And an especial development of the spiritual life, one characteristic experience of Religion, will be in the imitation of Him Whose peculiar glory it was that He 'went about doing good.'[1] Here Christianity can appeal with its great apologetic to the world, while it can show that it is ceaselessly labouring

[1] Acts x 30.

for its good. So Tertullian in his Apology upbraids the folly of the heathen persecutors, who in slaying Christians were slaying the benefactors of the race, those, namely, who as priests of humanity had access to the Father of all, in the mighty power of intercession. The Church can appeal once more to her mission work as a strong example of this goodness as a mighty power within her, as a sign and token of her great religious life. What power but supernatural grace can impel a man, without hope of distinction or reward, to risk his life, and spend his days in banishment, that he may bring home to the heathen the unsearchable riches of Christ? So it is with the long list of agencies in which the Church seeks to do good: they witness to a great power within, which impels men, like their Master before them, to minister to the necessities of the world. It is a force, wherever we see it, which is eloquent of the presence of God within, when men see the poor no longer treated like Lazarus at the gate, as advertisements of a benevolence, which would have the credit for good-nature, if it refuses to take any real trouble for the welfare of the world's outcasts. When the penitent are no longer scorned, and driven away from the Master's feet, by those who can appreciate neither the needs of penitence nor thankfulness for merciful deliverance from sin; when little children are taken up in the arms of the Church, as they nestled in the arms of the Saviour when He was on the earth; when the blind, and the lame, and the afflicted are treated as if they were Christ Himself,— the Church can appeal with some confidence to these developments of benignity and goodness, which are the fruit of the Spirit, as showing that in the Church we

have after all the truest form of the Religion of
humanity, and that Religion, when it has worked itself
out, or when, in the phrase used by S. James, 'it is
finished,' bringeth forth goodness.[1]

The fruit-bearing tree of human life fructified by the
Spirit is not exhausted yet. Faith, or Fidelity, will be
another sign of the supernatural life within, another
channel in which the vigorous sap finds a vent for its
life and fertility. The spiritual man is a man who can
be trusted, who is faithful in all his undertakings and
true to his promises. We know in the ordinary world
the mercantile value of fidelity and, as the average man
of business will tell us, how terribly rare it is. It is
not an easy thing to find trustworthiness in a region
where interest and passion conflict. It is a great thing
therefore that Religion should be able to exhibit a life
in which fidelity to principle, steadfastness in duty,
faithfulness as regards a trust, are more than an obligation, however solemn,—where they have become an
integral part of the man's very nature. The spiritual
man has learned from his earliest years the service
which is perfect freedom. He has been pledged all
along his life by solemn vows, from his birth at Baptism,
through his renewal at Confirmation, it may be in the
wedded life, it may be in the ordained life, it may be
in the religious life. He has known all his days
what it is to walk evenly between the hedges of God's
Law, to find His commandment exceeding broad, as
he is guided by the eye of His divine Leader. '*Quem
nosse vivere, cui servire regnare est.*' He is in no
danger of thinking restraint to be slavery, nor, on the
other hand, liberty to be licence. As all through his

[1] S. James i 15.

life, binding himself with rules, and resolutions, and pledges, he has learned the value of discipline, so he has learned the value of a course of action which enters on great difficulties pledged to faithfulness. We have already seen how sin gains its dominion by an overmastering of the will, so that a life which has habituated itself to obedience to principle, and faithfulness to promises, enters into the seductions and difficulties of the world with a greater hope of success, because it comes to the duties and conflicting interests in which it is engaged, as one trained to obey and follow out duty to the end. Faith, in the sense of adherence to resolution, obedience to law, regardfulness of promise, is a virtue which even the world can admire. Faithfulness will commend, as few other virtues can, the life which exhibits it, not as an effort, but as an instinct, as the product of a life lived close to God in the Spirit.

Once more, the fruit of the Spirit is Meekness; the same quality which our blessed Lord praises in the Sermon on the Mount, and attaches to it that reward in the spiritual sphere which almost sounds paradoxical, but is an echo of the words of the Psalmist, 'The meek-spirited shall possess the earth, and shall be refreshed in the multitude of peace';[1] while He points to it as one of the most salient features of His own life, 'Learn of Me, for I am meek.'[2] At first the world is frightened away by counterfeits, and disgusted with that which it takes for little-mindedness; at first the loud voice, and the commercial pushing of a mercantile rivalry drive meekness into a corner. But the time comes when a recognition takes place of humility, as a supernatural, as a master virtue. Self-

---

[1] Ps. xxxvii 11.   [2] S. Matt. xi 28.

assertion depends on the wielding of the world's ordinary weapons, and will gain sometimes the world's prizes; but the world does not know how to grapple with humility, before which its ordinary weapons of praise and blame fall pointless, or rather seem to increase the bright vigour which they were meant to destroy. Here is a virtue so rare, that it is very seldom seen in its perfection, but when it is seen there is no power like it. It means that the soul which possesses it has learned in the power of the Holy Spirit to put on one side all the lowering and obscuring pettiness of human nature, to sink self, and let the grace of God which is within come to the front. So says Ruskin, 'We are not humble when we think meanly of ourselves, but when we think truly.'

Then, yet again, there is a last fruit, a last manifestation of Religion, of life in the Spirit, which is known as Temperance. Here again, as by an instinct, the life led in the Spirit has learned the power and the beauty of self-control. The life which is lived under this constraining power has learned, according to the force of the Latin term, to keep properly mingled in their due place and proportion all such valuable ingredients as passion, impulse, sense, feeling, pleasure, and pain. It would be comparatively easy to suppress, to go forward with a crushed body, maimed ambition, numbed intellect; but the hard thing is to bring to the work of life the whole composite being, in which no disproportion, no undue assertion of one part over the other is allowed. A man who, in the truest sense of the word, is temperate, proclaims to the world, beaten and tossed by passion, and baffled by desire, that there is a force in Chris-

THE EXPRESSION OF RELIGION

tianity which it cannot afford to despise. A force which can temper the composite nature of man, and bring all its passions into line, is a master-power which will succeed, where other systems have grievously failed.

Such, in brief outline, is the development of Religion as it meets us in the life of goodness; its expression in the region of human life, just as worship was its expression towards God.

A glance backwards at Religion as we have endeavoured to view it in its ordinary meaning to a Christian man, will show us at once what a complete system it is which is put before us, and how intensely difficult it is of realisation. The very difficulty we experience in learning the language of Religion, which is Prayer, will show us this, and the extreme difficulty in using it when learned. There is no experience so common among religious people as this, that Prayer, which apparently is so simple in theory, is so extremely hard in practice. And what people experience in prayer extends equally to other parts of Religion. Nothing is so difficult as to get people to realise that Religion is a real work, taxing most severely the mental, spiritual, and even the physical powers of man. Religion cannot be taken up as a by-work, or used on certain occasions, or put on as a Sunday dress; it must be concerned with the whole life: whether we eat or drink or whatsoever we do, all must be done to the glory of God; and Religion must be honoured, loved, and followed up with earnest effort.

The Christian Religion is not a form of imaginative instinct, by which a man stretches out mute hands to God, or at the best thinks it safe, in case there be a Supreme Being, to erect an altar 'to the unknown God.' We have seen that God has spoken, has drawn back the curtain which veils Him, and through long ages, by the Patriarchal system, by the Law and by the Prophets, has prepared gradually the sacred precinct within which we have access to Him.

We have seen that it is not, and never can be, an immaterial thing to us, how much or how little we receive of what God has willed to reveal. If God has spoken, at least we are bound to listen. The periodical difficulties which beset people's minds as to the recitation of the Athanasian Creed, are a curious example of the indifferent easiness with which men are prepared to receive the divine command; while the prevailing cult of undenominationalism would be utterly disastrous, even if it were not insincere. Men do not believe in undenominationalism in anything about which they are in earnest, and at least in those subjects which concern their pockets as well as in those which concern their health, they seek always for the best, the most precise, and the most useful knowledge. But, on the other hand, no Religion which is worthy of the name can afford to ignore morality, or stand outside the problems which affect the possessor of such a complex nature, in which Body, Soul, and Spirit, all have their spheres of working, and all have to be provided for. When there is a breach between orthodoxy and morality, there is a mistake somewhere, and calamity is not far distant. But while Religion provides for the full discharge of the moral duties, we have seen further, that Christianity has wider fields of experience in higher regions, that the spies who visit her Promised Land bring back the rich fruits on their shoulders of Faith, Hope, and Charity, the great theological virtues. And if any fail in their purpose, and faint at the greatness of the task, there is the Ideal which they are allowed to copy, the great example which they are invited to imitate, in the life of Jesus Christ. 'Which of you convinceth Me of sin?' is still the challenge to the world. 'Learn of Me' is the invitation which only God could give. 'Follow Me' is the advice which only man could offer. Those who have parted with His Religion, and have emptied His precepts so that they become meaningless sentiments, are still struck by this unique Personality as it appears in the pages of history. Here was the skilful musician, who once in the history of the world drew out of the instrument of human nature varieties and combinations of sound never heard before; who fulfilled every part of human nature with a dignity which it had never known, and elevated it to a height of which it was not thought to be capable.

At the same time we have not hidden from ourselves the serious obstacles which beset the path of all who strive to follow out Religion. An attempt to dismiss the devil to the mediæval nursery, to bury the world in a mass of exploded church prejudice, to reinstate the flesh as human nature: these may do very well as theories for those who regard the battle from the outside; but those who are scaling the steep heights of Religion know too well that the devil is no childish ghost, the world no pettish nickname, and the flesh the very reverse of a friendly power. All these have been discussed at length with the seriousness which they deserve; while as closely connected with them, we have tried to pierce the dark clouds of doubt, the pall of smoke and dust which hangs over the fray, and depresses and misleads even where it can do no harm to the Christian warrior fighting the hard battle of life.

As of old the prophet of Dothan showed to the youth terrified at the stern aspect of the foes which seemed to surround them, that those that were on their side were more than those that were on the side of their enemies; so we have seen the divine help shown forth in the Atonement, and still active in the Church; whereby once for all Satan has been cast down, and sin deprived of its power; while the Church extends on all sides her wonderful network of grace.

Here is a study which will be amplified in subsequent volumes of this Library, as the beauty and strength of the Sacramental system is examined in its separate component parts. Naaman still despises Jordan, and thinks the rivers of Damascus more likely to be fruitful in results than such a humble stream. It seems utterly unlikely that Jericho will fall before the ark, and not before the siege train. Still Naaman relents; still a Joshua arises who can command assent. And leprosies are cleansed, and cities fall, and the wisdom of God is justified of her children; while the voice of Religion mounts up from all creation, in its most conscious and beautiful form from man who is the head, in worship, which loses itself in adoration and love; and Religion justifies itself to man, as being well worthy of his every effort, and the highest expression of his noblest powers, because it helps him to be himself, free from the alien occupation of adverse foes, free from the damaging blight of innate taint, ready for His pardoning, merciful approval, Who, when crowning our merits, will be crowning His own all-priceless gifts.

Printed by T. and A. CONSTABLE, Printers to Her Majesty
at the Edinburgh University Press

www.ingramcontent.com/pod-product-compliance
Lightning Source LLC
Chambersburg PA
CBHW022104230426
43672CB00008B/1277